Early Modern Literature in History

General Editors: **Cedric C. Brown**, Professor of English and Dean of the Faculty of Arts and Humanities, University of Reading; **Andrew Hadfield**, Professor of English, University of Sussex, Brighton

Advisory Board: **Donna Hamilton**, University of Maryland; **Jean Howard**, University of Columbia; **John Kerrigan**, University of Cambridge; **Richard McCoy**, CUNY; **Sharon Achinstein**, University of Oxford

Within the period 1520–1740 this series discusses many kinds of writing, both within and outside the established canon. The volumes may employ different theoretical perspectives, but they share an historical awareness and an interest in seeing their texts in lively negotiation with their own and successive cultures.

Titles include:

Mary Floyd-Wilson and Garrett A Sullivan Jr (*editors*)
ENVIRONMENT AND EMBODIMENT IN EARLY MODERN ENGLAND

Andrea Brady
ENGLISH FUNERARY ELEGY IN THE SEVENTEENTH CENTURY
Laws in Mourning

Mark Thornton Burnett
CONSTRUCTING 'MONSTERS' IN SHAKESPEAREAN DRAMA AND EARLY MODERN CULTURE

Jocelyn Catty
WRITING RAPE, WRITING WOMEN IN EARLY MODERN ENGLAND
Unbridled Speech

Dermot Cavanagh
LANGUAGE AND POLITICS IN THE SIXTEENTH-CENTURY HISTORY PLAY

Danielle Clarke and Elizabeth Clarke (*editors*)
'THIS DOUBLE VOICE'
Gendered Writing in Early Modern England

Katharine A. Craik
READING SENSATIONS IN EARLY MODERN ENGLAND

James Daybell (*editor*)
EARLY MODERN WOMEN'S LETTER-WRITING, 1450–1700

John Dolan
POETIC OCCASION FROM MILTON TO WORDSWORTH

Tobias Döring
PERFORMANCES OF MOURNING IN SHAKESPEAREAN THEATRE AND EARLY MODERN CULTURE

Sarah M. Dunnigan
EROS AND POETRY AT THE COURTS OF MARY QUEEN OF SCOTS AND JAMES VI

Teresa Grant and Barbara Ravelhofer (*editors*)
ENGLISH HISTORICAL DRAMA, 1500–1660
Forms Outside the Canon

Andrew Hadfield
SHAKESPEARE, SPENSER AND THE MATTER OF BRITAIN

William M. Hamlin
TRAGEDY AND SCEPTICISM IN SHAKESPEARE'S ENGLAND

Elizabeth Heale
AUTOBIOGRAPHY AND AUTHORSHIP IN RENAISSANCE VERSE
Chronicles of the Self

Constance Jordan and Karen Cunningham (*editors*)
THE LAW IN SHAKESPEARE

Claire Jowitt (*editor*)
PIRATES? THE POLITICS OF PLUNDER, 1550–1650

Arthur F. Marotti (*editor*)
CATHOLICISM AND ANTI-CATHOLICISM IN EARLY MODERN ENGLISH TEXTS

Jean-Christopher Mayer
SHAKESPEARE'S HYBRID FAITH
History, Religion and the Stage

Jennifer Richards (*editor*)
EARLY MODERN CIVIL DISCOURSES

Marion Wynne-Davies
WOMEN WRITERS AND FAMILIAL DISCOURSE IN THE ENGLISH RENAISSANCE
Relative Values

The series Early Modern Literature in History is published in association with the Renaissance Texts Research Centre at the University of Reading.

Early Modern Literature in History
Series Standing Order ISBN 0–333–71472–5
(*outside North America only*)

You can receive future titles in this series as they are published by placing a standing order. Please contact your bookseller or, in case of difficulty, write to us at the address below with your name and address, the title of the series and the ISBN quoted above.

Customer Services Department, Macmillan Distribution Ltd, Houndmills, Basingstoke, Hampshire RG21 6XS, England

English Historical Drama, 1500–1660

Forms Outside the Canon

Edited by

Teresa Grant and Barbara Ravelhofer

First published 2008 by
PALGRAVE MACMILLAN
Houndmills, Basingstoke, Hampshire RG21 6XS and
175 Fifth Avenue, New York, N.Y. 10010
Companies and representatives throughout the world

PALGRAVE MACMILLAN is the global academic imprint of the Palgrave
Macmillan division of St. Martin's Press, LLC and of Palgrave Macmillan Ltd.
Macmillan® is a registered trademark in the United States, United Kingdom
and other countries. Palgrave is a registered trademark in the European
Union and other countries.

ISBN-13: 978–1–4039–4849–6 hardback
ISBN-10: 1–4039–4849–6   hardback

This book is printed on paper suitable for recycling and made from fully
managed and sustained forest sources. Logging, pulping and manufacturing
processes are expected to conform to the environmental regulations of the
country of origin.

A catalogue record for this book is available from the British Library.

A catalog record for this book is available from the Library of Congress.

10   9   8   7   6   5   4   3   2   1
17   16   15   14   13   12   11   10   09   08

Printed and bound in Great Britain by
CPI Antony Rowe, Chippenham and Eastbourne

For Anne Barton

Contents

Acknowledgements   viii

Notes on the Contributors   ix

1 Introduction   1
   Teresa Grant and Barbara Ravelhofer

2 The Early Tudor History Play   32
   Janette Dillon

3 The Reformation of History in John Bale's Biblical Dramas   58
   Andrew W. Taylor

4 Seneca and the Early Elizabethan History Play   98
   Michael Ullyot

5 History in the Making: the Case of Samuel Rowley's *When
   You See Me You Know Me* (1604/5)   125
   Teresa Grant

6 The Stage Historicizes the Turk: Convention and
   Contradiction in the Turkish History Play   158
   Mark Hutchings

7 News Drama: the Tragic Subject of Charles I   179
   Barbara Ravelhofer

Index   202

Acknowledgements

The editors would like to thank the contributors for their excellent essays and hard work. We are very grateful to Andrew Hadfield and Cedric Brown for their extremely useful comments which helped to improve the collection immeasurably, as did those of the anonymous external reader. We would like to thank Hannah Ridge and (especially) Justine Williams, both students at Warwick University, for help at crucial stages in the book's production. We would also like to express our appreciation to the staff at Palgrave Macmillan: Paula Kennedy, who has been a patient and helpful editor throughout a long gestation period, and Christabel Scaife, who offered constant support on matters small and large.

Notes on the Contributors

Janette Dillon is Professor of Drama in the School of English Studies, University of Nottingham. She has published widely on medieval and early modern drama and literature, including recently *Performance and Spectacle in Hall's Chronicle* (Society for Theatre Research, 2002) and *The Cambridge Introduction to Early English Theatre* (Cambridge University Press, 2006).

Teresa Grant is Associate Professor in Renaissance Theatre and Director of Graduate Studies of the Centre for the Study of the Renaissance at the University of Warwick. She has published on early modern drama and literature, including recent essays in *The Myth of Elizabeth* (ed. Doran and Freeman, Palgrave Macmillan, 2003) and *A Cultural History of Animals* (ed. Kalof and Resl, 2007). She is currently preparing a monograph for Cambridge University Press on the uses of animals on the early modern English stage and is a general editor of *The Oxford Complete Works of James Shirley* (forthcoming).

Mark Hutchings is Lecturer in the School of English and American Literature at the University of Reading. The focus of his research and teaching is drama in performance, principally the early modern theatre, and he has a particular interest in perceptions and representations of the Ottoman Empire in English literature. Publications include 'Acting Pirates: Converting Robert Daborne's *A Christian Turned Turk*', in *Pirates? The Politics of Plunder, 1550–1650* (ed. Jowitt, Palgrave Macmillan, 2006), a jointly authored book with A. A. Bromham, *Middleton and his Collaborators* (Northcote House, 2006), and an edition of *Three Jacobean 'Turkish' Plays* for Manchester University Press (forthcoming). He is guest editor of a special issue of Shakespeare, 'Shakespeare and Islam' (Routledge, 2008).

Barbara Ravelhofer is Lecturer in English Literature at Durham University and Research Associate at the Centre for History and Economics, University of Cambridge. She has written on European spectacle of the Middle Ages and the Renaissance, virtual theatre, stage design, early modern attitudes to animals, Byron, editorial questions, and plagiarism. Her recent book, *The Early Stuart Masque: Dance, Costume, and Music*

(Oxford, 2006), studies illusionistic theatre of the Renaissance. She is a general editor of *The Oxford Complete Works of James Shirley* (forthcoming).

Andrew W. Taylor is Fellow and Director of Studies in English at Churchill College, Cambridge. His research focuses on sixteenth-century humanism and he has recently published essays on Henry Howard, Earl of Surrey (in *The Review of English Studies*), and Nicolas Bourbon and the epigram (in *Translation and Literature*). He has also contributed essays on biblical translation and commentary for *The Oxford History of Literary Translation in English* (forthcoming).

Michael Ullyot is Assistant Professor in English at the University of Calgary, Canada. His research is on the rhetoric of exemplarity and biographical self-consciousness, particularly in the Sidney, Essex, and Prince Henry circles. Recent publications include an edition for the John Nichols Project (University of Warwick), and essays in *Fantasies of Troy: Classical Tales and the Social Imaginary in Medieval and Early Modern Europe* (ed. Shepard and Powell, Toronto, 2004) and in *Books and Readers in the Middle Ages and the Renaissance* (ed. Moulton, Belgium, 2004).

1
Introduction

Teresa Grant and Barbara Ravelhofer

> History will be kind to me for I intend to write it.
>
> W. Churchill

> A historian is just an unsuccessful novelist.
>
> H. L. Mencken

Definitions

Every introduction to a collection about the 'history play' must perforce grapple with the thorny issue of definitions. Critical attention will probably never result in a satisfactory agreed answer to the question 'What is a history play?' To the present day, 'history play' and 'historical drama' are interchangeable definitions used to categorize such newly emerging subgenres as the 'women's history play in America', the 'contemporary British history play', or, indeed, the 'Third Reich history play'.[1] Yet scholars of the early modern period most commonly associate the term with Shakespeare's history cycles of the 1590s. G. K. Hunter defined it as 'a play about English dynastic politics of the feudal and immediately post-feudal period', in short, 'a play about barons' which appealed to a patriotic audience while also highlighting governmental weaknesses.[2] Critics have argued that the genre faded away as the Stuart regime continued, with John Ford's *Perkin Warbeck* (1633) often cited as the last 'history play' of note.[3] In an influential essay D. R. Woolf has blamed 'social and technological change' for the demise of the chronicle, and with it, the history play which relied on the former as a source. In Woolf's view, the weighty descriptive narratives progressing by calendar year were superseded by cheaper newsbooks, almanacs, antiquarian writing and analytical histories inspired by Tacitus and Machiavelli; this

variety of new forms provided historical information in a more flexible fashion, catered for a wider stratum of readers and thus relegated
the comparatively expensive folio chronicle to the status of a niche
product.[4] In this argument 'history play' appears to be synonymous with
'chronicle play'; the question remains whether dramatists could not
have – like their audience – moved on to different providers of information, to fashion a new kind of historical drama. Plays which do not
fit into a Shakespearean paradigm are thus often excluded; this affects
not only works composed before the 1590s, but also those written after
1616, and works which couch their concerns in different formats, rely
on different sources, or perform 'history' in different ways. As recent
studies have begun to revise our understanding of what may constitute
early modern historical drama we think that a more catholic approach
to the genre is timely.[5]

In its own time the 'history play' attracted such different labels as
'comedy', 'interlude' or 'show'.[6] Despite the huge number of English
kings who paraded through his playhouse, Henslowe only once ever
recorded a 'history' in his diary.[7] Furthermore, we must consider the
socio-economic dimension of generic attributions. Statistics suggest that
titles of early modern publications were as much a printer's or bookseller's ploy to attract buyers as a reflection of the work's literary content.
Generic meanings shifted in the process, as Peter Berek observes: for
instance, 'tragedy', initially a marker of drama, endowed, by the mid-
seventeenth century, royalist champions with heroic credentials irrespective of whether the text in question was a play. The term 'history'
peaked in publications printed between 1590 and 1616 (42.5 per thousand *ESTC* titles, including non-dramatic works), yet continued to be
used frequently between 1648 and 1662 (36.8). As Berek concludes from
such figures, the terminology of printed plays created a metaphorical,
theatrical vocabulary for a wider public discourse.[8]

Benjamin Griffin has noted that the terms 'history' and 'story' were
indiscriminately used in the early modern period.[9] Aristotle, of course,
had already provided the Renaissance with an explanation of what
the poet shared with the historian, despite avowed differences: '[the
historian] relates actual events, [the poet] the kinds of things which
might occur [...] poetry relates more to the universal, while history
relates particulars'. 'Herodotus' work', apparently, 'could be versified
and would be just as much a kind of history in verse as in prose'.[10]
Simple enough, until one discovers a little later that 'even should [the
author's] poetry concern actual events, he is no less a poet for that,
as there is nothing to prevent some actual events being probable as

well as possible'.[11] In other words, historical narrative and poetic fiction can intersect, one with a factual, another with a moral claim to truth. This encouraged artistic licence: both chroniclers and playwrights of the sixteenth century frequently used the rhetorical device of *prosopographia*, 'quoting' speeches at length as if they had actually happened that way.[12] Even the typography of early English translations of Thucydides reflected the use of this device, the orations separated from the narrative by page breaks and titles thus, 'The Oration of the Corcyriens bifore the counsayle of the Athenyans'.[13] Puttenham's definition of this trope is revealing: 'these be things that a poet or maker is wont to describe sometimes as true and natural, and sometimes to feign as artificial and not true, *viz.* the visage, speech and countenance of any person absent or dead [...] as Homer doth in his *Iliad*, diverse personages, namely Achilles and Thersites, according to the truth and not by fiction'.[14] But this is a habit that later commentators heavily criticized in Thucydides; Thomas Heywood reports, for instance, that Diodorus

> sticketh not secretly to carpe at the method of [Thucydides's] Orations, as doth Trogus Pompeius against Lyvy and Salust: saying, That they exceeded the bounds of History, by inserting their direct and indirect orations, For (as Cicero saith) nothing can be more pleasing in History than simple and significant brevity.[15]

So, in the good company of Aristotle, Puttenham and Polonius, we must accept, we think, the notion of the simultaneous 'tragical-comical-historical-pastoral'.[16] Several plays in this collection demonstrate a tragical-historical bent. For instance, the king's execution provided the 1649 pamphlet play *Charles I* with historical authority, while the title page proclaimed the piece a 'famous tragedie'. The play's deliberate parallels between the fates of Charles and his followers George Lisle and Charles Lucas, likewise executed, argue for tragic universality. The same can be said of the tragical-historical *Osmond the Great Turk*, where the repetition and repositioning of the 1453 Irene myth creates its own universality. Plays with historical subjects and comic shape are equally common, though perhaps we will be disappointed if we always look for a closing marriage in the comical histories of the period. In this collection, Janette Dillon notes the emblematic and allegorical marriages represented in the plays at Henry VIII's court and Teresa Grant the diplomatic marriage between England and the Holy Roman Empire with which Rowley's *When You See Me You Know Me* (1605) ends. And, of course, there are marriages not treated in this collection: Thomas Dekker's *The*

Shoemaker's Holiday (1599) concludes with a literal wedding for Lacie and Rose and there is a figurative marriage between Elizabeth and the city of London in Thomas Heywood's *If You Know Not Me You Know Nobody*, Part 1 (1605). Perhaps it is because most comical histories do lack the closure of real marriages that these are replaced with other ceremonies, as a way of finalizing the play. The repetitive episodic tableaux of John Bale's counter-cycle, the ritualized 'future perfect' in *When You See Me*, and other such effects in early modern plays, operate to create a realm of the already remembered. The *catastrophe* of comedy is, according to the fourth-century AD critic Evanthius, 'the resolution of the course of events so that there is a happy ending which is made evident to all by the recognition of past events'.[17] Evanthius thus stresses the backward-looking logic of comedy. Bale's biblical plays, at once tragedies of the human condition and comedies of redemption, look back towards origins as much as they project into the future. There is another possible genre which intersects with the 'history' of early modern plays. Griffin and Taylor have argued for saints plays and (counter-) cycle plays respectively as ecclesiastical and biblical history plays.[18] The roots of tragicomedy have been traced to these medieval forms. If the comic ending of tragicomedy is brought about by miraculous intervention, then, it has been argued, plays which rely on miracles to 'save' their saint or resurrect Christ also have a strong claim to be called tragicomedy.[19] This could also encompass such actions as presenting King Charles as a martyr, especially with the hope of royalist body politic renewal, and the final unwarranted forgiveness God gives to man in Bale's *God's Promises*.

Benjamin Griffin has further argued that 'Englishness' and 'pastness' are the genre's essential features, a proposition which, as Paulina Kewes points out, makes the 'history play' shorthand for the '*English* history play' and leaves us with a large number of historical plays in search of a genre.[20] Kewes also observes that this might narrow our understanding of notions of history and identity in the early modern period: for the 'history play' may not just deal with English but Welsh, Scottish and Irish identities, and plays based on foreign history may say as much about British identity as they do about the country in which they are ostensibly based.[21] Hence, plays treated in the present collection feature London and Colchester, but also Constantinople and Jerusalem. Foreign locations invite reflection on issues closer to home. Thus, revisiting the scenes of the Bible, Bale's plays create an allegorical kind of location: the Holy Land is 'everywhere' physically and 'always' temporally. While a literal location in biblical territory, it is also a space which the reader or spectator inhabits; in direct contrast to the Everyman genre of the late Middle Ages, these plays claim literal as well as allegorical truth.[22]

Griffin's other stipulation, 'pastness', also needs some discussion. The plays considered here differ widely in the time passed between the event recreated and the recreation of the event – 1500 years in the case of Bale's biblical plays; months for dramatic responses to the death of Charles I in 1649; 'real time' for festivities at Henry VIII's court in the 1520s which were themselves part of the historical event. As David Bergeron has observed, Lord Mayor's shows, royal entries or masques 'not only reflect and represent history but also *make* history, thereby adding an extraordinary dimension to the historical characters and themes represented in the fiction'.[23] Lord Mayors, courtiers and citizens play themselves. Paradoxically the entertainments are memorialized at the very moment they take place, as they present a running commentary which fixes the historical event in text and/or performance, a commentary possibly made available in subsequent print or manuscript versions for wider public consumption and instruction. Dale Randall notices that 'history plays [...] generally ended up with major scenes involving impressive ceremonies and eye-fixing tableaux'.[24] Slowed, formal, memorable scenes can fix a moment of history in performance. Historical drama often searches for closure. It instinctively memorializes the history related, often locking its relevance and meaning in emblematic stillness, so as to channel a more definite course for the future. The ceremonies greeting the newly crowned Elizabeth I in Thomas Heywood's *If You Know Not Me You Know Nobody*, Part 1 (1605) (though this is a play this collection only treats in passing) are exemplary of this strategy, and so are some court productions of the 1630s. For instance, with topical characters representing regional subjects and (on one occasion) a backdrop showing the city of London, William Davenant's late masques celebrated Charles I and Henrietta Maria as if they were already monuments ('live still, the pleasure of our sight').[25]

The performance of historical drama could be regarded as history-in-the-making[26] shaped by collective memory. According to Maurice Halbwachs and Jan Assmann, every culture forms a 'connective structure'. Celebration and textual tradition are powerful connectives; rituals and feasts influence the way a culture feels about the past and the future.[27] Re-enacting events of the past, a group performs and commemorates collectively. The shared experience creates a feeling of identity, binding the participants together and excluding outsiders. For J. G. Pocock, 'there have been as many pasts as there were social and professional groups with an interest in recalling it', and we concede that a dramatic response is as creative of, as reactive to, historical 'fact'.[28] For instance, although no reliable account reveals what Elizabeth wore and said at the Tilbury camp in 1588, plays and pamphlets invented, and perpetuated, a legend: a Pallas on horseback, Elizabeth was (with a little help from Heywood and others) thought to have addressed her troops with a rousing speech.[29] Yet it is fair to claim that, within the context of historical drama, a group, though diversified, shares the experience of a play or show. As Peter Womack puts it, history plays stage an 'imagined community' of the nation, handling several models of communal cohesion from dynastic to national. They offer protagonists up to audiences for understanding, identification, but also dissent.[30] Playwrights thus incorporated local detail and communal interests and agendas into their works. Samuel Rowley's *When You See Me You Know Me* (pr. 1605), for instance, emphasizes a history of conflict-solving and cooperation between commoner, judiciary and court. In this way historical drama may provide models of conduct (or deterrents), and promote a future, perfected, arrangement for the community. The English stage provided a lively forum for creating such nationalist, religious and political identities between 1500 and 1660.

Types of early modern history

The sixteenth and seventeenth centuries were exciting times for writing and playing history, though modern critics have argued long and hard about how quickly and completely this period can be said to have experienced a 'historical revolution'.[31] The Reformation had led to a profound reversal of historical consciousness as it necessitated a rethinking of the relationship between secular, ecclesiastical and biblical history, and the accuracy of each. Early modern historiography was heuristically and conceptually torn between the possible alternatives of antiquarian discourse, chronicle writing, legendary fiction, providential interpretation and pragmatic application. These conceptual struggles had a profound impact on two particular aspects of historical writing – the understanding of historical time, and with it the validity of history's lessons for the present age.

One classical, cyclical model of history, widely received in the early modern period, was based on the idea of gradual decline: epochs plotted similar courses, yet each repetition introduced a more degraded state which inexorably alienated the course of history from the initial perfection of creation.[32] Hesiod, via Book I of Ovid's *Metamorphoses*, had a huge impact on many writers, including Thomas Heywood, who began his tellingly named dramatic trilogy with *The Golden Age*, continued with *The Silver* and *Brazen Age*, and suitably concluded with *The Iron Age* (c. 1609–13). Desperate for the innocent and learned classical past, commentators turned to fictions of political usefulness: in poems Queen Elizabeth-Astraea heralded the return of Arcadian Eden.[33] The Judaeo-Christian tradition, on the other hand, emphasized an end to be hoped for – the promised land, be that earthly or heavenly – and with it linear history and Time. Teleological in their outlook, medieval cycle plays represented the plan laid down for humankind by God which the Church was following. Reformation historians coloured the teleological model with eschatological notions. Post-Reformation playwrights looked towards the prophetic books of the Bible, reminding their audiences of the apocalypse.

A peculiarly dual understanding of historical time, cyclical yet linear, operates within much historical writing of the early modern period.[34] Precisely because history is not merely a matter of the past, it can instruct us; hence the historian's particular mission – and responsibility. In Philip Sidney's words, 'the historian [...] denieth that any man for teaching of virtue, and virtuous actions is comparable to him', yet he also risks remaining 'captived to the truth of a foolish world', and becoming 'a terror from well-doing, and an encouragement to unbridled wickedness'.[35] When history is supposed to teach by example, time demands to be read as concurrently past, present and future: this is apparent in several essays in the collection. In many plays lessons of the memorialized past are played out in the present to create and validate the future: a hereditary principle is at work when Tudor courtly spectacle insists on a continued, rightful English domination of European politics; or when pre-1660 royalist plays imagine the restitution of the Stuart line.

History's exemplarity was so widely accepted by the sixteenth century that playwrights found ready defence for their art. As John Harington said about Thomas Legge's *Richardus Tertius* (1579), it deterred onlookers with tyrannical instincts from following their inclinations.[36] Moral compunctions as to the dramatic nature of the history presented were countered by claims that, far from simply indulging an idle audience, plays served as a didactic vade-mecum, 'sour pills of reprehension, wrapped up in sweet words'.[37] It is because of history's patently improving qualities that Thomas Nashe slyly uses drama 'borrowed out of our English Chronicles' to defend all types of plays: 'what can be a sharper reproof to these degenerate effeminate days of ours', he asks rhetorically, than England's venerable forefathers, 'raised from the grave of oblivion, and brought to plead their aged honours in open presence'.[38]

On the other hand, writers often prudently denied any exemplarity in their 'historical' narrative or drama, insisting on history-as-progress. For them, the flow of time was a river of no return. Such protestations, though, demonstrate that the present might yet be understood as a repeat performance of the past. The Roman historian Tacitus (*c.* 56–*c.* 117 AD) had already learnt as much, for in his accounts of the earlier Caesars, contemporaries saw veiled criticism of Domitian's current tyrannical regime. Elizabethan and Jacobean authors were well aware of the Janus-faced nature of Tacitean history – possibilities could turn into a predicament.[39] Ben Jonson's *Sejanus* (*c.* 1603) captures this poignantly in the figure of the Roman historian Cordus: he is charged with sedition, which his accusers 'will prove from thine own writings, here, / The annals thou hast published; where thou bit'st / The present age', and not even his defence that his studies are exclusively concerned with dead men who fought their battles long ago can save his books from being burnt.[40] Exploring thorny issues such as how one should deal with tyrannical rule, Fulke Greville encountered similar problems. After the fall of the Earl of Essex, Greville destroyed his play *Antony and Cleopatra* because 'many members in that creature (by the opinion of those few eyes, which saw it) having some childish wantonnesse in them, [were] apt enough to be construed, or strained to a personating of vices in the present Governors, and government'.[41] Politic history, even when tackling legendary rulers, did not always exculpate the author from the charge of unwarranted interference in current affairs: John Hayward's *Henry IIII* (1599) and the famous performance of a play about Richard II in 1601 sparked Star Chamber trials in which Hayward and the Earl of Essex were both accused of 'intent of [...] treason'.[42] An epistle in Hayward's work makes it very clear that its author understood historical examples to have a definite present purpose:

> Among all sortes of humane writers, there is none that have done more profit, or deserved greater prayse, then they who have committed to faithfull records of Histories, eyther the government of mighty states, or the lives and actes of famous men: for by describing the order and passages of these two, and what events hath followed what counsailes, they have set foorth unto us, not onely precepts, but lively patterns, both for private directions and for affayres of state.[43]

The Star Chamber's reaction leaves little doubt that the 'lively patterns' in Hayward's history were taken quite literally, 'it being plainly deciphered [...] for what end and for whose behalf it was made'. *Henry IIII* was seized, and Hayward was committed to the Tower.[44]

And it was not just the works of Tacitus which offered a useful paradigm and method for the early modern writer of history, dramatic or non-dramatic. Authors were alive to the differences between classical historians, and to the particular usefulness of each. Montaigne, for instance, commenting on the difference between Tacitus and Seneca, saw the former as more useful for the current conditions in France:

> It is not a book to read, but a volume to study and to learn... It is a seminary of morall, and a magazine of pollitique discourses, for the provision and ornament of those, that possesse some place in the managing of the world... I deeme Tacitus, more sinnowy, Seneca more sharpe. His service is more proper to a crazed troubled state, as is ours at this present: you would often say, he pourtrayeth and toucheth us to the quicke.[45]

This idea – that Tacitus contains valuable practical lessons, 'more precepts, than narrations' as Montaigne terms it – is echoed by Thomas Heywood in the 'Preface to the Reader' to his 1608 translation of Sallust: 'for men of eminency, Magistrates and Judges, no Historiographer, can be read with like profit [as Tacitus]'.[46] The rest of Heywood's preface gives us examples from and the strengths and weaknesses of the most famous classical, medieval and then-contemporary historians, thereby amounting to a useful digest of ongoing early modern discussions, their qualities and usefulness. Heywood collects reputable historians into three main groups:

> the first being wel qualified by nature, but better by learning, have bin called unto Magistracie. The second sort have wanted learning, and yet proved verie sufficient by the adjuncts of Nature and experience: and the latter being somewhat helped by Nature, and wanting experimentall imploiement, have notwithstanding by their industrie and integritie in their collection of History, even equalled those who have spent the greatest portions of their daies in the Counsell-house of Princes.[47]

But he also warns his readers about traits which make some historians less worth reading, singling out for particular criticism incompetence (those 'unexperienced in all affaires of importance, and uterly unlearned') and 'rayling' or too much passion ('him suspect of flattery, by praising himselfe, his favourites and Countrymen, and bitterly taunting his opposites, or enemies').[48] There are echoes of Montaigne's essay 'Of Bookes' in much of Heywood's preface, though Montaigne argues more for the importance of experience: 'the only good histories are those that are written by such as commanded, or were imploied themselves in weighty affaires, or that were partners in the conduct of them, or that at least had the fortune to manage others of like qualitie.'[49] But Montaigne, commending 'plaine and well-meaning Froisard' specifically, also recognizes the value of a history written without guile:

> I love those Historians that are either verie simple, or most excellent. The simple have nothing of their owne to add unto the storie, and have but the care and diligence to collect whatsoever come unto their knowledge, and sincerely and faithfully to register all things, without choice or culling, by the naked truth leave our judgement more entire and better satisfied.[50]

Indeed, the main plank of the seventeenth-century Jesuit René Rapin's criticism of Tacitus is an accusation that this historian makes 'Policy the universal motive', imposing his own personal predilection for stratagem upon 'all Sorts of Matter' rather than allowing each person in his narrative to 'act by their own proper character'.[51] Rapin prefers Livy, whose 'Skill in Modelling... not to be parallel'd in any other Historian, strik[es] upon all his Subjects the Colours they were naturally disposed to bear.'[52] J. H. Whitfield has argued that Tacitus superseded Livy as the preferred model for historians in sixteenth-century Italy, and the Tacitean fashion starting in about 1590 seems to suggest that this was also true in England.[53] Rather curiously, Heywood's introduction does not have a marginal tag for Livy as it does for every other historian one could name, though he does mention Livy in passing, to criticize him for being 'too prolix... in other men's praises' and to commend his 'reprehension' as being 'modest and grave'.[54] What the discussions above prove without any question is that early modern writers enjoyed a lively debate over historians, and, though author-based trends might be discernible as responses in specific eras to current political circumstances, one's choice of favourite historian was also a personal taste.

Playwrights and history

Since so much of Thomas Heywood's dramatic output was histor-ical drama of one sort or another, it is probably no surprise that he also indulged in translating classical history.[55] And surely his long preface to his translation of Sallust should offer us interesting insight into how this playwright felt about the task of writing history? The epistle is concerned with what is good and bad about history, but should we rightly apply its strictures to the writing of drama as well as prose 'histories', another genre in which Heywood dabbled?[56] Especially vexing, of course, is Heywood's discussion of the possibility of 'truth'. He reports the allegedly Turkish notion that

> no Historiographer can write truly upon report, much lesse will [the Turks], who were either in action, or in place over the action; every man being bewitched to tell a smooth tale to his owne credit; Or suppose, he be of an unpartial spirit, yet either the fear of great personages, or passion, or mony, will prevaricate his integrity.[57]

Though Heywood reckons that this is an extreme position, he (following Aristotle) advises the reader to take a middle course between believing everything and nothing. But he also argues for history which takes proper regard of witnesses, deeming this capable of conferring the 'apparancie of truth' even 'on seeming incredulities'.[58] This at least offers something approaching 'truth'. He shares this notion with John Foxe, the author of the *Acts and Monuments*, a source of his play *If You Know Not Me You Know Nobody*, Part 1. Foxe was much concerned when writing the histories of the Protestant martyrdoms of the sixteenth century to gather together the corroborating evidence of as many witnesses as he could. We have a number of the letters sent to Foxe containing martyrdom narratives and it has become apparent to scholars that he spent considerable energy cross-checking these to try to arrive at the 'true' story, and altered later editions of the *Acts and Monuments* when the reliability of an account became questionable.[59] One is tempted to posit for Heywood, even in the dramatic works, an attempt to be 'true': certainly in *If You Know Not Me* he follows Foxe's narrative carefully and, if the play is compared to other treatments of Foxean material such as Samuel Rowley's *When You See Me You Know Me*, it is apparent that Heywood gives greater respect to the facts and the chronology of his source. However, Thomas Dekker, another dramatizer of Foxean matter, states unrepentantly that he does not think flouting chronology a flaw in historical drama:

> And whereas I may...be Critically taxed, that I falsifie the account of time, and set not down Occurrents, according to the true succession, let such (that are so nice of stomach) know that I write as a Poet, not as an Historian, and that these two doe not live under one law.[60]

Much as electing one's personal favourite among historians was a matter of taste, so it seems, for the dramatist, was respecting the laws of historical time. He could choose to be more poet than historian, as it suited him.

Heywood is not the only writer of early modern drama to have left us his animadversions on the topic of history or historical drama, though his preface is some of the most expansive evidence we have. In 1954, Irving Ribner claimed not only that 'the Elizabethans left us [little contemporary evidence] which is of value', but that the early moderns '[did not conceive] of history as a separate dramatic form'.[61] Neither of these claims is, in fact, strictly true. Many playwrights wrote prefaces to, or included scenes in their plays, which give us some indication that they did consider the 'history' play as a distinct genre, and what they thought was proper to this genre. But, crucially, they also give us evidence that mixed genres were commonly accepted and that they were, as we are in this collection, more broad-minded than twentieth-century critics have suggested. For every Philip Sidney abhorring mongrel tragicomedy, there is a playwright happily mixing genres. Even Ribner's claim that 'the famous introduction to *A Warning for Fair Women*...does nothing to define the History play' needs to be challenged.[62] It *does* give us some important information about the history play and helps us to understand how contemporaries thought about them, if it does not actually produce a definition. The induction dramatizes a row between Tragedy, and Comedy and History about whose play is going to be staged that day. The play starts with the stage direction 'Enter at one doore, Hystorie with Drum and Ensigne: Tragedie at another, in her one hand a whip, in the other a knife.'[63] Of course, these attributes indicate the contents of the two dramatic genres, though it is made clear later by both History and Comedy that Tragedy, as we see her, is actually personating an executioner: 'the common Hangman unto Tyranny' (A2ᵛ) and 'a common executioner' (A2ʳ), as her fellow Muses taunt her.[64] And if Tragedy is a person – the hangman – then the drum and ensign carried by History imply that she is a soldier, offering a clear distinction between what Tragedy calls the 'fopperie' (A2ʳ) of History, and tragic 'passions that must move the soule, / Make the heart heavie, and throb within the bosome' (A2ᵛ). Tragedy consistently lumps together Comedy and History, allowing them both to have 'some sparkes of wit...to tickle shallow injudiciall ears' (A2ᵛ), but the overwhelming impression that the costuming in this section gives is that History deals with wars, while Comedy, playing a fiddle (so personating a clown) treats of merry tricks. But, of course, the date of the play – 1599 – has an effect on the way History is represented, coming as it does at the end of the period in which Shakespeare's history plays were written and performed for the same company who staged *A Warning*. That History has been hogging the stage is a complaint specifically made by Tragedy:

> 'Tis you have kept the Theatres so long,
> Painted in play-bils, upon every poast,
> That I am scorned of the multitude. (A3ʳ)

There is no doubt that an audience in 1599, accustomed to 'three rusty swords...fight[ing] over York and Lancaster's long jars', would readily associate soldiers with a history play in the Shakespearean manner.[65]

A possible association of soldiers with history, but more strongly with tragedy, is evident in Robert Wilson's *The Cobler's Prophecie* (1594). This play also introduces Comedy, History and Tragedy onto the stage together, though in this case they are called by the proper names of their respective Muses – Thalia, Clio and Melpomine [sic].[66] On entering, a 'Souldier' assures Clio that he is at her command (though this may be a formal gesture meant for all the Muses present). But when Melpomine realizes his vocation, she tells him that he is 'the better welcome unto [her]' (C2ʳ), arguing here for an identification of war with tragedy. Thalia's blunt rejoinder 'Not so to me' (C2ʳ) underscores the difference between Comedy and Tragedy, though not with History. The conceit of this part of the play is that Thalia is trying to write a pageant but doesn't have a pen to hand. She asks both Clio and Melpomine to lend her one, but Clio hasn't got one either, and Melpomine says that her pens 'pierce too hard for your writing' (B4ᵛ). Writing style is an ongoing theme: Melpomine explains to the soldier later that 'my pens are too sharpe to fit her stile' (C3ʳ), and the soldier notes that Clio's ink is dry (a reference to the pastness of her histories, and perhaps also a jibe at the dryness of the style). In the end, Thalia elects to make her pen from an ostrich quill because the comic men about whom she is going to write resemble ostriches – greedy, forgetful and 'froward' (C2ᵛ). Wilson gives us a much clearer idea about the contents of history plays than the token drum and ensign of *A Warning to Faire Women* did:

> Sould: What did you register when you did write?
> Clio: The works of famous Kings, and sacred Priests,
>   The honourable Acts of leaders brave,
>   The deeds of Codri, and Horatii
>   The love Licurgus bore to Spartans state,
>   The lives of auncient Sages and their sawes,
>   Their memorable works, their worthy lawes.
>   Now there is no such thing for to indite
>   But toyes, that fits Thalia for to write.
> Sould: A heavie tale good Lady you unfold,
>   Are there no worthie things to write as were of old.
> Clio: Yes divers Princes make good lawes,
>   But most men overslip them,
>   And divers dying give good gifts,
>   But their executors nip them. (C3ʳ)

In 1594, therefore, there is a less clear connection between war and history than later in the decade. What is more evident is the worthy and honourable – one might even suggest 'moral' – nature of the deeds registered, according with history's traditionally educative purpose. But as this collection seeks to show, especially according to playwrights, 'history' in this period is a fluid and unfixed entity which encompasses as many different meanings as there are commentators.

The jaundiced eye which Clio casts upon the present age is a Ciceronian commonplace: *O tempora! O mores!* But some commentators, with Montaigne, thought that nothing much had changed – and history based on Tacitean models encouraged the notion that historical times were just as bad as the current. In the 1630 university play *Pathomachia* Pride and Malice decide that the popular notion that 'the Vices of this Age are more grevious then those of the former, and therefore the Vertues must needs be the fewer' is a misconception. In fact, says Malice, it is only a matter of perception:

> Those emptie declaimers or [sic] against the Vices in this Age of whom you speake, are onely some impatient Male-contents, and Men that want the reflexive eye of Historie, for (to omit the Babilonish, Ægyptian, and Persian vanitie, and the Greekish Sects, and

Heresies) let me instance in the Romanes onely. Did not *Romulus* kill
his Brother? Was not *Numa Pompilius* an Hypocrite?[67]

His catalogue of Roman wickedness, *ab urbe condita*, extends up to
Gregory VII. So the 'reflexive eye' of history, according to this play,
should teach you to read your own time rightly – obviously a useful
skill.

Some early modern plays are more specific about what kind of source
material was used in the preparation of historical drama. John Ford,
famously, in the prologue to *Perkin Warbeck*, admits that he 'shews a
Historie, couch't in a Play'.[68] Ford commends his play to the reader not
only because his 'historie of noble mention [is] knowne, / Famous and
true' but especially because it is 'most noble, 'cause our owne: / Not
forg'd from Italie, from Fraunce, from Spain, / But Chronicled at Home'
(A4^v). Ford was lucky to stumble across such rich material as late as
1634, or so Thomas Heywood might have thought. In 1613, Heywood
was justifying his choice of material for *The Silver Age*, a collection of
dramatized classical myths, thus:

> Since moderne Authors, moderne things have trac't,
> Serching our Chronicles from end to end,
> And all knowne Histories have long bene grac't,
> Bootless it were in them our time to spend
> To iterate tales oftentimes told ore.[69]

This comment reflects the flurry of plays dealing with historical subjects,
and particularly with English historical subjects, which had been written
and performed between the very late 1590s and about 1608, many of
which Heywood himself had a hand in.[70] And by 1638, the possible
sources for historical plays were being listed humorously by a boastful
character in Thomas Randolph's *The Muses Looking-Glasse* who proves
himself particularly well-read by listing every single classical, foreign and
native historian one could name, including Tacitus, Sallust, Polydore
Vergil, Camden, Speed and Stowe's *Chronicles*.[71]

Types of sources

Geoffrey Bullough's monumental *Narrative and Dramatic Sources of
Shakespeare* (1957–75) has enforced an idea of playwrights' working
practices which privileges the written and the rigorous over more
fluid possible sources. In some instances we can identify, in proper

Bulloughian manner, a decisive, material source for the text of a history play. For instance, the Bible authorizes Bale's counter-cycle and *When You See Me* clearly relies upon John Foxe's prose history *Acts and Monuments*. The newsbooks and pamphlets which informed Interregnum plays on the execution of Charles I produced the curious effect of real-life drama becoming news, then becoming drama again.[72]

We have a wider understanding of what constitutes a source for historical drama: in our view, an important historical event or a city teeming with people can be as much a source as chronicles or Scripture. Going beyond Bullough's concept of a proper source, the essays in this collection also discuss ballads, folk tales and other forms of oral tradition, as well as communal memory. The oral need not chronologically precede the written, and written information has been introduced into oral discourse as frequently as vice versa.[73] What Heywood's prologue in *The Four Prentices of London* (1594) calls 'such historical tales as everyone can tell by the fire in winter' remained mostly unrecorded, given their very circumscribed local nature.[74] *When You See Me* probably depended on songs about King Henry VIII and the cobbler and Queen Jane and her baby before versions of these ballads appeared in print (we must accept that the record we have of them is necessarily mediated by this act of fixing).[75] Location provides another fruitful source for historical drama. Familiar settings, Adam Fox argues, were crucially important for a community as mise-en-scène for 'historical incidents or individuals of national renown'.[76] Thus, the city of London serves as identificatory dramatic backdrop, and this is how Dekker, Heywood and other playwrights who work with city interests in mind explore it in historical comedies and pageants.[77] The city is the impulse for and result of a memorial process that encodes history as simultaneously fluid and fixed. The 'text' of the city consists in buildings, streets (with all that they imply of movement and community), ceremonial, traditional games and the routines of manufacture, of 'crafts'. More self-consciously it registers itself in monuments, portraits and anecdotes, oral and scripted. History plays set in London explore these circumstances and appeal to Londoners as active readers of their own past. As the capital provides us with the greater part of the drama of this period, so must it also with the history for this drama. The giving and printing of London-based plays using their locations in this way helped to engender and spread a sense of London-as-England which tourists (and Londoners) still keep hold of today.

The impact too of another kind of source, drama itself, should not be neglected. The style and characterization of Senecan tragedy was transposed wholeheartedly into English humanist plays which sought to grasp history, native and non-native, with classical means – Legge's *Richardus Tertius* is just one earlier example. Alluding to *The White Devil* (1612) and *Women Beware Women* (1621), Lodowick Carlell's *Osmond the Great Turk* (1622) creates a quasi-oriental ambience by means of Jacobean tragic theatre, and models a female lead character after Webster's and Middleton's scheming heroines.[78] This Turkish history play thus activates alternating and sometimes opposed readings, and frequently frustrates playgoers and critics looking for a straightforward anti-Ottoman spectacle.

Our collection therefore surveys a range of different dramatic productions on a historical theme from the Tudor period to the Restoration. We examine not only straightforward plays in print or manuscript but also borderline phenomena such as reported historical drama and pseudo-dramatic pamphlets. With interludes, biblical (counter-)cycles, neo-Senecan drama and select Jacobean and Caroline plays as well as Interregnum dialogues, we present a variety of plays which engage with early modern historical method or thought. Progressing chronologically, some essays take a closer look at format, sources and performance contexts, while others focus on location, concepts of time and national identity.

The essays

The first essay of the present collection addresses terminological questions. Janette Dillon is interested in an early type of history play, distinct from those constructed in the 1590s, entertainments performed at the court of Henry VIII in 1518, 1522 and 1527. No scripted texts for these performances but only eyewitness descriptions survive, for which reason the word 'play' must be used with some care. Such reports constitute a fluid category, since they are difficult to separate from other elements which constituted the entertainment proper. As these performances included spoken text, contemporaries began to call them 'plays', thereby distinguishing them from masks, mummings and other such occasions which emphasized the non-verbal. This choice of terminology demands that Henry's festivities ought to be seriously considered in the development of historical drama. Dillon's plays are variously termed '*comedia*', '*farça*', 'disguisying', 'play' – all words which need examining for their unstable meanings whether in English or other languages. The audience makes the Henrician history play, the latter characterized by an international outlook and a distinct sense of the present: Dillon shows that the presence of learned diplomats at the court plays of Henry VIII's reign helped to create the history depicted. On such occasions the boundaries between past, present and future were deliberately blurred for political ends.

Recent studies have argued for saints plays and (counter-) cycle plays respectively as ecclesiastical and biblical history plays.[79] Andrew Taylor's essay in this collection is concerned with the three extant works of Bale's 'counter-cycle' of Protestant mystery plays – *God's Promises, John the Baptist's Preaching* and *The Temptation of Our Lord*. Written some time in the 1530s to displace the traditional Catholic mystery cycles, these 'interludes', which Bale also thought of in terms of classical genres of tragedy and comedy, sought to inculcate reformed religious doctrine through the dramatic articulation of biblical texts. For Peter Happé, the pre-Reformation mystery cycle 'facilitated the presentation of a sense of history and its periods [...] there were opportunities to show divine intervention in human history, as well as to the whole of history as a sort of pattern, a deliberate design'.[80] Bale's plays too present a deliberate divine design of human history; but their version of history corrects that handed down by the authority of the Roman church. Bale viewed the recovery of true religion from its degraded and corrupted state as an inherently dramatic process. Like other Reformation writers, he stressed the continuities between the early church and the reformed church so as to represent the Roman apostolic succession as a wrong turning, and the reformed church as reformed rather than new.

England's post-Reformation isolation and a Protestant preference for providential history encouraged some twentieth-century critics to think of England as the special recipient of God's merciful plan. The 'Elect Nation' was a term (now contentious) invented by William Haller in his *Foxe's Book of Martyrs and the Elect Nation* (1963) where he argued that Elizabethans began to understand themselves, like the Israelites, as another of God's 'chosen people'.[81] As early as the 1530s, Taylor shows, Bale's audiences were able to rediscover prophecy and God's promise through the biblically heightened poetry of drama. Bale's work is historically located within the religious politics of the Henrician Supremacy, but it also repositions the audience as critical participants in what is projected as the final, most significant moment in church history – the present.

Looking at classical and medieval sources, Michael Ullyot explores the role of Senecan drama in the development of the English history play. He addresses Thomas Norton and Thomas Sackville's *Gorboduc* (1561/2) and Thomas Legge's Latin *Richardus Tertius* (1579). As Ullyot argues, the dynastic character of Senecan drama is one reason for its choice as a stylistic model for history plays. History plays were written to be read in manuscript and print as well as to be performed and spoken.[82] With both purposes in mind, Ullyot investigates practices of reading, staging and composition at the Inns of Court and the universities. The Inns of Court encouraged drama to improve their members' eloquence. Ullyot notes that reading history was considered particularly useful – its exemplarity certainly provided excellent material for debating practice – and one cannot help but suspect that Legge's mammoth work on the last Plantagenet was at least as effective on the page as the stage, and perhaps intended to be so.

Teresa Grant pursues the city of London with particular attention to Samuel Rowley's Jacobean history play *When You See Me You Know Me* (pr. 1605). Raphael Samuel distinguishes between the fixed, dated and chronological written source, and popular memory, which 'measures change genealogically, in terms of generations rather than centuries, epochs or decades'.[83] This sense of the anti-chronological may encourage creative misattributions. Adam Fox cites a wonderful example: 'wherever [John Byng, the eighteenth-century traveller] went the people attributed the destruction of any ruined building to Oliver Cromwell. Moreover, they tended to muddle the Lord Protector with his namesake, Henry VIII's first minister'.[84] Popular memory has a sense of then and now (and perhaps also 'later'), yet it conflates two public figures and telescopes them into a coherent but inaccurate past. Grant's essay examines how Jacobean historical drama marshals its sources, oral and written, and commits similar creative errors for a particular political outlook on James's England. As the supposed 'honeymoon' period of early in James's reign comes under closer scrutiny, critics are beginning to see the plays of that date as more critical of James than previously thought.[85] In particular, *When You See Me You Know Me* is infamous for its reordering and telescoping of historical events, distilled from Foxe's and Holinshed's works, to create a new historical reality which bears little relation to anything we would accept readily as 'fact'. Rowley's imaginative transpositions were carefully calculated to have particular effect on the *performance* of these historical fictions. Rowley's play seeks to reconstruct a communal recollection of Henry VIII, based on the historical narratives, in order to memorialize the house of Tudor at the very beginning of the Stuart dynasty. As Grant argues, this interaction of different sources creates a new stage monarch for changed times. While making imaginative use of chronicles, Rowley appears to follow the precepts of Tacitean history, adding a critical, analytical touch to his version of Tudor history. Rowley's Henry VIII and Prince Edward could be regarded as mirrors for any ruler; yet at the time of the 1604 performance their presentation could have been viewed as an exhortative example to King James and Prince Henry and, at the play's resurrection in 1613, as stinging criticism of one and moving elegy for the other. Tellingly, Nathaniel Butter, the printer of *When You See Me* (and much else in the period), went on to be engaged in Tacitean publications during the 1630s, publishing news-books and works on European history in veiled terms which enlightened the English public on the ongoing Thirty Years War.[86]

Mark Hutchings shows how English playwrights used Ottoman history to comment upon English affairs. Lodowick Carlell's *Osmond the Great Turk* (1622) may be regarded as an allegory of discontent with James's court which was distrusted and ridiculed at the time of its writing. The play demonstrates how English mythic tradition (in this case connected with the fall of Constantinople in 1453) willingly incorporated foreign history. *Osmond* thus combined a communal Anglo-Ottoman pastness with revealing asides aimed at the inadequacies of contemporary rulers. It is perhaps a commonplace now to note that 'otherness' forces one to define one's 'selfness', but this idea is crucial when trying to ascertain what should be rightfully termed a history play. Though other essays in this collection show that native history may foster nationalism more directly, it becomes apparent that indirect methods can be just as effective: as scapegoat villains in a 1518 entertainment at the court of Henry VIII the Turks usefully stood in antithesis to the Christian alliance between Rome, France, England and Spain, allowing fissures in that concord to be overlooked. The Reformation changed senses of national identity, particularly in England, and the previous conception of the 'nation of Christendom' mutated into what might be termed Protestant England's 'radical and isolated position in Europe'. Whether this led to a new, specifically English, national self-awareness is a moot point.[87] As Dillon shows, entertainments showcased England's pre-eminence among other European powers even before the Reformation, and historical drama may memorialize and embroider a glorious show of English wealth and sophistication as different from both Ottoman and other European cultures. Certainly, Turkish historical matter becomes increasingly popular as new dramatic expressions of English self-awareness emerge, among the latter the history play.

Barbara Ravelhofer's essay leads towards the end of our time frame, concluding the collection. In 1649, when the Commonwealth regime both entrenched and radicalized England's Protestantism, its English enemies represented Cromwell's regime as Ottoman (both harsh and sexualized), and the newfangledness in religion as tantamount to turning Turk. The form and aims of the history play had changed considerably over the preceding 150 years, but the emblematic usefulness of the Turkish 'other' still retained its force. The anonymous tragedies *Charles I* (1649) and *The Tragical Actors, or The Martyrdom of the Late King Charles* (1660), short, quasi-dramatic pamphlet dialogues (and one of them with anti-Ottoman undertones), were published once only and probably never performed in public. Ravelhofer examines the possibilities for historical drama at a time when theatrical performance was severely restricted and argues that forms which encourage private reading, or even private declamation, ought to be included in the debate. The execution of Charles I solicited dramatic responses both in England and abroad. But while Continental repertoire of the period openly rehearsed Charles's fall in school plays and *de casibus* spectacle, English compositions on the subject of murdered majesty pertain to the closet genre, mediated as theatrical news. With their heavy reliance on newsbooks, the pamphlet plays uncannily resemble their sources. With this aggressive satire, following hot on the heels of a historical event, the crypto-dramatists of the Civil War may have created a new type of historical drama – news drama which survives to the present day in satirical columns of journals and newspapers.

In both performance and post-performance documentation, early modern historical drama offered spectators ways to learn about Time. Audiences were invited to immerse themselves into the fiction of the play and to make its history their own. Distant historical subject matter strangely resonated with present concerns. Following Jan Kott, Grigorij Kozintsev famously declared Shakespeare 'our contemporary',[88] and the same might be said of Thomas Dekker, Thomas Heywood, Samuel Rowley or anonymous Civil War pamphleteers penning sarcastic playlets about grasping dictators. The Star Chamber no longer exists, and it is now safe to mention the Earl of Essex, but political decision-makers still query the purpose of history.[89] Our last essay appropriately concludes with the histrionic paper battles fought by Blairite monarchs and denizens of the Higher Education Funding Council for England. Here, we hope, begins our readers' lasting joy.

Notes

1. Rebecca Carson, 'The Transformation of History into Drama: the Women's History Play in America, 1900–1940', *Theatre Studies*, 43 (1998), 7–21; Richard H. Palmer, *The Contemporary British History Play* (Westport, CT and London:

Greenwood, 1998); Glen W. Gadberry, 'An "Ancient German Rediscovered": the Third Reich History Play', *Text and Presentation*, 12 (1992), 29–34.

2. G. K. Hunter, 'Truth and Art in History Plays', *Shakespeare Survey*, 42 (1989), 15–24 (15–16).

3. Thus, in *Historiography and Ideology in Stuart Drama* (Cambridge: Cambridge University Press, 1996), Ivo Kamps concludes his study with *Perkin Warbeck* and diagnoses 'the demise of the history play' after the early Stuart period (p. 10).

4. D. R. Woolf, 'Genre into Artifact: the Decline of the English Chronicle in the Sixteenth Century', *Sixteenth Century Journal*, 19/3 (1988), 321–54 (pp. 321, 323, 332). On Machiavelli's reception in early modern Europe see Sydney Anglo, *Machiavelli – The First Century: Studies in Enthusiasm, Hostility, and Irrelevance* (Oxford: Oxford University Press, 2005).

5. See, for instance, Eric Sterling, *The Movement Towards Subversion: the English History Play from Skelton to Shakespeare* (Lanham, MD and London: University Press of America, 1996), and Benjamin Griffin's excellent *Playing the Past: Approaches to English Historical Drama, 1385–1600* (Woodbridge: Brewer, 2001).

6. For early definitions see Irving Ribner, 'The Tudor History Play: an Essay in Definition', *PMLA*, 69/3 (1954), 591–609. According to Ribner, Elizabethans hardly distinguished History as genre separately from Tragedy or Comedy. Ribner argues for recent historical subject matter, as opposed to the medieval apocalyptic model, as an innovation in Tudor drama inspired by Continental influence. See also Arthur Kinney, 'Scottish History, the Union of the Crowns and the Issue of Right Rule: the Case of Shakespeare's *Macbeth*', in *Renaissance Culture in Context: Theory and Practice*, ed. J. R. Brink and W. F. Gentrup (Aldershot: Scolar Press, 1993), pp. 18–53, and Jean Howard, 'Other Englands: the View from the Non-Shakespearean History Play', in *Other Voices, Other Views: Expanding the Canon in English Renaissance Studies*, ed. Helen Ostovich et al. (Newark and London: Associated University Presses, 1999), pp. 135–53.

7. As observed by Peter Berek in 'Genres, Early Modern Theatrical Title Pages, and the Authority of Print', in *The Book of the Play: Playwrights, Stationers, and Readers in Early Modern England*, ed. M. Straznicky (Amherst: University of Massachusetts Press, 2006), pp. 159–75 (p. 161). The lost collaborative play *The Unfortunate General* (performed 1603?), was labelled 'frenshe hestorey' in several entries in January 1602/3. *Henslowe's Diary*, ed. R. A. Foakes (Cambridge: Cambridge University Press, 2nd edn, 2002), pp. 221–3.

8. Generic terms not only created 'a market for printed plays' but 'turn[ed] into a metaphorical resource for texts of other kinds'. All statistics and citation from Berek, 'Genres', pp. 160, 169.

9. Griffin, *Playing the Past*, p. 9.

10. Aristotle, *Poetics*, ed. and tr. Stephen Halliwell, Loeb Classical Library, vol. 199 (Cambridge, MA: Harvard University Press, 1995), pp. 58–9 (IX, 1451b).

11. *Poetics*, IX, 1451b, pp. 62–3.

12. A. R. Braunmüller comments on dramatic diction in Tudor and Stuart historiography in '*King John* and Historiography', *ELH*, 55/2 (1988), 309–32.

13. *The Hystory writtone by Thucidides* etc., trans. Thomas Nicols (London, 1550), sig. Diii^r.
14. George Puttenham, 'English Poetics and Rhetoric' (1589), in *English Renaissance Literary Criticism*, ed. Brian Vickers (Oxford: Clarendon Press, 1999), pp. 190–296 (p. 275).
15. Sallust, *The Two Most Worthy and Notable Histories*, tr. Thomas Heywood (London: John Jaggard, 1608), Preface to the Reader, sig. ¶3^v.
16. W. Shakespeare, *Hamlet*, ed. H. Jenkins (London: Methuen/Routledge, 1982, rpr. 1994), II.ii.394–5.
17. 'Evanthius: On Drama', *Classical and Medieval Literary Criticism: Translations and Interpretations*, ed. A. Preminger, O. B. Hardison et al. (New York: Ungar, 1974), pp. 41–45 (p. 45). The Latin reads 'catastrophae conversio rerum est ad iocundos exitus patefacta cunctis cognitione gestorum' (*Sexti Publii Terentii Afri comoediae cum comment. Aelii Donati Grammatici et Joannis Calphurnii Brixiensis* (Treviso: [s.n.], 1477, sig. A4^r).
18. Griffin, *Playing the Past*, and Andrew Taylor's essay in this collection.
19. See Nancy Klein Maguire (ed.), *Renaissance Tragicomedy: Explorations in Genre and Politics* (London: AMS, 1988).
20. Griffin, *Playing the Past*, p. 21. Paulina Kewes, 'The Elizabethan History Play: a True Genre?', in *A Companion to Shakespeare's Works*, Vol. II, *The Histories*, ed. Richard Dutton and Jean E. Howard (Oxford: Blackwell, 2003), pp. 170–93 (p. 172). See also Janette Dillon's essay in the present collection.
21. Kewes, The Elizabethan History Play', p. 172.
22. See Andrew Taylor's essay in the present collection.
23. David M. Bergeron, 'Pageants, Masques, and History', in *The Cambridge Companion to Shakespeare's History Plays*, ed. M. Hattaway (Cambridge: Cambridge University Press, 2002), pp. 41–56 (p. 55).
24. Dale Randall, *Winter Fruit: English Drama, 1642–1660* (Lexington: University Press of Kentucky, 1995), p. 98. See also Barbara Ravelhofer's essay in this collection.
25. Citation from William Davenant, *Salmacida Spolia* (1640), in *Inigo Jones: the Theatre of the Stuart Court*, ed. S. Orgel and R. Strong, 2 vols (London: Sotheby Parke Bernet, 1973), II, p. 734, l. 475. The masque also featured an ancient Scottishman, Englishman and Irishman, next to a farmer, a bailiff and other contemporary figures. One scene in *Britannica Triumphans* (1638) showed English houses with London and the Thames in the distance (II, no. 334, pp. 668–9). With Merlin and rebel leaders such as Jack Cade, the masque dramatized English history.
26. A term preferred by Janette Dillon in this collection.
27. Maurice Halbwachs, *Les cadres sociaux de la mémoire* (Paris: Alcan, 1925). Jan Assmann, *Das kulturelle Gedächtnis. Schrift, Erinnerung und politische Identität in frühen Hochkulturen* (Munich: Beck, 1992), pp. 16–18, 58. For a recent theoretical approach, see Pierre Nora, 'Between Memory and History: *Les Lieux de Mémoire*', *Representations*, 26 (1989), 7–24.
28. Patrick Collinson on John Pocock's 'England' (*National Consciousness, History and Political Culture in Early Modern Europe*, ed. O. A. Ranum (Baltimore: Johns Hopkins University Press, 1975), p. 99), in 'History', *A Companion to English Renaissance Literature and Culture*, ed. Michael Hattaway (Oxford: Blackwell, 2000), pp. 58–70 (p. 63). Hayden White's concept of culturally

produced historical fact has now become a critical commonplace, as, for instance, outlined in Kamps, *Historiography and Ideology in Stuart Drama*, p. 8.

29. In the 1633 rewritten Tilbury scene of *If You Know Not Me You Know Nobody*, the queen, 'Compleately arm'd', is accompanied by the Earl of Leicester, soldiers and standard bearers. Thomas Heywood, *If You Know Not Me You Know Nobody*, Part II, ed. M. Doran, Malone Society Reprints (Oxford: Oxford University Press, 1935), V.19, sig. K^r, ll. 2684–6. 1633 Quarto. The queen is not fully armed in the first version. See also Susan Frye, 'The Myth of Elizabeth at Tilbury', *Sixteenth Century Journal*, 23/1 (1992), 95–114.

30. Peter Womack, 'Imagining Communities: Theatres and the English Nation in the Sixteenth Century', in *Culture and History, 1350–1600: Essays on English Communities, Identities and Writing*, ed. David Aers (New York, London: Harvester Wheatsheaf, 1992), pp. 91–145 (p. 91).

31. This is a notion which has been refuted by more recent critics – see D. R. Woolf's 'From Hystories to the Historical: Five Transitions in Thinking about the Past, 1500–1700', *Huntingdon Library Quarterly*, 68/1–2 (2005), 33–70. F. J. Levy's study, *Tudor Historical Thought* (San Marino, CA: Huntington Library, 1967), has been built upon since by many critics, especially by Woolf in numerous articles and three important monographs: *The Idea of History in Early Stuart England: Erudition, Ideology and 'The Light of Truth' from the Accession of James I to the Civil War* (Toronto: University of Toronto Press, 1990); *Reading History in Early Modern England* (Cambridge: Cambridge University Press, 2000); and *The Social Circulation of the Past: English Historical Culture, 1500–1730* (Oxford: Oxford University Press, 2003). See also Thomas Betteridge's recent *Tudor Histories of the English Reformation, 1530–83* (Aldershot: Ashgate, 1999). For useful summaries of the historiographical arguments see Ivo Kamps, 'The Writing of History in Shakespeare's England', in *A Companion to Shakespeare's Works*, ed. Dutton and Howard, pp. 4–25; Collinson, 'History'; and a subtle point on writing chronicles in Bart van Es, *Spenser's Forms of History* (Oxford: Oxford University Press, 2002), especially 'Introduction'. Our book concentrates on history in performance and we deal with early modern historical thought as far as it is relevant specifically to play and playing.

32. For a fuller discussion see Dominique Goy-Blanquet, 'Elizabethan Historiography and Shakespeare's Sources', in *The Cambridge Companion to Shakespeare's History Plays*, ed. Hattaway, pp. 57–70 (pp. 58–60).

33. For Hesiod's influence on Elizabethan humanist writing see Goy-Blanquet, 'Elizabethan Historiography', p. 59.

34. As Goy-Blanquet has pointed out, pagan and Christian beliefs about history and time were combined in every possible variation during the early modern period ('Elizabethan Historiography', p. 59).

35. Philip Sidney, *An Apology for Poetry*, ed. Geoffrey Shepherd (Manchester: Manchester University Press, 2nd edn, 1973), pp. 105, 111.

36. See Michael Ullyot's essay in this collection.

37. Thomas Nashe, 'Pierce Penniless his Supplication to the Devil', in *The Unfortunate Traveller and Other Works*, ed. J. B. Steane (Harmondsworth: Penguin, 1972, repr. 1985), pp. 49–145 (p. 114).

38. Nashe, 'Pierce Penniless', pp. 112–13.

39. On the reception of Tacitus, see, for instance, J. H. M. Salmon, 'Stoicism and Roman Example: Seneca and Tacitus in Jacobean England', *Journal of the History of Ideas*, 50/2 (1989), 199–225.
40. Satrius, in Ben Jonson, *Sejanus His Fall*, ed. Philip Ayers (Manchester: Manchester University Press, 1990), Act III, ll. 383–5.
41. *Sir Fulke Greville's Life of Sir Philip Sidney*, intr. Nowell Smith (Oxford: Clarendon Press, 1907), p. 156, also cited in R. A. Rebholz, *The Life of Fulke Greville, First Lord Brooke* (Oxford: Clarendon Press, 1971), p. 131. Hugh Gazzard argues that the transition from closet to performed drama precipitated Samuel Daniel's difficulties with the authorities over another play, *Philotas*. ' "Those Graue Presentments of Antiquitie": Samuel Daniel's *Philotas* and the Earl of Essex', *Review of English Studies*, 51/203 (2000), 423–50. But Greville obviously considered that even keeping plays in your closet might be too dangerous.
42. This particular charge cited from the trial in connection with *Henry IIII*; see 'Analytical Abstract in Support of the Charge of Treason against the Earl of Essex', *Calendar of State Papers, Domestic Series, of the Reign of Elizabeth I, 1598–1601*, ed. Mary Anne Everett Green, vol. V (London: HMSO, 1869), p. 455, 22 July 1600. See also John Hayward, *The first and second parts of John Hayward's The life and raigne of King Henrie IIII*, ed. John J. Manning (London: RHS for the Camden Society, 1991), esp. pp. 17–34; W. Shakespeare, *King Richard II*, ed. Peter Ure (London and New York: Routledge, 5th edn, 1961; rpr. 1991), pp. lviii–lix, and Goy-Blanquet, 'Elizabethan Historiography', p. 61. For the play about Richard II, which may or may not have been Shakespeare's, see, most recently, Blair Worden, 'Which Play was Performed at the Globe Theatre on 7 February 1601?', *London Review of Books*, 10 July 2003, and the subsequent correspondence with Frank Kermode in the same publication. See also Cyndia Susan Clegg, 'Censorship and the Problems with History in Shakespeare's England', *A Companion to Shakespeare's Works*, II, pp. 48–69.
43. J[ohn] H[ayward], *The first part of the life and raigne of King Henrie the IIII*. (London: John Woolfe, 1599), sig. A3ʳ.
44. *CSPD, 1598–1601*, p. 451 (13 July 1600), p. 455 (22 July 1600) and p. 457 (26 July 1600).
45. Michel Eyquem de Montaigne, *Montaigne's Essays*, tr. John Florio, intr. L. C. Harmer (3 vols; London: Dent, 1965, repr. 1980), 'Of the Art of Conferring', III, viii, pp. 156–82 (p. 180).
46. Sallust, *The Two Most Worthy and Notable Histories*, tr. Heywood, sig. ¶¶2ʳ.
47. Ibid., sig. [first quire] 4ᵛ.
48. Ibid., sig. ¶ʳ.
49. Montaigne, *Essays*, II, x, pp. 92–108 (p. 104).
50. Ibid., p. 103.
51. Réne Rapin (1621–87) from *The Whole Critical Works of M. Rapin*, tr. Basil Kennet (London, 1731), reprinted in *Tacitus: the Classical Heritage*, ed. Ronald Mellor (New York, Garland, 1995), pp. 134–7 (p. 135).
52. Ibid., p. 135.
53. J. H. Whitfield, 'Livy > Tacitus', in *Classical Influences on European Culture A.D. 1500–1700*, ed. R. R. Bolgar (Cambridge: Cambridge University Press, 1976), pp. 281–93. See also Salmon, 'Stoicism and the Roman Example'.

54. Sallust, *The Two Most Worthy and Notable Histories*, tr. Heywood, sig. ¶4ʳ.
55. These include *Edward IV* (pr. 1600), *If You Not Know Not Me You Know Nobody*, Parts 1 and 2 (pr. 1605–6) and, arguably, his five *Ages* plays (pr. 1611–32). Others of his plays could be included in a loose grouping of the 'historical' – *The Fair Maid of the West* (pr. 1631), for instance.
56. Notably *Gynaikeion or Nine Books of Various History Concerning Women* (1624) and *England's Elizabeth, Her Life and Troubles* (1631).
57. Sallust, *The Two Most Worthy and Notable Histories*, tr. Heywood, sig. [first quire] 4ʳ.
58. Ibid., sig. ¶ᵛ.
59. We are grateful to Tom Freeman for a very helpful conversation about this.
60. Thomas Dekker, *The Whore of Babylon* (London: Nathaniel Butter, 1607), 'To the Readers', sigs. A2ʳ⁻ᵛ.
61. Ribner, 'Tudor History Play', 591.
62. Ibid. Interestingly, Quincy Adams argued that Thomas Heywood wrote this play and, though we have no proof of this, the discussions which take place in the induction do tie in with what we know about Heywood's interests in historical genre. See Joseph Quincy Adams Jr., 'The Authorship of *A Warning for Faire Women*', PMLA, 284 (1913), 594–620.
63. *A Warning for Faire Women* (London: Valentine Sims for Williams Aspley, 1599), sig. A2ʳ.
64. Ibid., sig. A2ᵛ; sig. A2ʳ.
65. Ben Jonson, *Every Man in His Humour* (1616) in *Five Plays*, ed. G. A. Wilkes (Oxford: Oxford University Press, World's Classics, 1988), Prologue, ll. 9; 11.
66. Robert Wilson, *The Coblers Prophecie* (London: John Danter for Cuthbert Burbie, 1594), sigs. B4ᵛ – C3ʳ.
67. Anon., *Pathomachia: Or the Battell of Affections* (London: Thomas and Richard Coats for Francis Constable, 1630), Act 2, scene 5. This is one of the few STC texts not yet on EEBO, but a keyed copy can be viewed on Literature Online at http://gateway.proquest.com/openurl?ctx_ver=Z39.88-2003&xri: pqil:res_ver=0.2&res_id=xri:lion&rft_id=xri:lion:ft:dr:Z000051126:0
68. John Ford, *The Chronicle Historie of Perkin Warbeck* (London: Printed by T. P. for Hugh Beeston, 1634), sig. A4ᵛ.
69. Thomas Heywood, *The Silver Age* (London: Nicholas Okes, 1613), sig. B1ʳ.
70. For a discussion of these plays see Teresa Grant's essay in this collection.
71. In Thomas Randolph, *Poems with the Muses Looking-Glasse: and Amyntas* (Oxford: Leonard Lichfield for Francis Bowman, 1638), pp. 56–7.
72. See Barbara Ravelhofer's essay in the present collection.
73. Albert Bates Lord, *The Singer of Tales*, ed. Stephen Mitchell and Gregory Nagy (Cambridge, MA: Harvard University Press, 2nd edn, 2000). Mary Carruthers, *The Book of Memory: a Study of Memory in Medieval Culture* (Cambridge: Cambridge University Press, 1990). Adam Fox, 'Remembering the Past in Early Modern England', *Transactions of the Royal Historical Society*, 9 (1999), 233–56.
74. Thomas Heywood, *The Four Prentices of London. A Critical Old-Spelling Edition*, ed. Mary Ann Weber Gasior (New York and London: Garland, 1980), p. 5; Fox, 'Remembering the Past', p. 234.
75. *English and Scottish Ballads*, ed. Francis James Child, 8 vols (Boston: Little, Brown, 1889) prints and thus 'fixes' several versions of ballads treated in the

present collection. This reminds us that, as Pocock said of history, there are
as many versions of each ballad as there were singers of it.

76. Fox, 'Remembering the Past', p. 234.
77. See, for instance, *The Theatrical City: Culture, Theatre and Politics in London, 1576–1649*, ed. D. L. Smith, R. Strier and D. Bevington (Cambridge: Cambridge University Press, 1995).
78. See Mark Hutchings's essay in this collection.
79. For instance, Griffin, *Playing the Past*, ch. 1.
80. Peter Happé, *John Bale* (New York: Twayne, 1996), p. 6.
81. William Haller, *Foxe's Book of Martyrs and the Elect Nation* (London: Cape, 1963); Judith Doolin Spikes, 'The Jacobean History Play and the Myth of the Elect Nation', *Renaissance Drama*, 8 (1977), 117–49; James Ellison, '*Measure for Measure* and the Executions of Catholics in 1604', *English Literary Renaissance*, 33/1 (2003), 44–87 (pp. 80–2).
82. As we are helpfully reminded by Kewes, 'The Elizabethan History Play', p. 189.
83. Raphael Samuel, *Theatres of Memory, I. Past and Present in Contemporary Culture* (London: Verso, 1994), p. 19.
84. Fox, 'Remembering the Past', 241.
85. For a further discussion see Teresa Grant, 'Drama Queen: Staging Elizabeth in *If You Know Not Me You Know Nobody*', in *The Myth of Elizabeth*, ed. Susan Doran and Thomas S. Freeman (Basingstoke: Palgrave Macmillan, 2003), pp. 120–42.
86. S. A. Baron, 'Butter, Nathaniel (*bap.* 1583, *d.* 1664)', *Oxford Dictionary of National Biography* (Oxford: Oxford University Press, 2004) http://www.oxforddnb.com/view/article/4224, accessed 1 December 2005.
87. For an argument in favour, see A. J. Hoenselaars, 'Shakespeare and the Early Modern History Play', *The Cambridge Companion to Shakespeare's History Plays*, ed. Hattaway, pp. 25–40 (p. 26).
88. Grigorij Mikhailovich Kozintsev, *Shakespeare: Time and Conscience*, tr. Joyce Vining (London: Dobson, 1967); first publication in Russian [*Our Contemporary William Shakespeare*] (Moscow: Iskusstwo, 1962).
89. Margaret Thatcher was heard to term the study of history a 'luxury' during a visit at the LSE in the 1980s. For the more recent debate on whether Charles Clarke, while in office as Labour Education Secretary, had described the subject of history as merely 'ornamental', see *The Guardian*, 9, 10 and 15 May 2003.

Bibliography

Anglo, Sydney, *Machiavelli – The First Century: Studies in Enthusiasm, Hostility, and Irrelevance* (Oxford: Oxford University Press, 2005).
Anon., *A Warning for Faire Women* (London: Valentine Sims for Williams Aspley, 1599).
Anon., *Pathomachia: Or the Battell of Affections* (London: Thomas and Richard Coats for Francis Constable, 1630).
Aristotle, *Poetics*, ed. and tr. Stephen Halliwell, Loeb Classical Library, vol. 199 (Cambridge, MA: Harvard University Press, 1995).

Assmann, Jan, *Das kulturelle Gedächtnis. Schrift, Erinnerung und politische Identität in frühen Hochkulturen* (Munich: Beck, 1992).

Baron, S. A., 'Butter, Nathaniel (*bap.* 1583, *d.* 1664)', *Oxford Dictionary of National Biography* (Oxford: Oxford University Press, 2004), http://www.oxforddnb.com/view/article/4224, accessed 1 December 2005.

Berek, Peter, 'Genres, Early Modern Theatrical Title Pages, and the Authority of Print', *The Book of the Play: Playwrights, Stationers, and Readers in Early Modern England*, ed. M. Straznicky (Amherst: University of Massachusetts Press, 2006), pp. 159–75.

Bergeron, David M., 'Pageants, Masques, and History', *The Cambridge Companion to Shakespeare's History Plays*, ed. M. Hattaway (Cambridge: Cambridge University Press, 2002), pp. 41–56.

Betteridge, Thomas, *Tudor Histories of the English Reformation, 1530–83* (Aldershot: Ashgate, 1999).

Braunmüller, A. R., 'King John and Historiography', *ELH*, 55/2 (1988), 309–32.

Calendar of State Papers, Domestic Series, of the Reign of Elizabeth I, 1598–1601, ed. Mary Anne Everett Green, vol. V (London: HMSO, 1869).

Carruthers, Mary, *The Book of Memory: a Study of Memory in Medieval Culture* (Cambridge: Cambridge University Press, 1990).

Carson, Rebecca, 'The Transformation of History into Drama: the Women's History Play in America, 1900–1940', *Theatre Studies*, 43 (1998), 7–21.

Child, Francis James (ed.), *English and Scottish Ballads*, 8 vols (Boston: Little, Brown, 1889).

Clegg, Cyndia Susan, 'Censorship and the Problems with History in Shakespeare's England', *A Companion to Shakespeare's Works*, Vol. II, *The Histories*, ed. Richard Dutton and Jean E. Howard (Oxford: Blackwell, 2003), pp. 48–69.

Collinson, Patrick, 'History', *A Companion to English Renaissance Literature and Culture*, ed. Michael Hattaway (Oxford: Blackwell, 2000), pp. 58–70.

Dekker, Thomas, *The Shoemaker's Holiday*, ed. J. B. Steane (Cambridge: Cambridge University Press, 1965).

Ellison, James, '*Measure for Measure* and the Executions of Catholics in 1604', *English Literary Renaissance*, 33/1 (2003), 44–87.

Foakes, R. A. (ed.), *Henslowe's Diary* (Cambridge: Cambridge University Press, 2nd edn, 2002).

Ford, John, *The Chronicle Historie of Perkin Warbeck* (London: Printed by T. P. for Hugh Beeston, 1634).

Fox, Adam, 'Remembering the Past in Early Modern England', *Transactions of the Royal Historical Society*, 9 (1999), 233–56.

Frye, Susan, 'The Myth of Elizabeth at Tilbury', *Sixteenth Century Journal*, 23/1 (1992), 95–114.

Gadberry, Glen W., 'An "Ancient German Rediscovered": the Third Reich History Play', *Text and Presentation*, 12 (1992), 29–34.

Gazzard, Hugh, ' "Those Graue Presentments of Antiquitie": Samuel Daniel's *Philotas* and the Earl of Essex', *Review of English Studies*, 51/203 (2000), 423–50.

Goy-Blanquet, Dominique, 'Elizabethan Historiography and Shakespeare's Sources', *The Cambridge Companion to Shakespeare's History Plays*, ed. M. Hattaway (Cambridge: Cambridge University Press, 2002), pp. 57–70.

Grant, Teresa, 'Drama Queen: Staging Elizabeth in *If You Know Not Me You Know Nobody*', *The Myth of Elizabeth*, ed. Susan Doran and Thomas S. Freeman (Basingstoke: Palgrave Macmillan, 2003), pp. 120–42.

Greville, Fulke, *Sir Fulke Greville's Life of Sir Philip Sidney*, intr. Nowell Smith (Oxford: Clarendon Press, 1907).

Griffin, Benjamin, *Playing the Past: Approaches to English Historical Drama, 1385–1600* (Woodbridge: Brewer, 2001).

Halbwachs, Maurice, *Les cadres sociaux de la mémoire* (Paris: Alcan, 1925).

Haller, William, *Foxe's Book of Martyrs and the Elect Nation* (London: Cape, 1963).

Happé, Peter, *John Bale* (New York: Twayne, 1996).

Hayward, John, *The first and second parts of John Hayward's The life and raigne of King Henrie IIII*, ed. John J. Manning (London: RHS for the Camden Society, 1991).

—— *The first part of the life and raigne of King Henrie the IIII* (London: by John Woolfe, 1599).

Helgerson, Richard, 'Shakespeare and Contemporary Dramatists of History', *A Companion to Shakespeare's Works*, Vol. II, *The Histories*, ed. Richard Dutton and Jean E. Howard (Oxford: Blackwell, 2003), pp. 26–47.

Heywood, Thomas, *If You Know Not Me You Know Nobody*, Part II, ed. M. Doran, Malone Society Reprints (Oxford: Oxford University Press, 1935).

—— *The Four Prentices of London. A Critical Old-Spelling Edition*, ed. Mary Ann Weber Gasior (New York and London: Garland, 1980).

Hoenselaars, A. J., 'Shakespeare and the Early Modern History Play', *The Cambridge Companion to Shakespeare's History Plays*, ed. M. Hattaway (Cambridge: Cambridge University Press, 2002), pp. 25–40.

Howard, Jean, 'Other Englands: the View from the Non-Shakespearean History Play', *Other Voices, Other Views: Expanding the Canon in English Renaissance Studies*, ed. Helen Ostovich et al. (Newark, London: Associated University Presses, 1999), pp. 135–53.

Hunter, G. K., 'Truth and Art in History Plays', *Shakespeare Survey*, 42 (1989), 15–24.

Jonson, Ben, *Five Plays*, ed. G. A. Wilkes (Oxford: Oxford University Press, World's Classics, 1988).

Jonson, Ben, *Sejanus His Fall*, ed. Philip Ayers (Manchester: Manchester University Press, 1990).

Kamps, Ivo, 'The Writing of History in Shakespeare's England', *A Companion to Shakespeare's Works*, Vol. II, *The Histories*, ed. Richard Dutton and Jean E. Howard (Oxford: Blackwell, 2003), pp. 4–25.

—— *Historiography and Ideology in Stuart Drama* (Cambridge: Cambridge University Press, 1996).

Kewes, Paulina, 'The Elizabethan History Play: a True Genre?', *A Companion to Shakespeare's Works*, Vol. II, *The Histories*, ed. Richard Dutton and Jean E. Howard (Oxford: Blackwell, 2003), pp. 170–93.

Kinney, Arthur, 'Scottish History, the Union of the Crowns and the Issue of Right Rule: the Case of Shakespeare's *Macbeth*', *Renaissance Culture in Context: Theory and Practice*, ed. J. R. Brink and W. F. Gentrup (Aldershot: Scolar Press, 1993), pp. 18–53.

Kozintsev, Grigorij Mikhailovich, *Shakespeare: Time and Conscience*, tr. Joyce Vining (London: Dobson, 1967).

Levy, F. J., *Tudor Historical Thought* (San Marino, CA: Huntington Library, 1967).

Lord, Albert Bates, *The Singer of Tales*, ed. Stephen Mitchell and Gregory Nagy (Cambridge, MA: Harvard University Press, 2nd edn, 2000).

Mellor, Ronald (ed.), *Tacitus: the Classical Heritage* (New York, Garland, 1995).

Montaigne, Michel Eyquem de, *Montaigne's Essays*, tr. John Florio, intr. L. C. Harmer (3 vols; London: Dent, 1965, repr. 1980).

Mumford, Lewis, *The Culture of Cities* (New York: Harcourt Brace, 1938).

Nashe, Thomas, 'Pierce Penniless his Supplication to the Devil', in *The Unfortunate Traveller and Other Works*, ed. J. B. Steane (Harmondsworth: Penguin, 1972, repr. 1985), pp. 49–145.

Nora, Pierre, 'Between Memory and History: *Les Lieux de Mémoire*', *Representations*, 26 (1989), 7–24.

Orgel, S. and R. Strong (eds), *Inigo Jones: The Theatre of the Stuart Court*, 2 vols (London: Sotheby Parke Bernet, 1973).

Palmer, Richard H., *The Contemporary British History Play* (Westport, CT and London: Greenwood, 1998).

Preminger, A., O. B. Hardison et al. (eds), 'Evanthius: On Drama', *Classical and Medieval Literary Criticism: Translations and Interpretations* (New York: Ungar, 1974), pp. 41–5.

Puttenham, George, 'English Poetics and Rhetoric' (1589), *English Renaissance Literary Criticism*, ed. Brian Vickers (Oxford: Clarendon Press, 1999), pp. 190–296.

Randall, Dale, *Winter Fruit: English Drama, 1642–1660* (Lexington: University Press of Kentucky, 1995).

Randolph, Thomas, *Poems with the Muses Looking-Glasse: and Amyntas* (Oxford: Leonard Lichfield for Francis Bowman, 1638).

Rebholz, R. A., *The Life of Fulke Greville, First Lord Brooke* (Oxford: Clarendon Press, 1971).

Ribner, Irving, 'The Tudor History Play: an Essay in Definition', *PMLA*, 69/3 (1954), 591–609.

Sallust, *The Two Most Worthy and Notable Histories*, tr. Thomas Heywood (London: John Jaggard, 1608).

Salmon, J. H. M., 'Stoicism and Roman Example: Seneca and Tacitus in Jacobean England', *Journal of the History of Ideas*, 50/2 (1989), 199–225.

Samuel, Raphael, *Theatres of Memory, I. Past and Present in Contemporary Culture* (London: Verso, 1994).

Shakespeare, William, *Hamlet*, ed. H. Jenkins (London: Methuen/Routledge, 1982, rpr. 1994).

—— *King Richard II*, ed. Peter Ure (London and New York: Routledge, 5th edn, 1961; rpr. 1991).

Sidney, Philip, *An Apology for Poetry*, ed. Geoffrey Shepherd (Manchester: Manchester University Press, 2nd edn, 1973).

Smith, D. L., R. Strier and D. Bevington (eds), *The Theatrical City: Culture, Theatre and Politics in London, 1576–1649* (Cambridge: Cambridge University Press, 1995).

Spikes, Judith Doolin, 'The Jacobean History Play and the Myth of the Elect Nation', *Renaissance Drama*, 8 (1977), 117–49.

Sterling, Eric, *The Movement Towards Subversion: the English History Play from Skelton to Shakespeare* (Lanham, MD and London: University Press of America, 1996).

Terence, *Sexti Publii Terentii Afri comoediae cum comment. Aelii Donati Grammatici et Joannis Calphurnii Brixiensis* (Treviso: [s.n.], 1477).

Thucydides, *The Hystory writtone by Thucidides* etc., trans. Thomas Nicols (London, 1550).

Van Es, Bart, *Spenser's Forms of History* (Oxford: Oxford University Press, 2002).

Whitfield, J. H., 'Livy > Tacitus', in *Classical Influences on European Culture A.D. 1500–1700*, ed. R. R. Bolgar (Cambridge: Cambridge University Press, 1976), pp. 281–93.

Wilson, Robert, *The Coblers Prophecie* (London: John Danter for Cuthbert Burbie, 1594).

Womack, Peter, 'Imagining Communities: Theatres and the English Nation in the Sixteenth Century', *Culture and History, 1350–1600: Essays on English Communities, Identities and Writing*, ed. David Aers (New York, London: Harvester Wheatsheaf, 1992), pp. 91–145.

Woolf, D. R., 'From Hystories to the Historical: Five Transitions in Thinking about the Past, 1500–1700', *Huntingdon Library Quarterly* 68/1–2 (2005), 33–70.

—— 'Genre into Artifact: the Decline of the English Chronicle in the Sixteenth Century', *Sixteenth Century Journal*, 19/3 (1988), 321–54.

—— *The Idea of History in Early Stuart England: Erudition, Ideology and 'The Light of Truth' from the Accession of James I to the Civil War* (Toronto: University of Toronto Press, 1990).

—— *Reading History in Early Modern England* (Cambridge: Cambridge University Press, 2000).

—— *The Social Circulation of the Past: English Historical Culture, 1500–1730* (Oxford: Oxford University Press, 2003).

Worden, Blair, 'Which Play was Performed at the Globe Theatre on 7 February 1601?', *London Review of Books* (10 July 2003).

2
The Early Tudor History Play

Janette Dillon

The history play is usually associated with the decade of the 1590s and with public theatres. David Bevington's pioneering work in *Tudor Drama and Politics* showed the genre to be clearly associated with England's wartime aspirations during that period, and to recede with the failing years of Elizabeth and the peace policy of James I from 1603.[1] Despite broad critical agreement about its central axis in the 1590s, however, the history play has never been easy to define, and there is a general lack of agreement about how it should be identified. The term 'history play' was not in use during the sixteenth century, and the term 'history' was used in so loose a way (often closer in sense to modern 'story') that its presence or absence in play titles is unhelpful in reaching a definition of dramatic genre.[2] Even the well-known divisions of Shakespeare's First Folio (1623), which have probably been most influential in creating the need to conceive of the history play as a genre, distribute plays into the categories of history and tragedy in ways that raise almost as many questions as they answer. Samuel Johnson in 1765 expressed the opinion that 'the players who in their edition [the First Folio] divided our author's works into comedies, histories, and tragedies' seemed not 'to have distinguished the three kinds by any very exact or definite ideas'.[3] Benjamin Griffin, who has most recently sought to pursue the question of definition at length, begins his chronology of the history play in the fourteenth century, choosing 'Englishness' and 'pastness' as 'the genre's essential features' and arguing for the inclusion of British saint plays as amongst the earliest examples of the genre.[4] Both 'Englishness' and 'pastness' are contestable criteria, however, especially the first (as I shall discuss further below); while the inclusion of saint plays, where none of the nine listed is extant and few can be unequivocally shown to denote a play (as opposed to a game or festivity), poses problems of a different kind.[5]

There is, however, a group of Tudor plays predating, and in many ways different from, the kind of play constructed in the 1590s, which I would argue have a stronger claim than saint plays to be considered as early history plays, and which merit further attention in terms both of their own specificity and importance and of the ways in which their differences from the Elizabethan form also highlight the different specificity of the later mode. Like the saint plays Griffin cites, they are no longer extant; but the extant records of performance are full enough to leave no doubt that they were certainly performed, that they can reasonably be described as 'plays' and that it is possible to construct a fairly detailed picture of what they were like. Neither 'Englishness' nor 'pastness' are criteria that can be applied in any straightforward way to admit them to the genre; but examination of these plays, together with a closer look at the defining features of later historical drama, will suggest that these criteria are too narrow to accommodate the kinds of performances that took historical matter for their content in the early modern period. Even by looking at those plays most regularly discussed as central to the genre, one might argue, for example, that the most central feature of a history play is that it should deal with actual events; and one might extend that argument to note that plays dealing with actual events usually do so in order to make their audiences think politically about the events shown and their lessons or legacy for the present day. The early plays I wish to consider fall outside the scope of Griffin's definition because their focus is international rather than purely English politics (though in every case their relevance for England is prominently displayed) and because the past they deal with is very recent and shades into the present. Yet some plays listed as history plays in Griffin's appendix (*1 Henry VI*, *King Lear*, *Macbeth*, *Cymbeline*, *If You Know Not Me You Know Nobody*, for example) are either international or British rather than, or as well as, English in focus, or deal with quite recent events.

The further ground on which the early Tudor plays might be dismissed from the category of history play is that they function in allegorical mode; yet most critics, including Griffin, admit Bale's *King Johan* to the genre of 'history play' despite its strongly allegorical bent. There is no inherent reason why allegory should be dismissed as a mode of representing real events unless its application is ambiguous, as it increasingly comes to be under Elizabeth, when the growth of censorship begins to create the need for a safety barrier between the play's apparent fiction and its political content. Where allegorical characters are also named as historical individuals, as they are in *King Johan* (in which, for example, Sedition is sometimes Stephen Langton and Dissimulation is alternately Raymundus and Simon of Swinsett) or where the allegory is otherwise open and explicit, allegory can function as a way of underlining rather than distancing the play's political message. I shall address each of these features, internationalism, 'presentness' and the allegorical dimension, within the context of performance.

The performances I propose to focus on here are three shows at the court of Henry VIII in 1518, 1522 and 1527 respectively.[6] One reason why these performances are not well known is that, as noted above, texts are not extant; and this feature also constitutes a reason for using the word 'play' with some care in this context. As descriptions of the pieces show, their boundaries can be quite fluid, making it difficult to separate them off from the other performed material that took place alongside them. On the other hand, it is precisely the presence of spoken text in these performances that leads contemporaries to begin to use words like 'play' to distinguish them from, for example, masks, mummings or disguisings, and which demands that they be taken seriously within any study of the formation of the 'history play'. The distinction between different forms, however, cannot be consistently or rigidly enforced. Terms for dramatic performance were used very loosely at the time all across Europe, as citations from foreign observers below confirm.[7]

Because these plays are neither very familiar in outline nor accessible as scripts, it is necessary to begin by summarizing what is known of their content and shape. The little we know of them is in narrative or documentary form, and derives from three sources: Hall's *Chronicle*; eye-witness letters written by foreign ambassadors; and the Revels Office accounts by Richard Gibson, Yeoman of the Revels until 1534. The reader wishing to flesh out the summary accounts provided below may therefore turn to Hall and to the Calendars of State Papers for the reign of Henry VIII for fuller details.[8] It must be borne in mind, however, that different accounts vary in their representation of each performance, and in the absence of any extant script there is no way now of establishing a definitive version.

The 1518 piece was performed in the Great Hall at Greenwich Palace on Friday, 8 October, following the signing of the Treaty of London, and the betrothal of the young Princess Mary, daughter of Henry VIII, to the infant son of Francis I. Earlier that day a solemn mass had marked the sealing of these agreements, and the Master of the Rolls had made an elegant speech in praise of the betrothal. The French guests had been feasted all day before being brought into the hall at night for the '*comedia*', as an Italian observer refers to it. (Though this word is translated as 'comedy' in the state papers, it doesn't necessarily carry the generic sense of English 'comedy', and can mean merely 'play'.) Hall's description implies that the first element is the company's vision, as they enter the hall, of 'a rock ful of al maner of stones, very artificially made', with five trees on top, bearing the arms of Rome, the Emperor, England, France and Spain, and a lady in its centre with a dolphin in her lap. Richly costumed ladies and gentlemen sit in the lower part of the rock. Ten armed knights issue out of a cave in the rock and tourney together, following which the ladies and gentlemen descend from the rock and dance. The rock then moves 'sodeynly' to receive the disguisers, closing again after they have re-entered. Finally, a figure called Report, riding a flying horse called Pegasus, comes in to explain the meaning of the show in French.

An anonymous Italian account in the Mantuan archives differs in several important respects from Hall, and paraphrases some of the script. The Italian writer describes the piece as opening with Turks beating drums and the entry of Report on his winged horse. The horse speaks, announcing that the whole world is singing on account of the newly concluded peace and marriage, the cue for a song by two children, probably two of the Chapel Children. The horse then announces the appearance of a fine castle, at which point a pageant car appears, with a castle, a rock and a gilded cave within the rock. The richly costumed ladies and gentlemen surround a little girl with a dolphin in her lap, and Report goes on to expound the tableau represented, concluding that all the world rejoices at this peace. The tourney is initiated by a Turk who challenges the truth of what Report has said, claiming that 'I, who am of the world, rejoice not at it'. When the tourney is over the pageant car returns to its place before the king, musicians play and the ladies and gentlemen descend to dance.[9]

Clarifying the meaning of the allegory was evidently a priority both of the performance itself and for those reporting it. Hall says that Report explained (in French) 'the meaning of the rocke and the trees, and the Tournay', and the Italian paraphrases the explanation: the rock is the rock of peace, the child-queen and the dolphin represent the marriage; the olive, the lily, the rose and the pomegranate represent the Pope, France, England and Spain respectively (and Hall adds that the Empire was represented by a pineapple). Their presence together on the rock of peace represents the amity between them, and the tourney demonstrates their united front against the pagans. Following the show, both accounts make clear, is a massive banquet (of one hundred courses, says the

Italian), and the king and courtiers shake comfits out of silver shakers over where the French are sitting. The king also gives away 52 silver gilt cups to the French and takes off his own rich gown of gold brocade to give to Admiral Bonnivet, the leader of the French embassy.

The 1522 piece was part of the entertainments for the Emperor Charles V, nephew of Queen Katherine of Aragon, on his visit to England to confirm an Anglo-Imperial alliance. It took place in the Great Hall at Windsor, and Hall on this occasion calls it 'a disguisyng or play'. The substance of it he condenses into less than a sentence: 'there was a proud horse which would not be tamed nor brideled, but amitie sent prudence and pollicie which tamed him, and force and puyssaunce brideled him'. Martin de Salinas, the Archduke Ferdinand's ambassador to the Imperial court, gives a much fuller account. He refers to it as a '*farça*', which is a general word for 'play', derived from French and sometimes applied to 'learned' as opposed to 'popular' plays (the distinction is comparable with that between *commedia grave* and *commedia dell'arte*). It was later replaced by '*comedia*' used in the same general sense as in Italian.[10] De Salinas's narrative concentrates mainly on reported speech, showing that spoken text was a very important aspect of the performance. It was performed by boy-players in French, he notes ('*hablaron en lengua francesa*'). Friendship, he reports, is first to enter, speaking of his great deeds in Roman times. When Prudence enters, Friendship welcomes him with great joy and forms an alliance with him. A third figure, Might, is also welcomed as a most desirable ally. Blacksmiths then enter, and a man leads on a horse so wild than none can manage him. The three allies make a bridle and encourage the man to mount the horse. He finds that the horse is now obedient, though he still holds his head very high. The allies then curb the horse further until he follows his master voluntarily wherever he goes. Both Hall and De Salinas condense the allegory into a sentence. Hall writes: 'This horse was ment by the Frenche kyng, and amitie by the king of England and themperor, and the other [persons] were their counsail and power'. De Salinas also says that: 'The horse is the King of France'. What he cannot say, he continues, is whether they have bridled and tamed him.[11] The dry reference to events outside the play is unmistakable, since in the play there is no doubting that he is tamed. The play is followed by a mask, dancing and supper.

In 1527 the play was part of the entertainments for the French embassy visiting to ratify the Treaty of Amiens and to invest Henry with the Order of St Michael on the same day as English ambassadors were investing Francis I with the Order of the Garter. The entertainments took place on Sunday, 10 November in the double banqueting house at Greenwich, built for the French embassy's arrival in May to negotiate peace terms and a marriage between Princess Mary and the second son of Francis I,[12] and refurbished for this November meeting, following a summer of ongoing negotiation between Cardinal Wolsey and Francis I in Northern France. Earlier in the day the investment ceremony had been followed by the celebration of mass, a great feast in the king's chamber and jousting in the afternoon. A banquet of 90 dishes was served in the banquet chamber, and the company moved through to the disguising chamber for the show. As in 1518, Hall begins by describing what they see when they enter the hall: a fountain at one end with a lady on top; a hawthorn tree and a mulberry tree on either side; and eight ladies sitting on benches of rosemary around the fountain. The play that followed on this occasion was in Latin and, according to Hall, 'in maner of a Tragedy'. The substance was as follows:

> the pope was in captivitie and the church broughte under the foote, wherfore S. Peter appeared and put the Cardinal in authoritie to bryng the Pope to his libertie, and to set up the church agayn, and so the Cardinall made intercession to the kinges of England and of Fraunce, that they toke part together, and by their meanes the Pope was delyvered. Then in came the French kynges chyldren, and complayned to the Cardinal, how the Emperour kept them as hostages and wold not come to no reasonable point with their father, wherfore thei desyred the Cardinal to helpe for their deliveraunce, which wrought so wyth the kyng hys mayster and the French kyng that he brought the Emperor to a peace, and caused the two yong princes to be delyvered.

Don Iñigo de Mendoça, the Imperial ambassador in England, summarizes it very similarly, though he was not invited to attend the play, so his report must be secondhand.[13] '[T]he whole argument', he writes, tended 'to show that the Emperor was an Enemy of England'. In fact, it seems that the *dramatis personae* and action of the play were probably much fuller and richer than either narrative suggests, since Richard Gibson's Revels account for this event survives, listing characters and costumes for the entertainment, including 'an oratur in apparell of golld'; Religion, Ecclesia and Veritas 'lyke iii wowessys [vowesses] in garmentes of syllke and vayelles of laun and sypers'; Heresy, False Interpretation and Corruptio 'lyke ladyes of beem [Bohemia] inperelld in garmentes of syllke of dyvers kolours'; 'the errytyke lewter [heretic Luther] lyke a party freer in russet damaske and blake taffata lewters wyef lyke a frow of spyers in almayn in red sylke'; Peter, Paul and James; the Dauphin and his brothers; Lady Peace, Lady Quietness and Dame Tranquillity.[14] Again the play was followed by masks and dancing.

This courtly context of performance, in which the boundaries of the play are relatively fluid and its shape is not fully understood except within the larger shape of the revels and ceremonies that precede and follow it, is perhaps the most dominant trait distinguishing the Henrician history play from the Elizabethan history play. Not only is the Elizabethan history play strongly associated with the public theatres, but there is very little evidence to associate any Elizabethan or Jacobean history play with court performance at all. To say this is of course to beg questions, since so many of the records of court performances fail to name the title or specify the kind of play performed. We cannot say with any certainty that Queen Elizabeth never saw a history play. Yet amongst the numerous titles recorded it is at least suggestive that the history play is apparently so conspicuous by its absence in the later period. No history play at all is recorded as performed at court during the reign of Elizabeth, and only three history plays, all Shakespeare's, are known to have been performed at the courts of James and Charles, 1603–42.[15] This absence of recorded interest in history plays at the court of Elizabeth I, together with their notable popularity in the London theatres of the 1590s, makes a pointed comparison with the Henrician plays under consideration here, which are fully incorporated into the wealth, ostentation and political agenda of courtly performance in the widest sense.

Within a courtly context, as we have seen, the boundaries between one form of entertainment and another, and between fictional and non-fictional performance, are not always clear, and this is not accidental, but intentional. Diplomatic negotiations are themselves quite appropriately seen by contemporaries as performances; and events confirming or celebrating important agreements form a continuum leading from the negotiating table to the banqueting table. In 1518, for example, the signing of the treaty leads naturally into the celebration of solemn mass, the oration in praise of peace, the allegorical representation of the agreement in a rich tableau and in chivalric action, the dancing of the maskers, the dancing of the wider court, the ongoing and recurrent feasting and the presentation of rich gifts to the French ambassadors. Legal, religious, festive and allegorical ways of confirming the agreement slide into one another in ways that allow both parties to display that agreement, to celebrate its advantages and to reinforce and insist

on their new-found sense of alliance through revelling publicly, osten-
tatiously and at length.

Despite the seamlessness of this festivity in one sense, however, it is
also the case that we can pick out the shape of the evolving history
play to varying degrees from within these narratives, depending on
how the reporters note the points at which one shape closes and
another begins. The 1518 entertainment contains strong elements of
mask and disguising in its form, blending traditions of pageant-car
tableau, emblematic movement and dance with speech; and the two
surviving accounts, as we have seen, differ in how they mark its beginning and ending. Hall's account, in which the guests enter the hall
and see the decorated rock, hovers between tradition and innovation
in that, while the rock and the maskers are familiar elements of the
mask and the disguising, the more usual way of beginning either of
these would be for the rock and its inhabitants to enter the hall to the
already-assembled company. Hall's description of its ending, however,
marked by Report's speech declaring 'the meaning of the rocke and the
tree, and the Tournay', differentiates it from the mask (in which the
maskers would normally move from scripted movement into dancing
with the company), though not necessarily from the disguising (to
which William Cornish had introduced the possibility of spoken text,
especially expounding the meaning of the pageant, in 1501). Sometimes,
indeed, where Hall's account of a disguising does not mention scripted
speech and constructs the ending as the point where the disguisers
return to the pageant-car and are conveyed out of the hall, Gibson's
accounts show that somewhere in the piece the meaning was made clear
'by proses [process] of speche'.[16]

In the Italian narrative, by contrast, a speech by Pegasus, the winged
horse, precedes the entry of the rock, which is, furthermore, revealed
by the lowering of a curtain. Pegasus announces his reason for coming
(having heard of 'this peace and marriage'); introduces a song by two
children in praise of both; and resumes his speech, which in turn cues
the entry of the pageant car:

> 'You will now see a fine castle. We shall see who will be able to explain
> it;' and immediately after a curtain had been lowered, a handsome
> triumphal car appeared, with a castle and a rock, all green within and
> gilded.

The use of a curtain, a feature clearly demarcating a point of transition within the evening's revels, is only documented at one earlier

entertainment, the Golden Arbour Disguising of 1511; and its next reappearance is in May 1527, when both Hall and Gasparo Spinelli, the secretary to the Venetian embassy, note its use.[17] The Italian also represents the ending of the 1518 piece differently from Hall, as marked by the descent of the ladies and gentlemen to dance before the company.

Both these accounts may be interestingly compared with Hall's descriptions of the later entertainments of 1522 and 1527, where, although the same slippage from one level of entertainment to the next remains visible, Hall's language marks the 'play' more clearly as an entity, making a strong distinction between 'play' and 'mask', one following the other, as two visibly separate entities. In 1522, he writes, there took place on the Sunday night 'a disguisyng or play'; and 'after this play ended was a sumptuous Maske'. In 1527 the play is similarly marked out from the rest of the evening as 'playd [...] by children in the Latin tongue in maner of Tragedy' and Hall describes the reaction to it before going on to recount what followed in a new paragraph:

> At this play wisemen smiled and thought that it sounded more glorious to the Cardinall, then true to the matter in deede.
>   When the playe was done, and .iiii. companies of maskers daunsed, the King [and others]...entered with noyse of minstrelsy and toke the ladies that sat about the fountayne and daunsed wyth them very lustely.

Other accounts of 1522 and 1527 are equally clear about the beginning and end of the play as constituting an entity and a generic shape in itself. Martin de Salinas, writing in 1522, says that a French *'farça'* took place as part of the celebrations after dinner. Having described its action, he concludes: *'E ansy hubo fin la farça'* ('In this way the *farça* ended'), and moves on to describe the dancing that follows. Don Iñigo de Mendoça, writing in 1527, describes the *farça* as following the dancing, summarizes its argument and moves on to a different subject altogether.

Two features in particular make it possible to define the play as a distinct entity in this way. One is spoken text; and in each of these performances it is additionally the case that the text of the play is in a language other than English, a point that will be returned to, though here it is sufficient to note the clarity with which the move into a different language frames the event as separate from what surrounds it. The second is content: the pieces are perceived as having a meaning or an agenda, and in each case that content centres on recent or contemporary international events and the meaning is political. While contemporaries struggle with fluid and variant terminology, ranging from farce to tragedy, it is this shared focus on actual, historical events and the shared sense of representing these events for a political purpose that invites us to consider them after the fact as history plays. They undoubtedly share the first of these features and arguably share the second with all later history plays, but there are some important distinctions in approach between the Henrician and the Elizabethan plays in question.

As noted above, these Henrician plays differ from what is usually conceived of as the 'characteristic' Elizabethan history play by virtue of their contemporaneity, their internationalism and the allegorical cast of their material. In pursuing these distinctions, it is worth considering first where our notions of what is 'characteristic' about the Elizabethan history play come from. The short answer, of course, is Shakespeare. Shakespeare wrote ten plays classified as histories in the First Folio and was very influential on the development of the genre during the 1590s. It is also the case that most scholars reading history plays by Shakespeare's predecessors tend to read them back through the lens of Shakespeare's work, not least because several of them are either direct sources for Shakespeare or deal with similar material. And both these factors in turn have contributed to the later sense of what constitutes a history play in the early modern period. Thus Shakespeare's characteristic focus on the reigns of individual English kings living prior to his own lifetime and on the reverberations for and within England of their actions is seen as typical of the genre.[18]

There are reasons why this focus on England, Englishness and earlier history made particular sense within the context of 1590s public theatre. The audience was popular and English; the language of the plays was English; England was at war; and censorship legislation, virtually non-existent in the reign of Henry VIII, sought to prevent the stage from meddling in contemporary politics. Yet public theatre from the 1580s to beyond the closing of the theatres also embraced plays that took contemporary or near-contemporary events as their subject and that sometimes adopted an international perspective. But plays such as *The Massacre at Paris* (1593), *The Battle of Alcazar* (1588–9), *Captain Thomas Stukeley* (1596), *A Larum for London* (*c.* 1594–1600) and *Sir John van Olden Barnavelt* (1619), are not routinely classified as history plays. By tacit agreement, it seems, scholars have decided to exclude from the definition of the history play those kinds of plays that least resemble the Shakespearean model.

Yet there can be no doubt that the early Tudor entertainments outlined above arise out of a powerful sense of history in the making, situating themselves in an active present that primarily represents the participants as shaping the future, while including a sense of the past that has worked to shape the present moment. Sometimes there can be a hovering between past and future arising out of the flexible functioning of allegory, which does not need to clarify how much of what it shows is past and how much is to come (a hovering comparable with the 'open-endedness' that has been identified as a feature of later history plays).[19] Thus Martin de Salinas, responding to the allegory of 1522, expresses doubt about whether the French king has really been tamed. Yet the play, as he describes it, though showing the taming of the French king, does not necessarily claim that this position has already been reached, since its allegorical cast removes it from any rigid equation with real events or real time. It may, on the contrary, seek to inspire its audience with the desirability and possibility of reaching the position it puts on view.

It is certainly the case that all three pieces have strong political agendas, and that the way they represent the past has everything to do with the way they wish to celebrate the present and influence the future. Their stance is typically optimistic, celebratory and hortatory, showing the aims and ideals of the assembled company as though they were already achieved. Thus the 1518 piece encourages a sense of alliance between English and French by whipping up their animus against the Turks in a staged combat showing France and England uniting in battle against them. No Turkish crusade ever took place, and, though some extant documents show quite detailed plans for it, the letters of Sebastian Giustinian, the Venetian ambassador, make clear that a measure of false rhetoric was an expected part of even the more serious proceedings regarding the phrasing of the treaty. His concern, given that Venice was exposed to a much more real Turkish threat than either England or France, was that the wording of the treaty should not provoke unnecessary hostility which might endanger Venice, while functioning as mere empty rhetoric for England and France, who might (and did) fail to carry through their proposed military action against Turkey. He thus negotiated for the removal of an anti-Turkish preamble, and found the English quite willing to concede the point.[20] The projected Turkish crusade, however, created the opportunity for spectacular viewing, inspiring collective good will amongst an international audience by uniting them in hostility to an outside group through imaginary combat with that group.

In 1522 and 1527, however, the relation between past and future and between the worlds of factual reality and dramatic fiction was differently nuanced. Martin de Salinas's reaction in 1522 reflects precisely on the non-fit between the play's represented action and action in the real world, past and present: 'The horse is the King of France. Whether they have bridled and tamed him he is unable to say.' But the 1518 performance demonstrates that the kind of political drama the court was beginning to commission might choose to stage imaginary futures for diplomatic reasons. De Salinas may or may not have been used to seeing a drama that could treat time in this fluid way. The 1527 play is an even more complex and interesting example of how the boundaries between past, present and future might be deliberately blurred for political ends. It brings together events that have taken place over the past two years with their projected outcomes in a way that seems not to have distinguished between their status within the dramatic narrative. The Emperor's capture of the Pope, dramatized early in the play, had taken place following the Sack of Rome in May 1527; a French embassy was in England negotiating an alliance at that same moment in May, an alliance now further confirmed by this November embassy; the Pope's escape from captivity the following month was to remove the possibility of a heroic rescue by an Anglo-French alliance;[21] and Francis I's sons, delivered as hostages to the Emperor as a condition of Francis's own release in 1526, were not finally returned to France until 1530. Once again, as in 1522, the recorded reaction is one that expresses a worldly-wise scepticism about the gap between fact and fiction: 'At this play wisemen smiled and thought that it sounded more glorious to the Cardinall, then true to the matter in deede'. Marco Antonio Vener was cynical at a more practical level, offering his opinion in a letter to the Doge and Signory of Venice that all the honours lavished on the French ambassadors on this occasion were part of a campaign aimed at getting help from France at a time of grain shortage in England.[22] These remarks, taken together with De Salinas's comment in 1522, suggest a well-informed, discriminating and sophisticated audience, who understood perfectly well that the role of this kind of entertainment was precisely to dress things up for the occasion rather than to provide a factual representation, and were well attuned to seeing and assessing the difference.

Even without these recorded reactions, we would be likely to judge the audience on these occasions as a sophisticated and knowledgeable one. Certain key features distinguish it markedly from the later audiences of history plays. Besides the fact that it was elite rather than popular, it was also international rather than English and notable for the presence within it of some of the key players represented allegorically on stage.[23] Cardinal Wolsey, for example, is represented quite explicitly by the figure of the cardinal in the 1527 play. Henry VIII is figured in three different ways in these three pieces: emblematically in the static image of the rose tree in 1518, allegorically as a character (or part of one) in the figure of Amity in 1522 and literally, as himself, in 1527. Amongst the international figures portrayed, those currently allied with England would be present either in person or represented by their ambassadors (Charles V in 1522; French ambassadors in 1518 and 1527). Those condemned and abused would usually not be present, and their ambassadors might be pointedly snubbed by the absence of an invitation or might stay away from choice, anticipating the tenor of what was to come. Thus De Mendoça, the Imperial ambassador in 1527, is absent from the performance and reports the performance reported to him with emphasis on its representation and abuse of the Empire, noting the role of Gattinara, the Emperor's Chancellor, in agreeing to peace, and reporting that 'the Spaniards were called *barbarians*, and the Emperor a *tyrant*'.[24]

A wide and international range of educated men, many with diplomatic experience, would also be present. Besides the English courtiers who fell into this category and would always be well represented at such an event, the international audience was wider than just the members of the visiting embassy and their entourage. In 1518, for example, many more countries were included in the treaty than simply the English and the French, and contemporaries wrote of it in terms of a 'universal peace'.[25] Though only the French embassy was there specifically with a view to signing the treaty with England at that point, both Spain and Venice had resident ambassadors at the English court by this time, and other international visitors might be present at any given time for a number of different reasons. We know from the Venetian ambassador's letters, for example, that Cardinal Lorenzo Campeggio (the papal legate) and the Danish ambassador were present in October 1518 in addition to the visiting French embassy and the resident ambassadors.

This internationalism had various constraints and effects on the nature of the plays produced. First, it meant that the language of the play was not, as it mainly was in popular theatre, the national vernacular. So, of these three plays, the first two are in French and the third in Latin; none is in English. Language in this kind of performance thus seems to be more a matter of fashion, compliment and cultural signification than of comprehensibility and accessibility, though the latter may have had some lesser relevance on occasion. More generally, French had long been the second language of the court in England; and Latin had an even longer history as the language of the European church, of international scholarship and of international diplomacy and correspondence. These wider contexts framed the more specific contexts of the events themselves and their distinctive, occasional, international flavour. Thus, while the use of French in 1518 may have included an aspect of courtesy and compliment to the visiting embassy, it cannot have had that precise flavour in 1522, when the French were the subject of the play's animosity. Perhaps on that occasion French was simply the most widely shared language amongst the gathered community of the English court and the Emperor's entourage; but it may also have carried some degree of compliment, despite the shared hostility towards France, since it was the Emperor's own first language.

The choice of Latin in 1527 represents more of an innovation. It was around this time that Wolsey was beginning to introduce performances of classical plays at court, but this was the first contemporary play to be performed at court in Latin.[26] It is likely, then, that the use of Latin on this occasion primarily signalled sophistication, high fashion and elegance, aiming to display the English court's capacity to match its European neighbours in stylish display. What emerges most clearly from the language of these court performances, by contrast with that of the later English history play, is the sense of England signalling its role as an international power addressing a courtly European elite, as opposed to an England addressing shared national concerns in the later public playhouses.

The shared perspective of international European diplomacy is also what allows and encourages allegory as a mode of dramaturgy in the early English history play. Images like the maiden embracing the dolphin or the bridled horse signify clearly not only because the visual medium cuts through any linguistic difficulties, but because the community reading those images shares the same concerns and can thus recognize the correspondences between the images and the political issues they mediate. To some extent this is a matter of recognizing familiar and relatively unchanging correspondences, such as that between France and the lily or England and the rose; but, at a more detailed and transient level, it is also a matter of forming part of a group that becomes familiar with certain allegorical features through exposure to the same images in different European contexts and venues. Thus, in November 1527, for example, many of those present at the Greenwich revels would already have seen images of the captured Pope and the peace-loving Cardinal over the preceding months since the Sack of Rome in May. On 13 June, a mere five weeks after the event, the French performed a play of *The Ruin of Rome* before a visiting English embassy at the Parisian court; and during July and August, while Wolsey was progressing from Calais to Amiens, street pageants at Boulogne, Montreuil, Abbeville and Amiens itself offered Wolsey images of himself as peacemaker.[27]

Hall's account of the pageants for Wolsey at Boulogne in 1527 gives some indication of how heavy-handed and obvious the allegory was:

> And at the gate was made a pageaunte in the whiche was a Nonne called holy churche, and thre Spaniardes and thre Almaynes had her violated, and a Cardinall her reskued, and set her up of newe agayne.

> Another Pageaunte, was a Cardinall gevyng a Paxe to the Kyng of England and the French kyng in token of peace, a nother Pageant was the Pope, liyng under, and the Emperour sittyng in his Majestie, and a Cardinall pulled downe the Emperoure, and set up the Pope.

His closing comment, furthermore, provides another example of just how confidently a knowing audience could dismiss such emphasis as the obvious flattery it was:

> When wise men sawe this Pagiaunt, thei smiled and saied, well, can the Frenche kyng flatter, for harde it were for one Cardinall to subdue him that hath pulled downe the master of all Cardinalles.[28]

Just as Martin de Salinas smiled at the notion that England and the Empire could bridle France, so 'wise men' on this occasion knew the distance between allegorical images and hard facts, and understood clearly that the one sought to enhance the other.

The allegorical mode combines crafted delicacy with hammer-blow clarity. The images themselves are elaborately worked out, the correspondences are part of an elite code that requires a relatively informed audience to interpret their visual language, yet within those parameters the message is delivered with unmistakable emphasis. Even a mere list of characters and costumes can make this emphasis clear: Luther costumed 'lyke a party freer' and his wife in German costume leave us in no doubt of the play's anti-Lutheran stance; and the Imperial ambassador's report that 'the Spaniards were called *barbarians*, and the Emperor a *tyrant*' suggests that this emphasis also extended to language. Allegory, in other words, was not in any sense a device for concealment, but a way of depicting a political stance very forcefully; and this is another distinguishing element between early and later Tudor history plays. Whereas, within the knowing and in some sense intimate sphere of the European elite, the purpose of allegory was precisely to appeal to the shared sense of what the gathered viewing community already knew and felt, its purpose in the later public theatre could sometimes be quite different.

By 1581 successive statutes and proclamations had sought to restrict the remit of popular drama, ruling against its tendency to deal with matters of politics and religion and seeking to restrict this kind of drama to elite circles, where it was felt to be safer to express such views (though the presence of ambassadors must also have influenced the kinds of material that could be performed at court on any given occasion). The first such statute, forbidding the performance or printing of plays contrary to religious doctrine, was passed later in the reign of Henry VIII, in 1540; and it may be no accident that it was passed so soon after the performance of Bale's *King Johan*, one performance of which is on record precisely because of the trouble it caused by arousing the audience to strong feeling against the Roman church (see further below).

In 1549 the Act of Uniformity forbade interludes containing matter 'depraving or despising' the new Book of Common Prayer; and later that same year, as a result of the Kett rebellion, which followed the assembly of a large crowd at Wymondham, Norfolk, to see a performance of some kind, a proclamation was issued warning people not to 'openly or secretly play in the English tongue any kind of interlude, play, dialogue or other matter set forth in form of play, in any place, public or private, within this realm' for a period of three months.[29] Further similar proclamations forbidding unlicensed playing of interludes or plays on religious subject matter were issued in 1551 and 1553. Language, which could be discussed with reference to court performances between 1518 and 1527 in terms of a diplomatic politics of courtesy and compliment, thus became a tool of class politics. If a play was performed in English, it was probably being performed to lower-class audiences, perceived by the authorities as volatile, dangerous and ready to rebel; hence, matter that could be freely performed in Latin, to a safely select audience, might not be allowed to be performed in English.

When Elizabeth came to the throne in 1558, she lost no time in issuing a proclamation 'Prohibiting Unlicensed Interludes and Plays, Especially on Religion or Policy' which outlawed any play 'wherein either matters of religion or of the governance of the estate of the commonweal shall be handled or treated, being no meet matters to be written or treated upon but by men of authority, learning, and wisdom, nor to be handled before any audience but of grave and discreet persons'; and by 1581 full powers to censor the performance of plays were invested in the Master of the Revels.[30]

It was under these conditions that players came to realize a different function for allegory, one that might protect them from both censorship and punishment; and thus it is that allegory ceases to play a role *within* the history play as history itself *becomes* the allegory. Within a regime which forbids plays to dramatize matters of contemporary politics or religion, the apparently literal dramatization of historical events and concerns can become a veil for dramatizing contemporary events and concerns. Elizabeth and her government of course knew this; and Elizabeth not only recognized Richard II as allegorically representing her ('I am Richard II, know ye not that?'), but also saw the Essex rebellion as partly incited by performances on the subject ('this tragedy was played 40 times in open streets and houses').[31] The writing and performance of history thus became an increasingly risky activity, and government edicts began to legislate specifically against the printing of historiography. Although legislation controlling performance never specifically singled out history plays (presumably because the injunctions against dealing with matters of politics or religion were already so inclusive, in addition to the absence of the term or category itself), one of the factors likely to have inhibited the production of history plays was the issuing of an injunction in 1599 against the printing of English histories unless first licensed by the Privy Council. John Hayward, whose *First Part of the Life and Raigne of King Henrie IIII*, dedicated to the Earl of Essex, was suppressed in that year, was himself investigated for seditious intention in 1599, imprisoned in the Tower following Essex's fall from the queen's favour in 1600 and not released until after the queen's death in 1603. As he wrote some years later,

> men might safely write of others in manner of a tale; but in manner of a history, safely they could not: because, albeit they should write of men long since dead, and whose posterity is clean worn out; yet some alive, finding themselves foul in those vices which they see observed, reproved, and condemned in others, their guiltiness maketh them apt to conceive, that, whatsoever the words are, the finger pointeth only at them.[32]

The difference between the two groups of history plays is thus not that one group had a political agenda while the other had not. Both groups had a political agenda, differently situated and addressed; the crucial and determining point of difference is audience. The early court play addressed a social and international elite, many of whom were active participants in the decision-making processes of international politics, while the Elizabethan commercial-theatre history play addressed a popular audience that included those seen by government as potentially disruptive and rebellious. Bale's *King Johan* represents something of a turning point for the history play in that it is the earliest extant history play that sought to bridge the gap between these two audiences. *King Johan*, performed in 1538–9, was certainly played in the household of Archbishop Cranmer before an elite audience of his guests; but the fact that Bale's company was sponsored by Thomas Cromwell suggests the probability that it may have been taken on tour very deliberately to play to a wider and lower-class audience. Cromwell recognized early on the power of drama to reach and teach a widely illiterate nation. He understood that drama could be a weapon of state propaganda as easily as a weapon of opposition and consciously organized a campaign of Reformist drama to try to gain popular acceptance for a radical religious policy. Records of performance by Cromwell's Men are wide and varied in terms of both topography and social class; and, while most records cannot be tied to a particular play, the one other certainly recorded venue for performance of *King Johan*, St Stephen's Church in Canterbury, would have reached a much wider audience than Cranmer's household.[33]

Yet the experience of sponsoring drama for purposes of government propaganda must have been a mixed one for those seeking, like Cromwell, to control it; for public performance is an unstable, unpredictable event, and performance before a popular audience especially so. Dramatists themselves, especially when they are actively committed to the cause in which they write, as Bale was, may seek to move further and faster than government; and some of the positions Bale adopts in his writing must have caused Cromwell some political embarrassment and may have seemed to call the wisdom of using drama for propaganda purposes into question. Indeed, without Cromwell's protection, Bale would almost certainly have been punished for heresy. By his own account Cromwell rescued him more than once from prosecution on account of his plays.[34]

It is hardly surprising, then, that government legislation increasingly sought to forbid dramatists and players to deal with questions of religion and politics, nor that the London authorities sought to control and restrict performances within the city. The relatively sudden growth of a mass popular audience in London with the establishment of permanent commercial playhouses created a newly volatile political situation which both sides had to learn to deal with. As dramatists and companies tried to negotiate prohibitive legislation via allegory and history, government reacted differently in different circumstances, sometimes issuing new proclamations and imprisoning or punishing offenders, sometimes turning a blind eye, as when the political or religious content toed the government's current line. History plays are always political acts. How they are received depends on what content is played to whom.

The early Tudor history plays examined here were more than political acts: they were negotiating tools, seeking to steer and affirm political decisions and international relations. They dealt freely and explicitly with all the matters forbidden to the later public theatre by statute and proclamation, and could do so precisely because the audience was so different. Whereas a mass popular audience made the history play a volatile and dangerous commodity, it was, before an international diplomatic audience, a useful and practical way of fixing alliances, expressing hostility towards oppositional or enemy groups and spelling out the directions of future policy. And, perhaps even more importantly, it was not merely a useful tool, but a magnificent one; and magnificence had its own functionality, to which clarity was probably secondary. A court that could mount the spectacular display within which these plays figured was by implication a major power, capable of committing the kind of resources that could make any international enterprise, including military enterprise, successful. And a court whose revels drew on the most exciting and innovative aspects of staging and dramatic form (as in the staging of indoor tourneying, the introduction of a curtain, the incorporation of classicism, and so on), and on the talents of some of the best craftsmen in Europe, was also demonstrating its worthiness to be considered alongside the courts of mightier states. The history play in the context of the early Tudor court thus functioned as part of a wider statement about how England saw itself as an international power and how it sought to project its foreign policy. Its emphasis was much more on the future than on the past. If we seek to distinguish the early Tudor from the later Elizabethan history play by way of their specific use of history, we might say that, whereas the Elizabethan form characteristically sought to use history to explore the nuances of the present moment, the early Tudor form sought consciously to shape history by showing how the forces of past and present could move into the future in practical and particular ways.

As Paulina Kewes has shown, the category of the history play, as used by modern critics, is a matter of shared practice rather than clear theoretical definition, and there is thus no justification for its over-rigid imposition:

> What is to be gained by drawing a line between dramatic works which should be described as history plays and those which should not? If we want to understand the place and uses of history in early modern drama, we should be willing to consider any play, irrespective of its formal shape or fictional element, which represents, or purports to represent, a historical past, native or foreign, distant or recent (sometimes very recent). It makes sense, in other words, to treat *Richard II, The Massacre at Paris, Julius Caesar*, and *James IV* as Elizabethan history plays, since all four portray, or – in the case of *James IV* – affect to portray, figures and events drawn from history: of medieval England (and Wales and Ireland), late sixteenth-century France, late republican Rome, and early sixteenth-century Scotland (and England) respectively.[35]

Kewes goes on to argue that we should properly consider history plays alongside 'other modes of staging history', such as coronation and mayoral pageants, jousts, Garter ceremonies and entertainments on royal progresses. The early Tudor entertainments examined here straddle the categories of 'play', 'pageant' and 'entertainment' instructively, showing us how, even as the category of 'play' is barely distinct, and only just beginning to emerge from within a broader category of court performance, it is nevertheless capable of transmitting to the audience a powerful sense of history in the making, situating itself in an active present that represents the participants as shaping the future, while including a sense of the past that has worked to shape the present moment. Whether or not we choose to include these plays within the category of the history play, a category which post-dates even the plays commonly seen as core to its identity, we must surely recognize that they have much to teach us about an early modern understanding of how history is made.

Notes

I am grateful to the Folger Library for providing the time and resources for me to begin researching this essay in August 2001.

1. David Bevington, *Tudor Drama and Politics: a Critical Approach to Topical Meaning* (Cambridge, MA: Harvard University Press, 1968).
2. See Benjamin Griffin, *Playing the Past: Approaches to English Historical Drama, 1385–1600* (Woodbridge: Brewer, 2001), Appendix B and cf. Paulina Kewes, 'The Elizabethan History Play: a True Genre?', *A Companion to Shakespeare's Works, Vol. II: The Histories*, ed. Richard Dutton and Jean E. Howard (Oxford: Blackwell, 2003), esp. pp. 170–1.
3. Samuel Johnson, preface to his edition of Shakespeare's plays (1765), in *Dr Johnson on Shakespeare*, ed. W. E. Wimsatt (Harmondsworth: Penguin, 1969), p. 63.
4. Griffin, *Playing the Past*, p. 21.
5. As Lawrence Clopper has pointed out, not all references to a '*ludus*' with a saint's name refer to a saint's play. 'None of the citations for Becket plays in the literature', he argues, 'is secure' (*Drama, Play, and Game: English Festive Culture in the Medieval and Early Modern Period* (Chicago and London: University of Chicago Press, 2001), p. 132; and see further ch. 3). Seven out of nine of Griffin's listed saint plays are these Becket citations. For further discussion of this question, see the contributions to *Early Theatre*, 2 (1999), 97–116.
6. These are not the only contenders for the category of 'history play' in the early period, but they are the best documented and the most directly comparable with one another. One might also compare them, for example, with the play performed at Gray's Inn at Christmas 1526–7 which Cardinal Wolsey read as aimed at him (see Hall in Janette Dillon, *Performance and Spectacle in Hall's Chronicle* (London: Society for Theatre Research, 2002), p. 121), or with the play performed in January 1528 at Wolsey's residence, following the Pope's release from captivity (see Spinelli's letter in the *Calendar of State Papers, Venetian*, ed. Rawdon Brown et al. (London: Longman, 1864–1947), IV, #225, pp. 115–16; *I Diarii di Marino Sanuto*, ed. Rinaldo Fulin et al., 58 vols (Venice: La R. Deputazione Veneta di Storia Patria, 1879–1902), XLVI, cols. 595–7; and cf. n. 21 below).
7. This is broadly true regardless of Hall's famous description of the mask as an innovation in England in 1512, and despite my own attempt to distinguish between mask and disguising below. See further Dillon, *Performance and Spectacle*, pp. 8–9, 43, 194 and W. R. Streitberger, *Court Revels, 1485–1559* (Toronto, Buffalo and London: University of Toronto Press, 1994), p. 4.
8. Hall's narratives may be found either in *Hall's Chronicle*, ed. Henry Ellis (London: Johnson, 1809) or in the edited selection given in Dillon, *Performance and Spectacle*, where commentary is also provided, including extracts from the other extant accounts. For the 1518 performance, readers should consult Ellis, *Hall's Chronicle*, p. 595; Dillon, *Performance and Spectacle*, pp. 65–7; and the anonymous Italian account summarized in *CSP Venetian*, pp. 466–7; for the 1522 performance Ellis, *Hall's Chronicle*, p. 641; Dillon, *Performance and Spectacle*, pp. 112–13; and the letter of Martin de Salinas in the *Calendar of State Papers Spanish*, ed. G. A. Bergenroth, Pascual de Gayangos and Martin A. S. Hume (London: Longman, 1862–1954), II, #437, pp. 444–5; and for the 1527 performance Ellis, *Hall's Chronicle*, p. 735; Dillon, *Performance and Spectacle*, p. 131; and the letter of Iñigo de Mendoça, the Imperial Ambassador, in *CSP Spanish*, III.ii, #240, pp. 458–9. Gibson's accounts are unpublished in full, but are summarized and extracted in *Letters*

and Papers Foreign and Domestic, of the Reign of Henry VIII, 1509–47, ed. J. S. Brewer, James Gairdner and R. H. Brodie (London: HMSO, 1862–1910; 1920). In the case of Hall, the fuller narratives surrounding these accounts are of relevance; and Sydney Anglo (*Spectacle, Pageantry, and Early Tudor Policy*, 2nd edn (Oxford: Clarendon Press 1997)), W. R. Streitberger (*Court Revels*) and Greg Walker (*Plays of Persuasion: Drama and Politics at the Court of Henry VIII* (Cambridge: Cambridge University Press, 1991), ch. 1) offer especially useful discussions of both the performances and the surrounding events.

9. I am very grateful to Daniela Ferrari, Director of the State Archive of Mantua, for sending me a copy of the manuscript of this letter (Gonzaga 579).

10. I am extremely grateful here to Clara Calvo and Angel Luis Pujante at the University of Murcia for advising me on the original Spanish of De Salinas's letter, and in particular on the implications of the different terms in use during the period. De Salinas's letters are published in Spanish in *El emperador Carlos V y su corte según las cartas de Don Martin de Salinas, embajador del infante Don Fernando (1522–1539)*, ed. Antonio Rodriguez Villa (Madrid: Fortanet, 1903). The translation in the *Calendar of Spanish State Papers* is rather loose, however, and I am indebted to Clara Calvo for a more literal translation of the Spanish.

11. The translation in the Spanish state papers is misleading here. Before the sentence stating that the horse is the King of France, the translator gives this sentence: 'The meaning of it is clear'. De Salinas in fact writes *'La moralidad della queda á v.md.'* ('The moral of it is up to you').

12. The marriage projected between Princess Mary and the Dauphin in 1518 did not come to completion. This time the proposal was to marry the Princess to either Francis I or his second son, the Duke of Orleans, depending on the outcome of further negotiations between Francis I and Charles V, which included a possible marriage contract between Francis and Charles's sister, Eleanor.

13. *CSP Spanish*, III.ii., #66, p. 182.

14. BL MS Egerton 2605, f. 22ᵛ. Sydney Anglo transcribes Gibson's account in full in *Spectacle*, pp. 232–3. See also the summary of Gibson's account in *Letters and Papers*, IV.ii, #3564, pp. 1604–6.

15. The three plays are *Henry V* (performed January 1605), *Richard III* (performed November 1633) and *1 Henry IV* (performed 1612–13, 1625, and possibly also 1631 and 1637). *2 Henry IV* may also have been performed in 1612–13. It is also just possible that *The Tragedy of the King of Scots*, performed at court in 1567, may have had some of the features of a history play. See John Astington, *English Court Theatre 1558–1642* (Cambridge: Cambridge University Press, 1999), Appendix: 'Performances at court 1558–1642'. The apocryphal story about Queen Elizabeth commanding Shakespeare to write a play depicting Falstaff in love would of course suggest her familiarity with one or more of the *Henry IV* plays and *Henry V*, but the earliest version of that story does not appear until 1702 (S. Schoenbaum, *William Shakespeare: a Compact Documentary Life* (Oxford, London and New York: Oxford University Press, 1977), pp. 196–7).

16. The quotation is from Gibson's account of the Twelfth Night disguising of 1515, 'the pavyllyon un the plas parlos' (PRO E36/217, f. 209).

17. Hall describes the occasion in 1511 as follows: 'Within a littell whyle after [the king's] departing, the trompettes at thende of the Hall began to blowe. Then was there a device or a pageaunt upon wheles brought in, out of the whiche pageaunt issued out a gentelman rychelye appareiled, that shewed, how in a garden of pleasure there was an arber of golde, wherein were lordes and ladies, muche desirous to shew pleasure and pastime to the Quene and ladies, if they might be licenced so to do, who was answered by the Quene, how she and all other there were very desirous to se theim and their pastime: then a greate clothe of Arras that did hange before thesame pageaunt was taken a waye, and the pageaunt brought more nere, it was curiously made and plesaunt to beholde' (Dillon, *Performance and Spectacle*, p. 40). For the May 1527 entertainment see Dillon, *Performance and Spectacle*, p. 125; *CSP Venetian*, IV, #105, p. 60; and Sanuto, *I Diarii*, XV, cols 265–70. On the use of the stage curtain see W. J. Lawrence, 'The Story of a Peculiar Stage Curtain', in *The Elizabethan Playhouse and Other Studies* (Stratford-upon-Avon: Shakespeare Head Press, 1912), pp. 111–21.
18. Richard Helgerson has recently illustrated the 'systematic and repeated' ways in which Shakespeare's history plays differ from those of his contemporaries ('Shakespeare and Contemporary Dramatists of History', *A Companion to Shakespeare's Works, Vol. II: The Histories*, pp. 26–47 (p. 43)).
19. See Susan Snyder, 'The Genres of Shakespeare's Plays', in *The Cambridge Companion to Shakespeare*, ed. Margreta de Grazia and Stanley Wells (Cambridge: Cambridge University Press, 2001), pp. 83–97 (pp. 91–2) and Kewes, 'Elizabethan History Play', pp. 177–8.
20. On the planned crusade, see e.g. *LP*, II.ii., #3815–17, pp. 1195–8. For the Venetian Ambassador's letters, see *Four Years at the Court of Henry VIII*, ed. Rawdon Brown, 2 vols (London: Smith, Elder, 1854), II.210–35.
21. On the circumstances of the Pope's escape, see further Judith Hook, *The Sack of Rome, 1527* (London and Basingstoke: Macmillan, 1972), ch. 14. The event also provoked another history play, this time staged at Wolsey's (see Streitberger, *Court Revels*, p. 135). It was Wolsey's last recorded revel before his fall.
22. *CSP Venetian*, IV, #208, p. 108.
23. In describing the audience as elite rather than popular I am making a broad distinction between the court and the public theatre. Yet, while it is undoubtedly the case that the highest social echelon in Europe constituted the dominant element in the court audience and was the group at whom the entertainment was primarily targeted, there is much work remaining to be done on the full range of those in attendance at court spectacles. Hall regularly blames the 'rude and common people' for stripping costumes and pageant-cars of their expensive ornaments after the performance (e.g. Dillon, *Performance and Spectacle*, pp. 24–5).
24. De Mendoça writes that all the ambassadors with the exception of himself have been invited to the festivities (*CSP Spanish*, II.ii, #66, p. 182).
25. The countries included are listed in the terms of the treaty, as set out by the Spanish Ambassador, *CSP Spanish*, II. #264, pp. 290–3. England and France are noted in clause 14 as the originators of the league.
26. It is uncertain who was responsible for the performance of a comedy by Plautus at court in March 1519, but Wolsey was certainly the driving force behind the performances of Plautus's *Menaechmi* in January 1527 and Terence's *Phormio* in January 1528.

27. On *The Ruin of Rome*, see *Letters and Papers*, IV.ii.#3171, p. 1444; and for fuller detail on the welcome shows for Wolsey see V. Jourdain, *Les Spectacles populaires à l'entrée du Legat d'Angleterre à Amiens (4 Août 1527)* (Cayeux-sur-Mer: P. Ollivier, 1910); Dillon, *Performance and Spectacle*, pp. 127–8, 247; and Anglo, *Spectacle*, pp. 225–30.
28. Dillon, *Performance and Spectacle*, p. 127.
29. *Tudor Royal Proclamations*, ed. Paul L. Hughes and James F. Larkin, vol. I (New Haven and London: Yale University Press, 1964), pp. 478–9.
30. *Tudor Royal Proclamations*, ed. Paul L. Hughes and James F. Larkin, vol. II (*The Later Tudors (1553–1587)*) (New Haven and London: Yale University Press, 1969) p. 115. This proclamation was issued on 16 May 1559.
31. Her remarks were made to William Lambarde, her Keeper of the Rolls, in 1601. See further *The First and Second Parts of John Hayward's The Life and Raign of King Henrie IIII*, ed. John J. Manning, Camden 4th series, 42 (London: Royal Historical Society, 1991), p. 2.
32. Hayward, *The Life and Raign of King Henrie IIII*, ed. Manning, p. 1.
33. A performance was also given in London, possibly, but not certainly, at Cromwell House. Paul White discusses Cromwell's programme and his use of Bale's company more fully in *Theatre and Reformation* (Cambridge: Cambridge University Press, 1993), ch. 1, and provides a map of the company's projected touring routes based on their recorded places of performance, predominantly across the East Midlands and East Anglia. Furthermore, while Cranmer's household must be considered an elite venue, it was, as was the court itself, more inclusive in practice than this implies. The social status of the deponents giving evidence after it reminds us of this diversity (see further White, *Theatre and Reformation*, p. 29). On Bale's *King Johan* in performance, see also Walker, *Plays of Persuasion*, ch. 6 and Dillon, *Language and Stage in Medieval and Renaissance England* (Cambridge: Cambridge University Press, 1998), ch. 4.
34. See *The Complete Plays of John Bale*, ed. Peter Happé, 2 vols (Woodbridge: Brewer, 1985–6), I.147.
35. Kewes, 'Elizabethan History Play', p. 188. Roslyn Knutson similarly observes that the Admiral's Men in 1595–6 may have had 'three kinds of historical drama through which to explore the stage as a site of epic action and heroic behaviour: the foreign history, English chronicle, and classical play' (*Playing Companies and Commerce in Shakespeare's Time* (Cambridge: Cambridge University Press, 2001, p. 60)). A. J. Hoenselaars has also lamented the critical neglect of the continental history play, emphasizing the degree to which it, as much as the dramatization of more purely English history, effected a writing of English nationhood ('Shakespeare and the Early Modern History Play', in *The Cambridge Companion to Shakespeare's History Plays*, ed. Michael Hattaway (Cambridge: Cambridge University Press, 2002), pp. 25–40).

Bibliography

Manuscripts

British Library, MS Egerton 2605.
Public Record Office, MS E36/217.
State Archive of Mantua, MS Gonzaga 579.

Printed works

Anglo, Sydney, *Spectacle, Pageantry, and Early Tudor Policy* (Oxford: Clarendon Press, 2nd edn, 1997).

Astington, John, *English Court Theatre 1558–1642* (Cambridge: Cambridge University Press, 1999).

Bale, John, *The Complete Plays of John Bale*, ed. Peter Happé, 2 vols (Woodbridge: Brewer, 1985–6).

Bevington, David, *Tudor Drama and Politics: a Critical Approach to Topical Meaning* (Cambridge, MA: Harvard University Press, 1968).

Brown, Rawdon (ed.), *Four Years at the Court of Henry VIII*, 2 vols (London: Smith, 1854).

Calendar of State Papers, Spanish, ed. G. A. Bergenroth, Pascual de Gayangos and Martin A. S. Hume (London: Longman, 1862–1954).

Calendar of State Papers and Manuscripts, Relating to English Affairs Existing in the Archives and Collections of Venice, ed. Rawdon Brown et al. (London: Longman, 1864–1947).

Clopper, Lawrence, *Drama, Play, and Game: English Festive Culture in the Medieval and Early Modern Period* (Chicago and London: University of Chicago Press, 2001).

Dillon, Janette, *Performance and Spectacle in Hall's Chronicle* (London: Society for Theatre Research, 2002).

— *Language and Stage in Medieval and Renaissance England* (Cambridge: Cambridge University Press, 1998).

Ellis, Henry (ed.), *Hall's Chronicle* (London: Johnson, 1809).

Griffin, Benjamin, *Playing the Past: Approaches to English Historical Drama, 1385–1600* (Woodbridge: Brewer, 2001).

Hayward, John, *The First and Second Parts of John Hayward's The Life and Raign of King Henrie IIII*, ed. John J. Manning, Camden 4th series, 42 (London: Royal Historical Society, 1991).

Helgerson, Richard, 'Shakespeare and Contemporary Dramatists of History', *A Companion to Shakespeare's Works, Vol. II: The Histories*, ed. Richard Dutton and Jean E. Howard (Oxford: Blackwell, 2003), pp. 26–47.

Hoenselaars, A. J., 'Shakespeare and the Early Modern History Play', *The Cambridge Companion to Shakespeare's History Plays*, ed. Michael Hattaway (Cambridge: Cambridge University Press, 2002), pp. 25–40.

Hook, Judith, *The Sack of Rome, 1527* (London and Basingstoke: Macmillan, 1972).

Hughes, Paul L. and James F. Larkin (eds), *Tudor Royal Proclamations*, 3 vols (New Haven and London: Yale University Press, 1964).

Jourdain, V., *Les Spectacles populaires à l'entrée du Legat d'Angleterre à Amiens (4 Août 1527)* (Cayeux-sur-Mer: Ollivier, 1910).

Kewes, Paulina, 'The Elizabethan History Play: a True Genre?', *A Companion to Shakespeare's Works, Vol. II: The Histories*, ed. Richard Dutton and Jean E. Howard (Oxford: Blackwell, 2003), pp. 170–93.

Knutson, Roslyn, *Playing Companies and Commerce in Shakespeare's Time* (Cambridge: Cambridge University Press, 2001).

Lawrence, W. J., 'The Story of a Peculiar Stage Curtain', *The Elizabethan Playhouse and Other Studies* (Stratford-upon-Avon: Shakespeare Head Press, 1912).

Letters and Papers Foreign and Domestic, of the Reign of Henry VIII, 1509–47, ed. J. S. Brewer, James Gairdner and R. H. Brodie (London: HMSO, 1862–1910; 1920).

Rodriguez Villa, Antonio (ed.), *El emperador Carlos V y su corte según las cartas de Don Martin de Salinas, embajador del infante Don Fernando (1522–1539)* (Madrid: Fortanet, 1903).

Sanuto, M., *I Diarii di Marino Sanuto*, ed. Rinaldo Fulin et al., 58 vols (Venice: La R. Deputazione Veneta di Storia Patria, Visentini, 1879–1902).

Schoenbaum, S., *William Shakespeare: a Compact Documentary Life* (Oxford, London and New York: Oxford University Press, 1977).

Snyder, Susan, 'The Genres of Shakespeare's Plays', *The Cambridge Companion to Shakespeare*, ed. Margreta de Grazia and Stanley Wells (Cambridge: Cambridge University Press, 2001), pp. 83–97.

Streitberger, W. R., *Court Revels, 1485–1559* (Toronto, Buffalo and London: University of Toronto Press, 1994).

Walker, Greg, *Plays of Persuasion: Drama and Politics at the Court of Henry VIII* (Cambridge: Cambridge University Press, 1991).

White, Paul, *Theatre and Reformation* (Cambridge: Cambridge University Press, 1993).

Wimsatt, W. E. (ed.), *Dr Johnson on Shakespeare* (Harmondsworth: Penguin, 1969).

3
The Reformation of History in John Bale's Biblical Dramas

Andrew W. Taylor

Preacher, propagandist, playwright

Introducing the autobiographical *The Vocacyon of Johan Bale* (1553), Happé and King aver that, 'during his long career as an ecclesiastical reformer, he demonstrated varied capabilities as a prolific author, editor, preacher, dramatist, controversialist, antiquary, scholar, collector of books and manuscripts, historian, biblical commentator, and evangelical bishop'.[1] Bale is indeed a difficult figure to contain: yet although his diverse reforming endeavours complicate a narrative of his developing thought, these belie the sustained and single-minded engagement with religion and the past. His early and politically uninterested study of his religious order, the Carmelites, anticipates the monumental biobibliographical patriotism of his *Summarium* (1548) and *Catalogus* (1557–9), profound responses to the English Reformation and the need to reconfigure history.[2] This chapter explores the workings of Bale's historical imagination in the biblical drama initially conceived either during or immediately following his conversion, which he himself stated was not before Henry VIII's Act of Supremacy in 1534 (although some put it as early as 1531).[3]

Bale's later conversion separates him from Tyndale, Coverdale, Frith, Barnes, Latimer, Joye and other figures whose writings fostered the early Reformation. When he made up lost ground, it was more in a Reformed than a Lutheran direction. But while evangelical cells discussed Lutheran doctrine in the 1520s, Bale's travels to the Low Countries and France seem to have left this yet faithful Carmelite untouched by the 'new learning'; he seems to have been more receptive to the local examples of religious drama which would later inform his biblical trilogy, *God's Promises*, *John Baptist's Preaching* and *The Temptation of Our Lord*. Bale left his

Carmelite house at Ipswich in 1536, where he was Prior (perhaps even to marry), probably through the encouragement of Thomas, first Baron Wentworth, a Suffolk nobleman sympathetic to religious reform whose manor was at nearby Nettlestead. He assumed secular office at Thorndon in Suffolk that year, where his evangelical commitment to preaching the Word of God, encouraged by the reformist Ten Articles of July, disturbed some of his conservative parishioners. The 'small contentacion' some of them shared with traditionalists later at Kilkenny in Ireland (see below) resulted in him being reported to the authorities, imprisoned at Greenwich, and interviewed by Stokesley, Bishop of London, who required him to explain his preaching against the worship of saints, purgatory and unbiblical ceremonies. Here, Bale's roles as historian and dramatist seem to have contributed to his release: John Leland, the King's Antiquary, who already knew of Bale's complementary work on English writers as the Dissolution destroyed the great monastic repositories, interceded on his behalf. Bale's *Catalogus* (1. 702) records that this had also been encouraged *ob editas comoedias* – on account of 'published' comedies: Thomas Cromwell recognized that Bale's abilities as a writer and performer of polemical drama could be put to good use in his campaign against papal authority and Catholic doctrine. Although evidence of the activities of Bale's troupe is patchy, it suggests that Cromwell backed several theatrical tours of the Lord Privy Seal's Men, 'Bale and his felowes', in 1538–9: playing complemented the printing and preaching of the new order.[4] When Cromwell fell in 1540, Bale's departure overseas was immediate.

The *Vocacyon*'s Pauline account of his election and suffering for righteousness includes his latest tribulations in Ireland as Bishop of Ossory in 1552–3. The following episode indicates that Bale still thought his three biblical 'mystery plays' useful:

> On the .xx. daye of August / was the Ladye Marye with us in Kilkennye proclamed Quene of Englande / Fraunce and Irelande / with the greatest solempnyte that there coulde be devysed / of processions / musters and disgysinges / all the noble captaynes and gentilmen there about beinge present. What a do I had that daye with the prebendaryes and prestes abougt wearynge the cope / croser / and myter in procession / it were to muche to write.
>
> I tolde them earnestly / whan they wolde have compelled me therunto / that I was not Moyses minister but Christes / I desyred them that they wolde not compell me to his denyall / which is (S. Paule sayth) in the repetinge of Moyses sacramentes & ceremoniall

s[c]haddowes (Gal. v). With that I toke Christes testament in my hande / and went to the market crosse / the people in great nombre folowinge. there toke I the .xiii. chap. of S. Paule to the Roma. declaringe to them brevely / what the autorite was of the worldly powers & magistrates, what reverence & obedience were due to the same. In the meane tyme had the prelates goten .ii. disgysed prestes / one to beare the myter afore me / and an other the croser / makinge .iii. procession pageauntes of one. The yonge men in the forenone played a Tragedye of Gods promises in the old lawe at the market crosse / with organe plainges and songes very aptely. In the afternone agayne they played a Commedie of sanct Johan Baptistes preachinges / of Christes baptisynge and of his temptacion in the woldernesse / to the small contentacion of the prestes and other papistes there.[5]

Here Bale's 'history of self' dramatizes his personal refusal of traditional religious ceremony, which he equates with priestly disguises, the arrogance of men's traditions and the theatricality of Catholic rite he attacked so vehemently elsewhere. He preached first from Paul and then had his biblical drama continue the work of conversion, which, if he assumed the role of Prolocutor, would have brought the pulpit and the stage into contiguity. *God's Promises* extends his condemnation of the Catholics as Mosaic in their adherence to traditional sacraments and spurious claims to righteousness before God. As he asserts his identity as Christ's minister rather than Moses's, we feel the force of biblical history in the fashioning of this narrative: the original Gospel account of Christ's fulfilling of the Law to perplex the scribes and Pharisees interprets the present circumstances. His pursuit of true religion seeks assurance in its conformity to biblical paradigms, and shapes accordingly both its narrative understanding and the rhetoric of its antagonistic discourses. As we shall see, Bale's biblical trilogy similarly negotiates the return to biblical sources in the rewriting of religious drama. The Bible, located in history but potentially the interpreter of history, was for Bale the only legitimate source for this. His Protestantism also brought these conditions of Scripture to bear in his dramatic writing to encourage the reshaping – for him the restoration – of Christian identity, one which included the recognition of the believer's place in the true history of the church. His drama also fosters a sense of participation which cannot easily be separated from his historical understanding of true religion and the epochal struggle which defined it.

We know the three biblical plays from the editions of Dirik van der Straten, responsible also for Bale's *Three Laws* and *Summarium* in 1547–8. These publications seem likely to have constituted an attempt to attract homecoming patronage soon after the accession of Edward VI. Bale spelled out their concerns with wordy title-pages for the presses at Wesel:

> A Tragedye or enterlude manyfestyng the chefe promyses of God unto man by all ages in the olde lawe, from the fall of Adam to the incarnacyon of the lorde Jesus Christ.

> A brefe Comedy or Enterlude of Iohan Baptystes preachynge in the wyldernesse openynge the craftye assaultes of the hypocrytes with the gloryouse Baptyme of the Lord Jesus Christ.

> A brefe Comedy or enterlude concernynge the temptacyon of our lorde and saver Jesus Christ by Sathan in the desart.[6]

Whatever their relationship to earlier visions of a complete cycle, at the time of their printing they were seen as a distinct group and may have been rewritten towards greater conformity; the final exchange between Moseh Lex and Christi Lex in *Three Laws* celebrates Edward as king and prays 'for Quene Kateryne, and the noble Lorde Protectour' (2040). Generic distinctions aside – their significance is as slender, perhaps indiscriminate, as that of *history* – these plays were all 'compyled' by Bale. Poised between the anonymity of the corporate cycle plays and the assertion of authorship of writers of humanist interludes like Heywood, Rastell or Medwall, Bale's attitude perhaps reflects in part his dramatic reinvestment in the higher authority of Scripture, partly his role as evangelist.[7] John Watkins notes incisively that 'Bale's critique of drama belongs to his more generalized assault on allegory as both a hermeneutic and a rhetoric. Dismissing everything but the literal sense as false, he resists any situation in which one thing, whether an actor or a literary trope, represents something other than itself... nominalist directions that resist the universalism of narratives about Mankind and Everyman.'[8] Where the earlier *Three Laws* may be seen as having appropriated the morality play for the polemical representation of the assaults on religious devotion (here 'Mankind' never makes it into the allegorical space), so his biblical plays react critically to the tradition of the miracle play and its representation of ecclesiastical authority and teaching. Bale's far greater closeness to his biblical source contrasts with the inclusion of non-biblical scenes and the elaboration of fictional dialogue and narrative in the traditional fare. Moreover, this closeness to

Scripture articulates a temporal gap between the present of performance and the biblical past, yet without collapsing totally the contemporary application as allegory, work available to the viewer as well as performed by the play. Where *Three Laws* polemically exploits the morality play, in *King Johan*, another play of the earlier 1530s, 'moral allegory yields to a historical allegory in which characters and episodes in the fiction correspond to specific people and events in history'.[9]

Variation in the generic labels these plays attract in part reflects the transforming energies of Bale's aggressive appropriations of form. But where the biblical plays seem at first more restrained and accommodated, closer to the medieval tradition than anything else he wrote, Bale's representation of biblical material is likewise informed by this shift towards 'historical allegory'.[10] Bale's alternative to tradition, mystery cycles involving the whole community in the playing of 'romantic, legendary material', sought to return them to biblical sources in a movement which conspicuously renegotiated the relationships between sacred and secular history.[11] Habits of allegorical interpretation are thus redirected towards a typological reading of biblical figures which alters the relationship between sacred and secular, or rather absorbs the secular into the sacred: typology here registers the very historicism found in *King Johan*, where John and Henry VIII, rather than being represented as reducible to one symbolic identity, appear as distinct markers of a period of historical struggle. How Bale's drama participates has found various expression: White, for example, avers that 'The dramatic world of his plays interrelates and depicts biblical and historical past with historical present', while Blatt states, 'All Bale's plays are historical as well as biblical in the sense that he uses the Bible as a chronicle, and considers right-minded chroniclers to utter gospel truth'.[12] But if it may be said of *Three Laws* that it 'depicts Catholic clergy as a contemporary manifestation of a timeless spiritual evil corrupting God's laws through the ages', the relationship between present, past and immutable divine truth is one differently accented in Bale's biblical trilogy.[13] Given Bale's continued commitment to the plays' utility, it is worth considering some elements of Protestant historical thought with which he engaged between the mid-1530s and early 1550s.

Reforming history

The strongest scheme of revolutionary Protestant historiography is apocalyptic, a linear rather than cyclical reading of history of which Bale became a leading exponent. His *Image of Both Churches* was the first commentary on the Book of Revelation in English, parts one (completed during 1541) and two were published in 1545, the third part in 1547, in which he asserted that the Book of Revelation constituted

> a full clearance of all the chronicles and most notable histories which hath been writ since Christ's ascension, opening the true nature of their ages, time, and seasons [...] it containeth the universal troubles, persecutions and crosses, that the church suffered in the primitive spring, what it suffereth now, and what it shall suffer in the latter times by the subtle satellites of antichrist, which are the cruel members of Satan.[14]

In his dedicatory epistle to Edward VI for his edition of Leland's *Laboryouse Journey* (1549), he repeated how the biblical text 'is a light to the chronicles, and not the chronicles to the text'.[15] Although Bale's adoption of an apocalyptic interpretation of history is generally considered the product of his first period of exile, his engagement with Protestant patterns of sacred history originated with his conversion and may have been part of it. Although Lutheran apocalyptic thought only took root in the early 1530s, with its influence on English thinkers generally considered to lie towards the next decade, John Frith's translation of Luther's *De Antichristo* as *The Revelation of Antichrist* (1529) is a salient exception.[16] Moreover, Luther recorded the change in his own understanding in the preface he supplied for Robert Barnes's *Vitae Romanorum Pontificum* in 1535, a book of great interest to Bale:

> Though I was not at first historically well informed, I attacked the papacy on the basis of Holy Scripture. Now I rejoice heartily to see that others have attacked it from another source, that is, from history. I feel I have triumphed in my point of view as I note how clearly history agrees with Scripture. What I have learned and taught from Paul and Daniel, namely that the Pope is Antichrist, that history proclaims, pointing to and indicating the very man himself.[17]

Where chronicle and biblical texts are brought into dramatic contact in Bale's handling of *King Johan*, the biblical trilogy seems to lack the chronicle component allowing discussion of the representation of Bale's apocalyptic thought. However, as we shall see, the three plays are of interest both for their development of doctrinal speech in a dramatic setting, but also for how Bale adumbrates a new historical orientation, involving the audience in their Protestant moment.

The *Vocacyon* affords us a compressed view of the linearity of Bale's mature historical thought, the development of which is thought to have occurred predominantly during his first exile 1540–7:

> And brevely to saye sumwhat of the Christan churche of oure realme / in those dayes called Britaine / and now named Englande / what originall it had and from whens /what continuaunce / what darkeninges / what decayes / what falle / and what rayse againe.[18]

Bale begins with Adam, then invokes Abel's sacrifice of the 'firstlinges of his flocke' as witness of his righteousness, a foreshadowing of Christ's Atonement. The importance for Bale of the continuity between the Old and New Testament lies not merely in the congruence between the two parts of the Bible, but as an analogue of the moment of spiritual crisis faced by Christians in his own time. When Bale asserts that, 'S. Johan sayth / that the lambe was slayne from the worldes beginninge / [Apo. 13], that is to saye / in promise / in faith / & in misterie of their sacrifices', it is in order to establish the godliness of the English prior to Christ's fulfilment of that promise of salvation: 'And therupon Gildas in Excidio Britannie, concludeth / that the inhabitours of the realme / have alwayes had knowlege of God / almost sens the worldes beginninge'. Bale's rejection of the authority and doctrine of the Catholic church necessitated the representation of Augustine's mission as the moment of corruption.

> Untruly therfore are we reported of the italyane writers / and of the subtylle devysers of sanctes legendes / that we shulde have our first faythe from Rome / and our christen doctryne / from their unchristen bysshoppes. From the schole of Christe hymselfe / have we receyved the documentes of oure fayth. From Jerusalem / & not from Rome / whom both Peter & also Christe hath called Babylon / for that she so aptly therunto agreeth in ministerying confusion to the world.

The reader is swept quickly from King Lucius's conversion by 'the preachinge in Britaine' of Timothy, a disciple of St Paul, to a general statement of the health of the English church before Roman influence: 'Nurrished / brought up / & continued was this Brittish churche in the doctrine of faithe / without mennes tradicions / by the wurthie doctours of that age.' But then,

> Though the kinges of Britaine in that age / Arviragus, Marius, Coillus, Lucius, and Severus, with others / were not all Christened / yet were

they no cruell persecuters of Christes congregacion / that we reade of. In the generall quyetnesse provided to the churche by the forenamed Constantine, Arrius, Pelagius, Leporius, and one Tymothe, partly by subtile allegories / and partly by open heresies greatly obscured the glory therof. Anon after there folowed a certen kinde of monkery / with an heape of ceremonies / but yet without blasphemouse superstitiouns / till Antichrist had fashioned them to his execrable use.[19]

Saxon conquest was God's punishment for disobedience, then 'an other swarme of monkes / much wurse than the other [...] lyke laysye locustes sprange fourth of the pytt bottomlesse'. Augustine, the traditional father of the English church is thus transfigured into 'the Romish monke', harbinger of 'their owne fantastical doctrines / vaine tradicions / & supersticiouse ordinaunces. So that they made Gods heavenly wurde / to seme to the people / darke / rough / harde / & unpleasaunt for their ydle bellyes sake'.[20] The 'sophisticall sorceryes' of the school doctors and the four orders of friars (Augustinian, Carmelite, Dominican and Franciscan) banished the Christian religion by overwhelming the church with 'the most filthye sinagoge of Sathan', its 'false wurshippinges', 'monstrouse buggery for a professed virginitie', the last charge pervading his pungent *The Actes of Englysh Votaryes* (1546). From 'the registre of the visitacions of the cloysters of Englande', Bale claims documentary authority for his appraisal of the worsening state of the true Church, corrupted first by monkish mingling of Christian and pagan philosophy, but worse still through the institution of transubstantiation in the mass.

This boldly plotted decline of Christian doctrine and worship under Roman influence answers the question posed to evangelicals, 'Where was your church before Luther?' Bale's nationalist answer is based in English history and as such constitutes part of the response required by Henry VIII's break with Rome in 1534. The empire of Britain is combined with its own deep ecclesiology to assert both religious and political independence and sufficiency in opposition to subsequent foreign intrusion, the source of that depravity and fraud which religious and political reform now counters. But as Bale's *Vocacyon* reaches the present, it proclaims the ultimate significance of this decline:

Now truly in this lattre age and ende of the worlde God shewinge great mercy to his elected heritage / hath gathered them togyther from the parels of perdicion / by the voyce of his holye Gospell. Yea / lyke as by Hieremie the prophete before the exile into Babylon / by Johan Baptist / Christe / and his Apostles folowers before the division and first ruyne of the Romish empire / he called his disparsed remnaunt / so doth he now agayne before his generall comminge to judgement / [c]all tog[y]ther his churche of true belevers / by the godly preachers of thys age.[21]

Although there is some justice in seeing in the work, 'the comforting theme that the suffering of English Protestants under Queen Mary is only the latest incident in a cyclical pattern of suffering followed by providential deliverance, which underlies the history of the true church from its earliest origins', the pattern of Bale's account leading up to his own entry into the narrative has apocalyptic strains which intimate a more specific meaning for the present suffering witnesses to the faith.[22]

In contrast, Tyndale's polemical employment of the term 'Antichrist' in the attacks on papal corruption and false doctrine in the *Parable of the Wicked Mammon* stands typically in the Wycliffite tradition: 'Antichrist is a spiritual thing; and is as much to say as against Christ: that is one that preacheth false doctrine contrary to Christ. Antichrist was in the Old Testament... he was also in the time of Christ and his apostles... Antichrist is now and shall (I doubt not) endure till the world's end.'[23] There is, then, a distinction between identifying the pope as Antichrist and claiming that the historical moment of that identification is significant in an apocalyptic chronology. Yet, if Bale's thought shifted under the influence of certain continental reformers, we can view his dramatic works as anticipations of those first explicit expressions of that English apocalyptic tradition so thoroughly explored by Bale's later associate, John Foxe, in his *Acts and Monuments*.[24] We should also keep Firth's caveat firmly in view: 'Since both or either of these meanings [of Antichrist] could be implied, the early reformers had trouble in making themselves clear.'[25] The degree of millenarian interpretation also depended on the immediate polemical or apologetic needs: Bale sometimes still sounds like a Wycliffite in writings later than those in which he shows close acquaintance with such works as Francis Lambert's *Exegeseos in sanctam diui Ioannis Apocalypsim Libri VII* (1539). There are finally also problems in placing Bale's dramatic texts in the chronology of his work. His manuscript *Anglorum Heliades*, written for John Leland in 1536, lists only *King Johan* and *Three Laws* – those *comoediae* perhaps – among sundry others no longer extant (or never written) which suggest a concerted effort towards an evangelical counter-cycle.[26] The biblical trilogy, like *Three Laws*, was printed a decade after the title-pages' claim of compilation in 1538.[27] Although we have firmer knowledge of the performance of *King Johan* in 1538 and 1539 from letters and records of payment to players – its playing before Cranmer has been widely discussed – unequivocal evidence does not survive to indicate that these other four dramatic texts were performed during this period. The notion of a 'counter-cycle' may be no more than a tantalizing fiction. Furthermore, in printed publication they emerge as much closet dramas or texts to be distributed and read as scripts for a troupe – both degrees and dates of revision may never be known.

Protestant historical thought was thus various, but whether Wycliffite or apocalyptic, cyclical or linear, it opposed the place in history of the medieval church. The cycle form, as Happé summarizes, 'facilitated the presentation of a sense of history and its periods [...] there were opportunities to show divine intervention in human history, as well as to see the whole of history as a sort of pattern, a deliberate design'.[28] The following offers a discussion of how Bale's biblical imagination historically replotted the sacred drama with which his own both directly competed and against which it protested. If the New Testament is foreshadowed by the Old, then both may be seen as foreshadowing the moment identified by evangelicals as a new fulfilment of this dispensation after a period of suppression by a false church. Furthermore, the perceived need to break with the immediate past was not simply revolutionary: it was predicated on a return to origins, to the pristine exemplarity recorded in the Bible, traces of which had been preserved in the true church through time. Reformation was analogous to the fulfilment of Old Testament prophecy in Christ, and we shall see how this biblical exemplarity was one historically located in relation to the present. The true church was to be restored, and its contemporary struggle understood through past struggles.

God's Promises

Bale's biblical drama begins with man's first transgression. Miller gives the following admirably terse account of the structure of *God's Promises*:

> The seven scenes are parallel. Each scene consists of a dialogue between God and a prophet. Each dialogue develops through attack on mankind by God, defense of mankind by the prophet, debate between God and the prophet, a promise said by the prophet, and, finally, an antiphon begun by the prophet and taken up by choir and organ. This pattern of scene, dialogue, attack, defense, debate, promise, sign, praise, and antiphon is exact enough to prove Bale painstaking with it, especially in contrast with his general absence of articulation in other plays.[29]

The seven ages recapitulate the division of history in *Three Laws*: three ages under the Law of Nature, three under that of Moses, and the seventh age of the Law of Christ. This Pauline-Augustinian tripartite sequence Nature-Law/Moses-Gospel/Christ was to be found in works like the medieval *Speculum Sacerdotale*.[30] Seven prophet plays of a traditional *processus prophetarum* are compressed into seven almost anti-dramatic acts: for Happé, 'his intention is more emblematic' – no story, no plot.[31] Although the play has been less sympathetically judged as expressing Bale's 'conscientiously deadly subordination of drama to sermon', it seems unique among his extant corpus in not sacrificing plot to propagandistic ends, despite its attack on image-making.[32] Pater Coelestis interviews Adam Primus Homo, Justus Noah, Abraham Fidelis, Moses Sanctus, David Rex Pius, Esaias Propheta and Joannes Baptista, a choice praised by Blackburn as 'the six most appropriate figures he could have selected...[They] show that Bale understood each of them to be in some special sense a prefiguration of Christ in one or other of His special offices.' The series approaches that in Vincent of Beauvais's *Speculum Naturale*, yet this adds an eighth age of joy and forgiveness.[33] In contrast, Bale is far more concerned with the discovery of the Gospel both as the fulfilment of prophecy and through recovery in his own day.

The structure of *God's Promises* is repetitive but clearly designed for the emphatic imposition of the continuity of God's special relationship with true believers throughout time. Thus each of the seven acts closes with an anthem celebrating the renewal of God's promise of salvation: Bale's interest in the historical sequence of the prophets leads him to reorder the antiphons appropriately.[34] The printed text defines closely the musical and stage business. Bale used the antiphons from the *Breviary*, the 'Great O's' double antiphons which traditionally follow the *Magnificat* in the week before Christmas Eve (17–23 December), to register the restoration of man to God's grace. It has been suggested that this play was specifically composed for Advent, perhaps Bale's first at Thorndon, and that it is particularly suited to performance in a church.[35] Whether on not it was played at the appropriate time in the church calendar, liturgical awareness would have underlined how seven days are keyed to seven ages from Creation to Incarnation, and in pointing towards the Nativity perform a prophetic function which becomes part of the play's persuasion towards recognition or conversion. Bale's modification of the usual order of the seven antiphons (1567234) restores them to their chronological sequence in biblical history. These antiphons also underline the foreshadowing of the New Testament by the Old, providing a musical framework in which the traditions of liturgy are redirected across time to their historical origins as recorded in Scripture.

The inclusion of Latin liturgy, together with an English alternative, complicates simple notions of a reformer's rejection of the Latin Vulgate in favour of the English Bible: Bale understood that liturgy could produce desirable effects, exploiting the audience's registering of the sound of Latin as the likely quotation of sacred text.[36] Official sponsorship of vernacular liturgy might have been part of the diplomatic wooing of Lutherans in 1537 – ironically, the English Litany appeared in 1544 during a period of conservative retrenchment – yet Bale could easily have added English versions when he prepared his copy for the press in 1547. Moreover Bale's inclusion of both Latin and vernacular texts perhaps indicates the potential accommodation of the play to different audiences.[37] Bale could deploy liturgical language dramatically as part of his attack on the obfuscations and mystique of false religion: Latin in *King Johan* and *Three Laws* signals corrupt priestly authority which facilitates the spiritual and fiscal exploitation of the laity. But in *God's Promises*, whether in Latin or English, the antiphons mark each Act's final pristine contact between man and God: as Adam states,

> I have it in faythe   and therfor I wyll synge
> Thys Antheme to hym   that my salvacyon shall brynge.

> (*God's Promises*, ll. 177–8)

The text states that the prophet's solo is taken up by the chorus, yet this may not have been more than one or two further voices from the small touring troupe. The plays could have been performed more privately as pious 'interludes' within the houses of noblemen sympathetic to religious reform even after the prohibition of public performance in the 1540s.[38]

In considering the particular nature of the native tradition of the late-medieval mystery play, Happé notes that, 'several, perhaps the majority, of the cycles we know about offered a sweep of human history from the Creation to Doomsday. Continental cycles were more likely to concentrate upon the Passion.'[39] This history was the Old Testament, with the New, important beyond all measure for Christian doctrine and faith, providing only a brief chronological extension after which post-biblical chronicle extends to the present. Bale's adaptation of the Prophet Play within the cycle tradition asserts the Protestant doctrine of divine election based on the historical covenant between God and his elect.[40] In the years immediately before his capture and execution in 1536, and just as Bale would have engaged wholeheartedly with Protestant writing,

Tyndale's soteriology became increasingly covenantal under the influence of Reformed thought, in which both testaments are understood as one unified statement of God's promise of salvation.[41] In the preface to his translation of the Pentateuch (1530), Tyndale had already interpreted the Old Testament's doctrine of salvation, concluding that believers in ancient Israel were justified in a twofold fashion: 'The new testament was ever, even from the beginning of the world. For there were always promises of Christ to come, by faith in which promises the elect were then justified inwardly before God, as outwardly before the world by keeping of laws and ceremonies.'[42] The latter were abrogated under Christ. Blatt, in her relation of the dilation of the fifth Act to Judges 3–10, has demonstrated Bale's treatment of the Bible as a 'chronicle' for David, and this can be shown likewise for the rest of the prophets in *God's Promises*.[43] The history of the righteous and the unrighteous is shoe-horned into each of the prophet's narrations to provide a seemingly uninterrupted account of the whole of biblical time. It is this comprehensiveness and continuity which points towards doctrinal significance not only within the biblical sequence of the *processus*, but for extrapolation to the present. This apparent plotlessness is the plot.

The *Praefatio* by Baleus Prolocutor opens with a consideration of historical events, asserting an interesting distinction between ephemera, including the play's performance, and the immutability of divine truth:

> If profyght maye growe,   most Christen audyence,
> By knowlege of thynges   whych are but transytorye
> And here for a tyme,   of moch more congruence
> Advauntage myght sprynge   by the serche of causes heavenlye

(God's Promises, ll. 1–4)

The play's epigraph is from John 1, in which the eternal nature of Christ is confirmed: 'Thys lyght yet shyneth in the darkenesse, but the darkenesse comprehendeth it not'. Bale carefully has this idea resound at the end of the prologue:

> Yea, first ye shall have   the eternall generacyon
> Of Christ, lyke as Johan   in hys first chaptre wryght;
> And consequentlye   of man the first creacyon
> The abuse and fall   through hys oversyght;
> And the rayse agayne   through Gods hygh grace and myght,

> By promyses first   whych shall be declared all,
> Then by hys owne sonne   the worker pryncypall.
>
> (*God's Promises*, ll. 22–8)

The novelty of the drama which follows, both formally and in its insistent doctrinal emphasis on repentance and faith, would have struck an audience raised on a diet of extra-biblical elaborations. Bale as Prolocutor very likely provided himself with further metadramatic rhetoric to persuade the audience not only to assent to the play's doctrinal content but to move them to distinguish themselves from those who would deny it, the spiritually blind who 'yet' fail to perceive the light in the darkness:

> Yow therfor, good fryndes,   I lovyngely exhorte
> To waye soche matters   as wyll be uttered here,
> Of whome ye make loke   to have no tryfleinge sporte
> In fantasyes fayned,   not such lyke gaudysh gere;
> But the thynges that shall   your inwarde stomake stere
> To rejoyce in God for your justyfycacyon,
> And alone in Christ   to hope for your salvacyon.
>
> (*God's Promises*, ll. 15–21)

The opposition between inwardness and outward works is repeatedly stressed. Equally, 'tryfleinge sporte in fantasyes fayned' pointedly demands a mimetic distinction between Bale's play and the falsifying extra-biblical elaborations of traditional mystery plays, especially their underwriting of priestly authority and its role in the economy of salvation.

With characteristic efficiency and directness, the first dialogue immediately delivers on the promise of the prologue, 'They come that therof wyll shewe the certytude' (l. 35).

> And thys lyght shall shyne   amonge the people darkened
> With unfaythfulnesse,   yet shall they not with hym take,
> But of wyllfull hart   hys lyberall grace forsake.
>
> (*God's Promises*, ll. 54–6)

Like the successive Acts, the first opens with a prologue of Pater Coelestis in the presence of the human advocate. God looks forward across time to anticipate the 'plages of coreccyon' required as punishment for human unfaithfulness. Adam's pleading for forgiveness is met by implacable condemnation, to which Adam responds with flimsy mitigation: 'that I was left to myne owne lybertye'. God replies archly, 'Then thu art blamelesse, and the faulte thu layest to me?' (ll. 84–5). Adam, resisting the temptation to absolve himself, nevertheless moves the argument to his current fallen state and the issue of dependency:

> Lorde, now I perceyve   what power is in man,
> And strength of hymselfe   whan thy swete grace is absent;
> He must nedes but fall,   do he the best he can,
> And daunger hymselfe   as apereth evydent.
> For I synned not   so longe as thu wert present
>
> (*God's Promises*, ll. 92–6)

So much for Adam's free will. But Bale's interest lies elsewhere: Adam's repeated statement of remorse is met with the implacable sentence, 'thu shalt dye'. Thrice God condemns, but on the fourth he replies, 'But art thu sory from bottom of thy hart?', responding seemingly to repentance finally achieved *de profundis* (we can imagine the intensification of Adam's pleading). Adam, as the first of the series of advocates, is then told of his new obligation of enmity to the serpent:

> Cleave to thys promyse   with all thy inwarde powre;
> Fyrmlye enclose it   in thy remembraunce fast;
> Folde it in thy faythe   with full hope daye and houre,
> And thy salvacyon   it wyll be at the last.
>
> (*God's Promises*, ll. 121–4)

In the exhortation that Adam trust to the 'sede' of Christ, who 'shall clere the of all thy wyckednesse past / And procure thy peace with most hygh grace in my syght', his salvation is shown to depend only on faith. Furthermore, the signs offered by the Father, that the serpent shall creep and woman suffer 'sorowe in paynefull propagacyon' (l. 141), are presented as the evident outward correlatives of the 'hydden thynge', a trust now of religio-political importance for Bale in opposing ecclesiastical traditions. Yet where Bale has Adam speak of man's 'inwarde powre', his Noah requests, 'brynge hym agayne of thy abundant grace / To the folde of faythe, he acknowlegynge hys trespace' (ll. 209–10), a statement congruent with the epilogue's condemnation of 'wyll workes':

> Where is now fre wyll   whom hypocrytes comment?
> Wherby they report   they maye at their owne pleasure
> Do good of themselves   though grace and fayth be absent,
> And have good intentes   their madnesse with to measure.
>
> (*God's Promises*, ll. 976–9)

In the *Image*, Bale later used Revelation 13:3 to attack the backsliding of English religion despite the defeat of papal authority, that wounding of only one of the beast's seven heads: 'When men shall defend free-will, and allow their popish mass to be a sacrifice satisfactory for the quick and the dead, labour they any other (think you) than the healing of the wound?'[44]

Adam, now alone, concludes the Act with a speech of praise which soon modulates into the forceful recapitulation of human depravity, guilt and repentance before God, the acceptance of just punishment, and the divine work of his 'swete lorde':

> I am enforced   to rejoyce here inwardelye,
> An ympe though I be,   of helle, deathe, and dampnacyon
> Through my owne workynge,   for I consydre thy mercye
> And pytiefull mynde   for my whole generacyon.
> It is thu, swete lorde,   that workest my salvacyon
> And my recover.
>
> (*God's Promises*, ll. 165–70)

The direct and simple relationship between faith and salvation is repeated before Adam's 'Antheme', in which Bale purposefully reinforces the message's continuous relevance across time, 'from the begynnynge to the ende' (ll. 180–1).

Once Adam has left the stage, Happé suggests a stage direction indicating the simultaneous entrance of Pater Coelestis and Noah. If the dramatic action is a two-hander, then it would make sense for Noah to appear as the next interviewee only after Pater Coelestis has delivered his introductory speech, thus affording time for a change of costume, however perfunctory (the briefest opportunity is for David in Act 5). Bale omits to put Noah's name in God's mouth until halfway through the Act, nor has the Prolocutor issued the roll-call for the procession of figures. Noah's identity could perhaps have been marked in some way; perhaps the sequence was highly predictable. On the other hand, the deferred naming of each figure which is repeated across the play helps to focus attention on the figures' words before their identities raise distracting expectations. Moreover, the intensity and narrowness of the dialogue of Noah with God is the play's *modus operandi*. Unlike the cycles at York and Chester, or of the Wakefield Pageants in the Towneley Cycle, Noah's faith is figured without artisanal distractions of the ark, the sensationalism of the flood itself, or the diverting comic recalcitrance of his peevish wife.[45]

God's complaint over man's continual transgression and vicious existence moves him to regret and a destructive urge. Noah's pleading for the merciful correction and restoration to faith of those fallen from godliness fails to quell God's anger, who considers it 'wylfull workynge...through mynde dyabolycall' (ll. 219–20). Comparison of Bale's lines with Tyndale's Old Testament (1530) reveals how the dramatist reshaped biblical phrases and divine speeches. When Pater Coelestis retorts to Noah's pleading, 'Thu knowest I have geven to hym convenyent space' (l. 211), we hear the echo of the Lord's words, 'I will give them yet space, an hundred and twenty years' (Genesis 6:3). A few lines earlier, Bale quotes directly, 'I wyll destroye hym [...] For it repenteth me that ever I made them here'.[46] Bale's rewriting of the biblical account as dramatic dialogue requires Noah's righteousness to be active and vocal rather than obedient and mute. Through Noah, Bale develops the theme of profound human impotence in the face of sin, but does so without Adam's penitential confession of personal culpability. When Pater Coelestis charges man with wilful malice rather than weakness, his judgement is unopposed by Noah, who shifts the ground of argument onto God's infinite mercy: 'But graunt hym thy grace as he offendeth so deply, / The to remembre and abhorre hys myserye' (ll. 228–9). Noah's arguments on behalf of mankind – the biblical account gives Noah no speech except his final curse against Canaan – result only in his salvation, and that of his wife and three sons and their wives, an elect and righteous community renewed through God's covenant, a matter Noah at first only partly comprehends:

Justus Noah Blessed be thy name, most myghtye mercyfull maker –
     With the to dyspute it were unconvenyent.
Pater Coelestis Whye doest thu saye so? Be bolde to speke thy intent.
Justus Noah Shall the other dye without anye remedye?
Pater Coelestis I wyll drowne them all for their wylfull wycked folye,

That man herafter therby   maye knowe my powre,
And feare to offende my   goodnesse daye and houre.

(*God's Promises*, ll. 249–55)

To this decision Noah can only manage, 'As thy pleasure is so myght
it alwayes be; / For my healthe thu art and sowles felycyte' (ll. 256–7),
a courteous equivocation and confession of dependency in the face of
God's seemingly limited resources of mercy. Noah's righteousness is
nevertheless a vocal one, rather than that of the obedient mechanical.

Through the small-scale dramatic effects of dialogue Bale subtly incul-
cates the division of the elect from the reprobate in terms of contemporary religious politics. With God retired, Noah's paean reasserts the
ground of salvation:

Thy promyse in faythe   is our justyfycacyon
As it was Adams   whan hys hart therin rested,
As it was theirs   whych therin also trusted
[...............]
Faythe in that promyse   preserved both me and myne,
So wyll it all them   whych folowe the same lyne.

(*God's Promises*, ll. 273–5, 288–9).

Bale uses Noah's closing speech to articulate a genealogy of the righteous, allowing mention, however fleeting, of Abel, Seth, Enos, Mathus-
alah and Enoch, all of whom were saved by 'faythe in that promyse'.
From the historical trace of righteousness, the closing antiphon of Noah,
like Adam's, addresses the present both in its lyric qualities and in the
conscious use of contemporary Christian liturgy. Biblical history, present
pressures on doctrinal elucidation, and affective deployment of song, all
combine in the complex effects with which Bale punctures and punctu-
ates the periods of his narrative. He clearly represents the plain message
of salvation through faith to have originated in Adam but to apply to
subsequently renewed claims of the righteous.

Bale also reorders the narrative so that in the Old Testament's account
of God's institution of the sign of His 'bond' or 'testament' (Tyndale's
1530 translation), the rainbow, occurs after the flood has receded:

And God said. This is the token of my bond which I make between me
and you, and between all living thing that is with you for ever: I will
set my bow in the clouds, and it shall be a sign of the appointment

between me and the earth: so that when I bring in clouds upon the earth, the bow shall appear in the clouds. And then will I think upon my testament which I have made between me and you, and all that liveth whatever flesh it be. So that henceforth there shall be no more waters to make a flood and to destroy all flesh.

The bow shall be in the clouds, and I will look upon it, to remember the everlasting testament between God and all that liveth upon the earth, whatsoever flesh it be. And God said unto Noe: This is the sign of the testament which I have made between me and all flesh on the earth. (Genesis 9)[47]

Where the biblical account avers merely that, 'Noe was a righteous man and uncorrupt in his time, and walked with God', Bale shows him as an adept counsellor who appeals effectively to the mercy of an omnipotent and potentially tyrannical God: 'remembre thy great mercye [...] I knowe that mercye with the is permanent, / And wyll be ever, so longe as the worlde endure [...] Beynge thy subject he is undreneth thy cure' (ll. 230–6). As Roston has observed,

> Bale's characters speak with the rational self-confidence of the Renaissance humanist, challenging the apparent cruelty of God and demanding justice as well as mercy [...] The timidity of the medieval figures has been replaced by a respectful dignity; they no longer cower, but sternly refuse to accept the stern decrees of God until they have wrung from him a contract in the form of a covenant sealed with an eternal seal.[48]

Furthermore, the collision between this rhetorical reshaping of God's interlocutor and the ostensibly punitive tyranny of Pater Coelestis, where the traditional representation of God had been more as a benevolent father, may reflect an aspect of the antithetical but complementary relationship of Law and Gospel in evangelical doctrine.

Traditional exegesis of the Old Testament developed a typology for its biblical figures and events whereby they were seen as foreshadowing the Christian dispensation of the New Testament in Christ. In *God's Promises*, Bale underscores his concern with God's covenant with mankind through a peculiarly repetitive and rigid drama which promotes doctrinal concerns at the expense of dramatic potential. But this biblical play seems to stand in unusual relation to the extra-biblical characterization which had developed in the mystery cycles, where figures like Noah and Abraham were cast in anachronistic costume, and whose speech was imbued with similarly current concerns. Covenant theology, even in its early form, modified the Christian's relationship with the Old Testament. The message of *God's Promises* is clear: God's covenant is renewed from generation to generation of true believers, those whose faith in the promise is their salvation. Their righteousness is tested in the face of God's Law, which condemns with justice, but through their pleading mercy and penitential recognition of sin, they are saved. Abraham, like Noah, initially calls on Pater Coelestis to remember,

> [.........] thy worde and promes
> And lose not the sowles   of men in so great nombre,
> But save thyne owne worke   of thy most dyscrete goodnes
> I wote thy mercyes   are plentyfull and endles;
> Never can they dye   nor fayle, thy self endurynge.
> Thys hath faythe fixed   fast in my understandyne.

> *(God's Promises*, ll. 323–8)

Abraham shows himself to be a wily horse-trader in his bargaining over the number of righteous inhabitants required for their city to be spared from His 'malyce'. As the number is renegotiated downwards from fifty to forty to thirty, Abraham becomes wary: 'I take upon me to moche, lorde, in thy syght?'; but the reply comes, 'No, no, good Abraham, for I knowe thy faythe is ryght' (ll. 371–2). Abraham is encouraged to continue the exchanges, finally reducing the number to a single righteous person is deemed sufficient reason. Although Abraham proclaims, 'Great are thy graces' (l. 386), the exchanges assert Abraham's righteousness as having motivated his successful request for the exercise of God's mercy. Where it is demanded of Abraham that he 'Prynt thys in thys in thy faythe and it shall thy sowle renue' regarding circumcision as the 'sure seale', he elaborates the doctrine in his soliloquy:

> I can not perceyve   but that thy mercye is endles
> To soch as feare the   in every generacyon,
> For it endureth   without abrevyacyon.
>
> Thys have I prynted   in depe consyderacyon;
> [...]
> Helpe have the faythfull   therof, though they be infect,
> They condempnacyon   where as it is reject.

> *(God's Promises*, ll. 407–10, 415–16)

The dramatic representation of active righteousness in Abraham is thus emphatically asserted across time: God's mercy for the god-fearing is endless and 'without abrevyacyon'. In its iterative structure and didactic referentiality, *God's Promises* follows prophetic advice to imprint the message deeply.

Successive acts begin with Pater Coelestis bewailing the current state of human affairs. Such repetition does not, however, work to annihilate the history of mankind between Adam and John the Baptist. In these narrations, Bale takes pains to outline the events which fall between the Acts. Thus between the third (Abraham Fidelis) and the fourth (Moses Sanctus) we hear *en passant* of Ismael, Esau, Laban, Dina, Ruben, Judas, Onan and Achan, whose specific sins prompt recall of their biblical stories. For variation the opening narration is uttered by David Rex Pius in Act 5, while in the previous Act, Bale has Moses recount his own story: the plagues in Egypt, the flight of the Israelites, the crossing of the Red Sea, and so on. If the first Act alone was not in itself supposed to 'your inwarde stomake stere / To rejoyce in God for your justyfycacyon' (ll. 19–20), it does establish the pattern which will be repeated in the six which follow, an inculcating regularity pursued with such rigour that an element of anticipation (and its fulfilment) are a central effect. Meeting expectation, teaching the audience through repetition and reinforcement, serves the proselytizing aim. Monotony is avoided through the reorientation of each prophet's episode towards dialogue with God enhanced with unexpected twists of debate and mitigating argument.

The *processus* also conveys the passing of time through the efficient importation of considerable amounts of biblical material to locate each figure in their narrative, finally to register the advent of Christ in God's mollified attitude towards Isaiah. The opening speech of Joannes Baptista in the seventh Act is a grand recapitulation, an exhortation not only for God to remember and consider, but for the audience to do so too: 'Graces of the lorde, and promyses lyberall / Whych he hath geven to man for every age' (ll. 952–3). Through the adumbrated theology of the covenant, the parade of prophetic examples plots biblical history to arrive both at Christ and the crisis of contemporary religious reform. Although this teleological drive finally overtakes the iterated righteousness of the prophets, *God's Promises* establishes the elect and performs its theological work before we finally hear Pater Coelestis's reassurance of Christ, 'most hygh grace wyll I sende' (l. 810). As Baleus Prolocutor states in the epilogue, 'Though they se afarre yet all they had one justyce, / One masse, as they call it, and in Christ one sacryfyce' (ll. 967–8); 'For one savynge helthe in Christ they all confessed' (l. 961).

Faith in the promise of Old Testament prophecy, heard and confirmed so often in the first play of the trilogy, then merges with the Promise itself, Christ's sacrifice and the availability of its redemptive work to the elect, 'the faythfull chosen sorte' (l. 13). Bale's metadramatic voice thus works rhetorically to present the drama as a representation of scriptural truth, thereby confronting the audience with the choice of acknow-ledging its faithful and saving teaching on free will or, in rejecting it, having to repel the charges of the 'madnesse' and 'darknesse' of the 'hypocryte'.

John Baptist's Preaching

The Prolocutor's last line disposes *God's Promises* as part of a larger scheme: 'More of thys matter conclude herafter we shall' (l. 982). The trilogy continues with two New Testament 'comedies', 'dramatic', Blatt avers, 'to the extent that the account in the Bible on which they are based is dramatic'.[49] This does not mean that they are merely a patchwork of biblical phrases, but that elaboration of doctrine and its dramatized opposition tend to resist the interpolation or invention of extra-biblical material. Bale's interest in John the Baptist derived in part from his pre-conversion gathering of information on the saint who had a particular connection with the Carmelite order. Yet within the discursive confines of the biblical trilogy, he significantly remodels the saint or miracle play, rethinking sainthood both in *King Johan* and *John Baptist's Preaching*. Of the latter Happé observes, 'Compar-ison with the relevant mystery plays shows that Bale's changes have both scriptural basis and a Protestant ideological commitment.'[50] John's preaching mission is articulated initially, following Luke 3, through the confession, conversion and baptism of three emblematic repres-entatives of the people: Publicanus, Turba Vulgaris and Miles Armatus. That Bale has them spell out their identities in response to John's inquiry, 'What are ye? Tell me ych persone severallye' (l. 100), intim-ates the continuation of the strict patterning of *God's Promises*. *John Baptist's Preaching* again emphasizes justification by faith alone, but unlike the first play in the trilogy, represents not only sinners in need of God's grace for salvation, but those hostile to this message.[51] Drawing on his representations of the ungodly in *Three Laws* and *King Johan*, Bale builds on Matthew 3:7 in his treatment of Pharisaeus and Sadducaeus. Their resistance to true doctrine is accommodated to the present concerns of religious reform: they complain against John's 'new learnynge' and perceive the threat to their livings (ll. 207, 210).

Protestant polemic quietly invades *John Baptist's Preaching*, growing subtly out of the play's biblicism. Where John repeatedly assaults the arrogant and sinful hypocrisy of outward works, his opponents harp against 'newe learnynge' (ll. 207, 253, 316) and 'newe lawes soch as we never hearde' (l. 252). As in the *Vocacyon*, false religion is associated with the righteousness of works and ceremonies. John's opponents are literal interpreters of the five Mosaic books; significantly, Bale had restrained himself from the extraneous consideration of the Law or idolatry in Abraham's portion of *God's Promises* (484–9) and its preoccupation with the faith of the elect. Significantly, John's doctrinal assault against Pharisaeus and Sadducaeus absorbs much of Christ's discourse in the Gospels, which lack the threats to the Baptist found here. *John Baptist's Preaching* accentuates the dramatized opposition both through having John resist this attempted ensnarement and by rendering more aggressively the denunciations of false religion and Antichrist, especially in terms of their theatricality, impersonation and disguise.

The interview of this second phase commences after Pharisaeus and Sadducaeus have overheard John preaching to the people (*alloquitur populum*), i.e. to the audience, following the third baptismal encounter. In response to their demand that John acknowledge that their 'relygyons are worshypfull', he retorts,

> Not so worshypfull   but moch more false and deceytfull.
> An outwarde pretence   ye have of holynesse.
> Whych is before God   a double wyckednesse.

> (*John Baptist's Preaching*, ll. 224–6)

John further challenges their authority in scriptural interpretation and dependency on the alleged fulfilment of the Law: 'corrupt with your pestylent tradycyons / For your bellyes sake' (ll. 231–2); 'outward workes ye have but in sprete nothynge at all' (l. 238). Although Pharisaeus covertly boasts, 'Tush, thu shalt se me undermyne hym very fynelye' (l. 212), John's plain-talking quickly ignites exchanges of rising intemperance which serve to convey the absolute incompatibility and antagonism of their positions: 'Before God ye are no better than Sodomytes' (l. 240), he retorts with a barb against the cloister as well as condemnation of their worldly and self-righteous preoccupations:

> Neyther your good workes,   nor merytes of your fathers,
> Nor fastynges, longe prayers   with other holy behavers
> Shall yow afore God   be able to justyfye,
> Your affeccyons inwarde   unless ye do mortyfye.

> (*John Baptist's Preaching*, ll. 265–8)

The debate centres finally on the meaning of Abraham's righteousness, whether to stand in his line or to share in his faith constitutes godliness. John replies to the literal-mindedness of his opponents:

> *Joannes Baptista* The Gentyles can he call   whom ye very sore despyse
>   To Abrahams true faythe,   and graces for them devyse.
>   No hart is so harde   but he can it mollefye,
>   No synner so yll   but he maye him justyfye.
> *Pharisaeus* Yea, he tolde the so: thu art next of hys counsell
>   And knowest what he myndeth   to do in heaven and in hell.
>   And forsoth thu art   a jolye Robyne Bell.
> *Sadducaeus* Wyth a lytle helpe   of an heretyke he wyll smell.

> (*John Baptist's Preaching*, ll. 291–8)

Bale's suggestion that the audience's recognition and profession of true religion will render them liable to persecution will be heard again in the prologue to *The Temptation of Our Lord*: 'To persecucyon lete us prepare us than, / For that wyll folowe in them that seke the truth' (ll. 18–19), and again in its epilogue: 'He is unworthye of hym to be a member, / That wyll not with hym some persecucyon suffer' (ll. 404–5). Bale binds together the Baptist's doctrine with the possibility of his fate. The audience, to whom John as well as the Prolocutor has been preaching, are tacitly positioned in the historical procession of witnesses to faith.

In the religiously charged atmosphere of the early English Reformation, the contemporary references serve finally not merely to apply the biblical drama to the present, but to establish the historical understanding of true religion. With the departure of the plotting Sadducaeus and Pharisaeus, John addresses the audience again to encourage application to the present of what is resolutely the dramatic and historically remote representation of biblical narrative: 'The nature of these is styll lyke as it hath be – / Blasphemers they are of God and hys veryte' (ll. 320–1). The Prolocutor repeats this in the epilogue, where his recapitulation of the themes of humility and penance, dependency on faith in

Christ rather than in men's traditions, ends by returning the drama to Scripture, reminding the audience of what should be considered 'new':

> The justyce of men   is but an hypocresye,
> A worke without fayth,   an outwarde vayne glorye.
> An example here   ye had of the Pharysees,
> Whom John compared   to unfruteful, wythered trees.
>
> Geve eare unto Christ;   lete mennys vayne fantasyes go,
> As the father bad   by hys most hygh commaundement.
> Heare neyther Frances,   Benedyct nor Bruno,
> Albert nor Domynyck,   for they newe rulers invent.
> Beleve neyther Pope,   nor prest of hys consent.
> Folowe Christes Gospell, and therin fructyfye,
> To the prayse of God   and hys sonne Jesus glorye.

> (*John Baptist's Preaching*, ll. 482–92)

'Ecclesiastical' history here stands against the history of the faithful. The Pharisees are, for example, a biblical type through which history may and (for Bale) must be understood. As 'interpretours the holy scriptures to treate', these latter-day Sadducees and Pharisees serve their own corrupt worldiness and false righteousness, the 'pestylent tradycyons' and 'false exposycons' of Catholic doctrine. But more than being merely typological, these figures are located historically and manifested repeatedly (indeed continuously) through history, a narrative commitment with which Bale confronts his audience and prompts Protestant historical consciousness.

The nexus between history and biblical interpretation is also evident in the role of the sacraments. In earlier mystery plays dealing with John's baptism of Christ, the action was often performed according to the official rite, an expression of how medieval drama existed primarily to give religious instruction, establish faith and encourage piety.[52] The emphases of the clerical authors were ultimately towards worship: 'In effect, the biblical narrative, expanded to include a number of non-scriptural episodes, was presented in such a way as to enlarge its mystery and to bring out the transcendental.'[53] In Reformed thought baptism becomes an act of remembrance, partly because the theory of election reduces the need for baptism to perform any kind of transformation.[54] Hence Bale has John explain what is immediately termed 'newe learnynge': 'My baptyme is a sygne of outwarde mortyfyenge; / A grace is hys baptyme of inwarde quyckenynge' (ll. 191–2);

and later, 'The baptyme of me is but a shadow or type; / Soch is thy baptyme as awaye all synne doth wype' (ll. 389–90). Bale here uses John as the priestly reformer of the sacrament; Cox sees this play as the closest Bale ever came to denying baptism's salvific effcacy.[55] Tyndale's preface to the New Testament (1534) asserts, 'The right way, yea, and the only way to understand the scripture unto salvation, is that we earnestly and above all things search for the profession of our baptism, or covenants between us and God.'[56]

In the Reformation the true church was no longer entered simply through baptism and universally recognized sacraments. Where the Towneley Cycle has been seen as forcefully restating Catholic sacramental teaching in the face of Lollard objections – and it is worth noting that religious drama was already engaged in fighting heterodoxy – Bale's drama counters those corrupting rituals and traditions lacking scriptural authority: he avoids the miraculous and focuses on biblical events and the words of Christ.[57] The Edwardian adminstration, showing early signs of its Reformed leanings, suppressed the Corpus Christi cycles in 1548 primarily because of their ceremonial components rather than merely their association with the 'old religion'.[58] As we shall see in *The Temptation of the Lord*, the human dimension of Christ is emphasized through the invention of discourse which portrays the victory over Satan as the triumph of language's proper use, of true over false speaking.[59] Similarly, where the mass was also traditionally thought of as a 'miraculous' recreation of past events, Zwinglian or Swiss reformers replaced notions of the Eucharist as the ritual re-sacrifice of the Real Presence with the historical contingency of Christ's death, once-for-all in a temporal as well as theological framework.[60] Lollard thought was anti-transubstantiationalist – Bale was a great preserver of their writings – but his movement beyond the Lutheranism of early English reformers towards Reformed theology may have occurred well before his first exile. Griffin has suggested how Reformed theology impacted on ritual dramas, arguing that, 'the significance of the reformed service lies not in the conversion of the Mass into theater but the conversion of its theatrical aspect into historical drama'.[61] Although the self-imposed constraints of Bale's biblical drama exclude the possibility of defining specific theological commitments within the broadly evangelical, the manner in which it handles the dramatic representation of the Bible does indicate a movement away from the dramatization of ritual towards the memorializing representation of biblical episodes as history, without denying its immutable significance and hermeneutic function in sacred history. We also find the historicism and biblicism of Bale's dramatic imagination at work in the limits imposed on the representation of Christ, who here introduces Himself as 'the ymage of hys substaunce' (339), and explains 'wherfor I am incarnate'.

After John's Trinitarian prayer, Baleus Prolocutor reappears to interpret 'Thys vysyble sygne', a term which extends from Christ through John the Baptist's role as preacher, to the dramatic performance itself. The importance of signs and their interpretation is signalled throughout the trilogy. But this semiotic preoccupation serves to stress an engagement with something no longer present:

> Johan was a preacher – note wele what he ded teache:
> [...]
> The waye that Johan taught   was not to weare harde clothynge,
> To saye longe prayers,   nor to wandre in the desart,
> Or to eate wylde locusts.   No, he never taught soch thynge.

> (*John Baptist's Preaching*, ll. 465, 472–4)

Bale implies that what John taught has just been faithfully represented. Equally, John's final exclamation serves to disengage the audience from the moment of celebration:

> O tyme most joyfull!   Daye most spendiferus!
> The clerenesse of heaven   now apereth unto us.
> The father is hearde,   and the holy Ghost is seane,
> The sonne incarnate   to puryfye us cleane.
> By thys we maye se   the Gospell ones receyved
> Heaven openeth to us   and God is hyghly pleased.

> (*John Baptist's Preaching*, ll. 446–51)

That climactic moment in history is made visible again through Bale's drama. But what are we to make of John's final exhortation, 'Lete us synge therfor togyther, with one accorde' (l. 452)? The direction, '*Et expansis ad caelum manibus canit Joannes*' (And with his hands outstretched John sings), seems to exclude participation in an antiphon most likely based on one for Trinity Sunday. Perhaps the audience looked on and listened, with the Prolocutor's immediate return as metadramatic interpreter reinforcing the play as the representation of a specific historical moment, irrespective of any eternal significance. Yet if the truth is eternal, its ephemeral revelation requires subsequent interpretation: Bale's final account of doctrinal corruption in *John Baptist's Preaching* leaves the audience with a brief but trenchant attack on the history of 'mennis tradycyons' and 'mennes vayne fantasyes' (ll. 466, 486) against the Gospel. As Cavanagh states in his study of the sixteenth-century history play, 'if the past may be revealed as a site of criminality, of false language, then how much more so does the interpretation of the past as sacred history: what could be more criminal than being the agent of Antichrist, damning souls for eternity'?[62]

The Temptation of Our Lord

A brefe Comedy or enterlude concernynge the temptacyon of oure lorde and saver Jesus Christ by Sathan in the desart, the third play in the sequence, opens by recalling the second.[63] The plot of *The Temptation* is, like that of *John Baptist's Preaching*, strongly influenced by biblical narrative, being primarily a set-piece dialogue inherited from the cycle tradition between Jesus Christ and Satan Tentator structured around the latter's three attempts at seduction: in the wilderness, on the pinnacle of the temple, and finally on the mountain.[64] It may have been from the medieval Carthusian biblical exegete Ludolphus (*Vita Jesu Christi*) that Bale inherited the notion that Christ's fulfilment of the Law (Exodus 34:28 gives Moses's prefiguration) was to increase Satan's doubt over his identity. But more significant is Bale's representation of Christ and his relationship to the audience. The nature of Christ's exemplarity is dependent on conceptions of Christ's nature, and the implications for the true followers of Christ's actions. Bale embarks on this consideration when Christ enters alone to address the audience as interpreter of his own fasting:

> Thynke not me to fast bycause I wolde yow to fast,
> For than ye thynke wronge and have vayne judgement.
>
> (*Temptation*, ll. 44–5)

Bale's Christ interprets Christ to redeem His true meaning. Once again, the historical dimension intrudes into the biblical scene: the attack against fasting is locally one on Catholic practice, but more deeply against a post-biblical tradition of misinterpretation. These words reinforce the exhortations of Baleus Prolocutor in his introduction:

> Lerne first in thys acte that we whom Christ doth call
> Ought not to folowe the fantasyes of Man,
> But the holy Ghost, as our gyde specyall;

> Whych to defende us   is he that wyll and can.
> To persecucyon   lete us prepare us than,
> For that wyll folowe   in them that seke the truth:
> Marke in thys processe   what troubles to Christ ensuth.

> > (*Temptation*, ll. 15–21)

The emphatic rejection of penitential fasting for righteousness as a 'fantasy' of man's tradition is immediately underscored by Satan's approach in the guise of a monk: (stage direction) '*Hic simulata religione Christum aggreditur*'. Satan's assumption of 'godlye pretence outwardly must I beare, / Semynge relygyouse, devoute and sad in my geare' (74–5), aligns him with the scheming Pharisaeus and Sadducaeus of the previous play. The attack against monks continues in Satan's ironic profession of humilty:

> Scriptures I knowe non   for I am but an hermyte, I.
> I may saye to yow   it is no part of our stody;
> We relygyouse men   lyve all in contemplacyon.
> Scriptures to stodye   is not our occupacyon;
> It longeth to doctours.

> > (*Temptation*, ll. 157–61)

But then for the second temptation at the temple, Satan shifts his ground to assert that Scripture is for Christ's leaping backwards off the pinnacle (with its echo of Tyndale's serpent to Eve, 'tush ye shall not die' (Genesis 3:4), and of Satanic vice in Pharisaeus's, 'Tush, thu shalt se me undermyne hym very fynelye' (*John Baptist's Preaching*, 212; also Infidelitas in *Three Laws*, 1196):

> Tush, scripture is with it,   ye cannot fare amys;
> For it is written   how God hath geven a charge
> Unto hys Angels   that if ye leape at large
> They shall receyve ye   in their handes tenderly,
> Least ye dashe your fote   agaynst a stone therby.

> > (*Temptation*, ll. 208–12)

Christ rebukes Satan for misusing Matthew 4:6 (and Psalm 90:11–12), offering a comprehensive analysis with scriptural authority of his factitiously truncated quotation which finishes with a critical interpretative distinction:

> The clause that ye had   maketh for non outwarde workynge,
> If ye marke the Psalme   thoroughly from hys begynnynge.
> [...........]
> To take of hys worde   an outwarde experyment
> Of an ydle brayne,   whych God neyther thought nor ment.
>
> (*Temptation*, ll. 239–40, 252–3)

The speech in which Satan offers Christ the world begins with his pungent assault on Christ's trust in God's word in the face of adversity. Its colloquial energy hints at impatience if not desperation:

> Forsake the beleve   that ye have in Gods worde,
> That ye are hys sonne,   for it is not worth a torde.
> Is he a father   that se hys sonne thus famysh?
> If ye beleve it   I saye ye are to folysh.
>
> (*Temptation*, ll. 293–6)

Here, as earlier in the play (ll. 169–72 for example), when Bale has Satan test Christ's fidelity to God, he also addresses the audience's own convictions with pointed allusion to the infamous fate of contemporary evangelicals: 'Preache ye ones the truth, the bysshopes wyll ye murther' (l. 122).[65] In *John Baptist's Preaching*, which the audience may have just seen, the figures of Sadducaeus and Pharisaeus are opponents of the 'newe learnynge', a phrase which ironically captures the profound reversal of historical consciousness associated with the Reformation. Of course Bale's polemical agenda purposefully colours the biblical narrative with anachronistic reference and allusion. But in Bale's dramatic writing there is a very different sense of anachronism from that which pervades medieval religious drama on biblical themes.

In his account of the ideological reversal effected by Luther, Anthony Kemp states,

> Tradition accumulates by denying its own accumulation, by declaring its innovations to be ancient and original. The result is a cognitive timelessness, without which Christianity, in its medieval form, could not exist. Luther's attack is made in medieval terms: what is wrong

with tradition is that it is not original, but a novelty, unsubstantial, the trick of the devil.[66]

Bale's biblical dramas subscribe to this Lutheran reversed evaluation of the *traditio imperii*, which had made the Roman church the ecclesiastical heir to the Empire. Protestant reformers who shared the humanistic commitments of Erasmians looked to the renascence of the past to mend contemporary ills. But where such use of classical antiquity has been interpreted as having induced to varying degrees a growing sense of belatedness and historical alienation from the very matter they sought to revivify, Protestants saw in Scripture, and in the apostolic church which immediately followed the Incarnation, the source of eternal and immutable truth which had been obscured through the generation of a false historical consciousness:

> The whole structure of history as developed by Eusebius, Augustine, and Osorius centred on the Church as the true repository, the reliquary, of the apostolic tradition. It was the chief of those icons of compensation that bridged the abyss between the believer and the Christ he had never known, both the abyss of time, through the doctrines of apostolic succession and of relics, and the abyss between earth and heaven, through the doctrine of the real presence.[67]

But for the reformers, for whom the bridge was really a primrose path, true doctrine was that which originated (and ended) in God's Word. Protestant ecclesiology thus uprooted the historical basis of the Church of Rome, while those who struggled against its usurped authority were ever fulfilling the historical destiny of the elect.[68]

Bale's *Temptation* seems therefore to offer a double vision in which the biblical narrative is implicitly offered as the representation of a historical past, while also possessing a new kind of dramatic exemplarity for the audience. Christ is shown to be both more and less human: the increased human dimension of Christ is throughout articulated in his manner of speech and its dramatic responsiveness to the modulating language of conflict. Making Christ a more human interlocutor not only allows Satan to be drawn out more dynamically, just as Bale's Christ predicted, but has also been seen as a purposeful extension of human obligation in a divine context.[69] To be God's son is to be faithful to God's word, whether as Christ or as a Christian: 'The strength of Gods worde myghtyly sustayned Moses' (l. 137). Thus the members of the true church must be sustained by fidelity to God's word in the face of temptation and oppression: 'Thy cruell assaultes shall hurt neyther me nor myne, / Though we suffer both, by the provydence dyvyne' (ll. 345–6). But in Christ's admonition against fasting, Bale explicitly warns of the limits of Christ's exemplarity, a limit which is an expression not merely of doctrinal origin, but of a new relationship to the biblical past.

The offer of worldly power, the vista of 'these kyngedomes and the incomparable treasure; / I, the lorde of them, may geve them at my pleasure' (ll. 299–300), is met with absolute disdain in Christ's plangent identification of Satan. His triumphant rejection invokes examples of Satan's prior convictions as fraudster: the world is not his to give, but God's who made it:

Thus dedyst thu corrupt   the fayth of Adam and Eve.
Thus dedyst thu deceyve   both Moses and Aaron,
Causynge them to doubt   at the lake of contradyccyon.
[............]
Provyde wyll I so   that thy kyngedom shall decaye;
Gods worde shall be hearde   of the worlde, though thu saye naye.

(*Temptation*, ll. 314–16, 325–6)

Bale's evangelical plays indeed preach the Gospel to fulfil the prophecy. Satan Tentator, frustrated by Christ, then turns from his failure to a prediction of the future which points towards the present as well:

Well than it helpeth not   to tarry here any longar;
Advauntage to have   I se I must go farther.
So longe as thu lyvest   I am lyke to have no profyght;
If all come to passe   I may syt as moch in your lyght.
If ye preach Gods worde   as me thynke ye do intende,
Ere foure yeres be past   I shall yow to your father sende.
If Pharysees and Scrybes   can do any thynge therto,
False prestes and byshoppes   with my other servauntes mo,
Though I have hynderaunce   it wyll be but for a season.
I dought not thyne owne   herafter wyll worke some treason;
Thy vycar at Rome   I thynke wyll be my frynde.
I defye the, therfor,   and take thy wordes but as wynde.
He shall me worshypp   and have the worlde to rewarde;
That thu here forsakest   he wyll most hyghlye regarde.
Gods worde wyll he treade   underneth hys fote for ever,
And the hartes of men   from the truth therof dyssever.

> Thy fayth wyll he hate,   and slee thy flocke in conclusyon.
> All thys wyll I worke   to do the utter confusyon.
>
> (*Temptation*, ll. 327–44)

Following Augustine, Wyclif, in his *De apostasia*, averred that the current crisis in the church had been predicted by Revelation 20, where Satan is to be loosed in the second millennium of the church, that is the sixth of the seven millennia of history between Creation and the final Apocalypse.[70] Interestingly, Bale leaves Satan free to wreak havoc on the church, corrupting it into anti-Christian practices under the guise of Catholic tradition. Where Augustine, writing in the sixth millennium, predicted, and Wyclif in the seventh thought he was experiencing, the loosing of Satan, as we have seen from Bale's *Vocacyon*, in the Protestant mind the Roman church was from its inception the agency of Antichrist. Where Augustine could not have foreseen the second thousand years of the Christian church, this sixth millennium was subsequently extended more and more problematically beyond that point when God was again to be absolutely present: as Kemp trenchantly observes, 'Medieval history transformed an infinite abandonment into an indefinite expectation.'[71] Bale's evangelical plays may therefore be seen as having rewritten the mystery tradition towards direct biblical representation which counteracts this sense of deferral.

Despite Blatt's observation that, 'It is only when they are seen in connection with *Three Laws* that the biblical plays gain the controversial significance which, otherwise, is largely left to the imagination of the spectators', the trilogy nevertheless resists tradition in pointedly reforming biblical drama towards sacred history.[72] Where their controversial elements are indeed subdued in comparison with his earlier Protestant plays, Bale's biblical dramas share their historical concern. Bale's biblicism is at the heart of his historical consciousness: in correcting what he considered to be corrupt in popular religious drama, Bale placed the Bible at the centre of his to imbue it with the significance of his biblical hermeneutics. This is not to imply that we need to have identified a specific strain of apocalyptic thought in Bale: Protestant understanding of history reshaped the religious significance of the past without necessarily foretelling an imminent Second Coming. His dramatizing of biblical episodes works to strip away the accretions of tradition which mark the suspension of 'medieval history'. Although Bale's biblicism is far from straightforward, the trilogy employs a rhetoric of self-display as a representation of Scripture, and incorporates, explicitly through the Prolocutor, its own interpretative paradigms. Their biblicism also presents itself as a necessary return to an origin obscured by man's traditions through time. The rejection of the *traditio* of the Roman church is a moment of radical reinterpretation of post-biblical history, but here only touched on lightly by Bale, perhaps to avoid too profoundly discolouring the biblical scenes with contemporary polemic. The plays are historical in that they do not allegorize the past (as understood by a believer in that aspect of scriptural truth), but also tentatively begin to hold up a light to the chronicles. The history of cycle drama is thus interpreted critically by Bale's evangelical intervention in which his dramatic representation of Scripture is preoccupied with the shadows, figures and signs – indeed the plays themselves participate directly in this semiotics. Thus the inclusion of the Prolocutor metadramatically represents the fresh interpretative pressures through which Bale sought to displace his audience from ritual habits of living and the sacred drama which reflected and sustained them. Bale sought not merely to reform but, through the suasions of affective drama, to restore his audience to true religion both with doctrine and through asserting their constitutive place in the drama of history.

Notes

1. John Bale, *The Vocacyon of Johan Bale*, ed. Peter Happé and John N. King, Medieval and Renaissance Texts and Studies (Binghamton, NY: Renaissance English Text Society, 1990), p. 1. The original was probably printed in London by Hugh Singleton under a false colophon.
2. John Bale, *Illustrium Maioris Britanniae scriptorum ... summarium* (Wesel: Dirik van der Straten, 1549); *Scriptorum illustrium Maioris Brytanniae ... catalogus* (Basel: Oporinus, 1557–9).
3. For example, Jesse W. Harris, *John Bale: a Study in the Minor Literature of the Reformation* (Urbana, Illinois: University of Illinois Press, 1940), pp. 69–71. In his *Summarium* (fols 229–30), Bale states, 'cum ante illius in Romanum Pontificem edictum, obstinatissimus papista fuerim'. See Richard Rex, 'John Bale, Geoffrey Downes and Jesus College', *Journal of Ecclesiastical History*, 49/3 (1998), 486–93. Rex considers Bale's conversion 'a protracted process' originating in the period *c.* 1530–4, while 'the completion of the process can hardly be located earlier than 1536, the year in which Bale left the Carmelites' (pp. 491–2).
4. The evidence is thoroughly explored in Paul Whitfield White, *Theatre and Reformation* (Cambridge: Cambridge University Press, 1993), chapters 2 and 5. For a 'Norfolk Troupe' in 1537–8, see Richard Beadle, 'Plays and Playing at Thetford and Nearby, 1498–1540', *Theatre Notebook*, 32 (1978), 4–11 (p. 7). See also John N. King, *English Reformation Literature* (Princeton: Princeton University Press, 1982), p. 48.

5. Bale, *Vocacyon*, p. 59. On the ongoing hostility encountered by Protestant preachers, see Christopher Haigh, 'The Recent Historiography of the English Reformation', in *The English Reformation Revised*, ed. Christopher Haigh (Cambridge: Cambridge University Press, 1987), pp. 19–33 (pp. 24–5).

6. For further bibliographical details, see *The Complete Plays of John Bale*, ed. Peter Happé, 2 vols (Cambridge: D. S. Brewer, 1986), vol. 2, pp. 125, 141, 150.

7. On the genre of the interlude, see Nicholas Davis, 'The Meaning of the Word "Interlude": a Discussion', *Medieval English Theatre*, 61 (1984), 5–15.

8. John Watkins, 'The Allegorical Theatre: Moralities, Interludes, and Protestant Drama', in *The Cambridge History of Medieval English Literature*, ed. David Wallace (Cambridge: Cambridge University Press, 1999), pp. 767–92 (p. 791).

9. Ibid., p. 791.

10. *Three Laws* could be seen as an anti-Catholic morality, *King Johan* more as an adapted saint play or anti-Catholic history play where biography vies with the morality structure.

11. Lois Potter, 'John Bale', in *The Revels History of Drama in English: Volume II 1500–1576*, ed. Norman Sanders, Richard Southern, T. W. Craik and Lois Potter (London: Methuen, 1980), pp. 177–85 (p. 178).

12. White, *Theatre and Reformation*, p. 34; Thora Balslev Blatt, *The Plays of John Bale* (Copenhagen: G. E. C. Gad, 1968), p. 63.

13. White, *Theatre and Reformation*, p. 27.

14. *Select Works of John Bale*, ed. H. Christmas, The Parker Society (Cambridge: Cambridge University Press, 1849), p. 253.

15. See also Bale's dedicatory epistle to Edward VI of his edition of John Leland, *The laboryouse journey and serche of J. Leylande for Englandes antiquitees* (London: Richard Jugge for John Bale, 1549), sig. Aiii[r]: 'continuall reading of bokes, specyally of auncyent hystories, after the necessarye search of the Byble scryptures'.

16. John Frith, *A pistle to the Christen reader The revelation of Antichrist. Antithesis, wherin are compared to geder Christes actes and oure holye father the Popes* ([Antwerp]: [Hoochstraten], 1529).

17. Robert Barnes, *Vitae Romanorum Pontificum* (Basel, 1535), translation from N. S. Tjernagel, *Henry VIII and the Lutherans: a Study in Anglo-Lutheran Relations from 1521 to 1547* (Saint Louis: Concordia Publishing House, 1965), p. 148.

18. Bale, *Vocacyon*, p. 45.

19. Ibid., p. 46.

20. Ibid., p. 47.

21. Ibid., p. 48.

22. Ibid., p. 7.

23. William Tyndale, *Doctrinal Treatises*, ed. Rev. Henry Walter, The Parker Society (Cambridge: Cambridge University Press, 1848), p. 42.

24. Katharine R. Firth, *The Apocalyptic Tradition in Reformation Britain* (Oxford: Oxford University Press, 1979), esp. chapter 2: 'From Exile to Exile: John Bale and the Two Churches'. See also Paul Christianson, *Reformers and Babylon: English Apocalyptic Visions from the Reformation to the Eve of the Civil War* (Toronto: Toronto University Press, 1978) and Richard Bauckham, *Tudor Apocalypse* (Abingdon: Sutton Courtenay Press, 1978), pp. 21–9.

25. Firth, *Apocalyptic Tradition*, p. 7.

26. Peter Happé, *John Bale* (New York: Twayne Publishers, 1996), p. 6.
27. 'Compyled by Johan Bale, Anno Domini 1538' in *God's Promises*; 'Compyled by Johan Bale, Anno 1538', in *John Baptist's Preaching* and *The Temptation of Our Lord*; 'Compyled by Johan Bale. Anno M.D.XXXVIII' in *Three Laws*.
28. Peter Happé, 'John Bale's Lost Mystery Cycle', *Cahiers Élisabéthains: Late Medieval and Renaissance English Studies*, 60 (2001), 1–12 (p. 4).
29. E. S. Miller, 'The Antiphons in Bale's Cycle of Christ', *Studies in Philology*, 48 (1951), 629–38 (p. 633).
30. L. P. Fairfield, *John Bale: Mythmaker for the English Reformation* (West Lafayette, Indiana: Purdue University Press, 1976), pp. 57–8.
31. Happé, *John Bale*, p. 110.
32. Potter, 'John Bale', p. 180; Rainer Pineas, 'The Polemical Drama of John Bale', in *Shakespeare and the Dramatic Tradition: Essays in Honor of S. F. Johnson*, ed. W. R. Elton and William B. Lang (Newark: University of Delaware Press, 1989), pp. 194–210 (p. 194).
33. Ruth Blackburn, *Religious Drama under the Tudors* (The Hague: Mouton, 1971), pp. 54–5.
34. Miller, 'Antiphons', p. 636. The traditional sequence is: (1) *O Sapientia* (17th); (2) *O Adonai* (18th); (3) *O radix Iesse* (19th); (4) *O clavis David* (20th); (5) *O oriens, spendor* (21st); (6) *O Rex gentium* (22nd); (7) *O Emmanuel* (23rd).
35. See White, *Theatre and Reformation*, pp. 149–62, for an extended consideration of the evidence for performance at St Stephen's, Hackington near Canterbury in September 1538, and how *God's Promises* might have been staged. Glynne Wickham, *Early English Stages 1300–1600*, 3 vols (London: Routledge & Kegan Paul), vol. 3, pp. 258–9.
36. Janette Dillon, *Language and Stage in Medieval and Renaissance England* (Cambridge: Cambridge University Press, 1998), pp. 104, 95.
37. Peter Le Huray, *Music and the Reformation in England 1549–1660* (London: Herbert Jenkins, 1967), pp. 3–5.
38. Happé, *John Bale*, p. 108.
39. Happé, 'John Bale's Lost Mystery Cycle', p. 4.
40. Murray Roston, *Biblical Drama in England: From the Middle Ages to the Present Day* (London: Faber & Faber, 1968), p. 62.
41. Carl Trueman, *Luther's Legacy: Salvation and English Reformers, 1525–1556* (Oxford: Clarendon Press, 1994), pp. 76, 106–13.
42. William Tyndale, *Exposition and Notes on Sundry Portions of The Holy Scriptures together with The Practice of Prelates*, ed. H. Walter, The Parker Society (Cambridge: Cambridge University Press, 1849), p. 417.
43. Blatt, *Plays of John Bale*, pp. 90–1.
44. Bale, *Select Works*, pp. 427–8.
45. See 'Processus Noe cum filiis', in *The Wakefield Pageants in the Towneley Cycle*, ed. A. C. Cawley (Manchester: Manchester University Press, 1958); *Medieval Drama*, ed. David Bevington (Boston: Houghton Mifflin, 1975), pp. 290–307. In the *Ludus Coventriae*, Noah's wife fulfils her typological role as the prototype of Mary.
46. William Tyndale, *Tyndale's New Testament: a Modern Spelling Edition*, ed. David Daniell (New Haven: Yale University Press, 1992), p. 21: 'he repented that he had made man upon the earth and sorrowed in his heart. And said: I will destroy mankind which I have made, from off the face of the earth:

both man, beast, worm and fowl of the air, for it repenteth me that I have made them. But yet Noe found grace in the sight of the Lord'.

47. Ibid., p. 24.
48. Roston, *Biblical Drama*, pp. 63–4.
49. Blatt, *Plays of John Bale*, p. 95.
50. Peter Happé, 'The Protestant Adaptation of the Saint Play', in *The Saint Play in Medieval Europe*, ed. Clifford Davidson (Kalamazoo, Michigan: The Medieval Institute Publications, 1986), pp. 205–40 (pp. 211–13, 222).
51. Pineas, 'Polemical Drama', p. 194.
52. Hardin Craig, *English Religious Drama of the Middle Ages* (Oxford: Clarendon Press, 1955), p. 15.
53. Peter Happé, ' "Erazed in the booke": the Mystery Cycles and Reform', in *Tudor Drama before Shakespeare, 1485–1590: New Directions for Research, Criticism, and Pedagogy*, ed. Lloyd Edward Kermode, Jason Scott-Warren and Martine van Elk (Basingstoke: Palgrave Macmillan, 2004), pp. 15–33 (p. 27).
54. White, *Theatre and Reformation*, p. 159. Happé, *Complete Plays*, vol. 1, p. 13, also notes that Bale downplays the ritual element, but observes (vol. 2, p. 145) that the traditional interpretation of Matthew 3:11 in the *Glossa Ordinaria* does not 'differ greatly' from Bale's.
55. John D. Cox, *The Devil and the Sacred in English Drama, 1350–1642* (Cambridge: Cambridge University Press, 2000), p. 84.
56. Tyndale, *Exposition and Notes*, p. 469.
57. Lauren Lepow, *Enacting the Sacrament: Counter-Lollardy in the Towneley Cycle* (Rutherford: Fairleigh Dickinson University Press, 1990), pp. 26, 50, 63.
58. Happé, ' "Erazed in the booke" ', pp. 24–5.
59. Ibid., p. 28.
60. Mary C. Erler, 'Spectacle and Sacrament: a London Parish Play in the 1530s', *Modern Philology*, 91 (1994), 449–54.
61. Benjamin Griffin, *Playing the Past: Approaches to English Historical Drama, 1385–1600* (Woodbridge: D. S. Brewer, 2001), p. 27.
62. Dermot Cavanagh, *Language and Politics in the Sixteenth-Century History Play* (Basingstoke: Palgrave Macmillan, 2003), p. 18.
63. *John Baptist's Preaching* and *The Temptation* were printed on continuous signatures by Straten in 1547–8; *God's Promises* was issued separately, being longer than the other two combined. The opening lines are, 'After hys baptyme Christ was Gods sonne declared / By the fathers voyce as ye before have hearde'.
64. See Peter Happé, '*The Temptation of Our Lord*: Bale's Adaptation of the Scriptural Narrative', *Theta*, 2 (1995), 57–78.
65. Although faithful Catholics could point to their own recent martyrs with equal justice.
66. Anthony Kemp, *The Estrangement of the Past: a Study of the Origins of Modern Historical Consciousness* (Oxford: Oxford University Press, 1991), p. 79.
67. Ibid., p. 72.
68. See R. A. Markus, *Saeculum: History and Society in the Theology of St. Augustine* (Cambridge: Cambridge University Press, 1970), p. 21; Avihu Zakai, 'Reformation, History, and Eschatology in English Protestantism', *History and Theory*, 26/3 (1987), 300–18 (pp. 305–6).
69. Happé, *John Bale*, p. 116.

70. John Wyclif, *Iohannis Wyclif: Tractatus de apostasia*, ed. Michael Henry Dziewicki (London: Trübner for the Wyclif Society, 1889), p. 46 (chapter 3).
71. Kemp, *The Estrangement of the Past*, p. 74.
72. Blatt, *Plays of John Bale*, p. 99.

Bibliography

Bale, John, *The Complete Plays of John Bale*, ed. Peter Happé, 2 vols (Cambridge: D. S. Brewer, 1986).
— *Illustrium Maioris Britanniae scriptorum... summarium* (Wesel: Dirik van der Straten, 1549).
— *Scriptorum illustrium Maioris Brytanniae... catalogus* (Basel: Oporinus, 1557–9).
— *Select Works of John Bale*, ed. H. Christmas, The Parker Society (Cambridge: Cambridge University Press, 1849).
— *The Vocacyon of Johan Bale*, ed. Peter Happé and John N. King, Medieval and Renaissance Texts and Studies (Binghamton, NY: Renaissance English Text Society, 1990).
Barnes, Robert, *Vitae Romanorum Pontificum* (Basel, 1535).
Bauckham, Richard, *Tudor Apocalypse* (Abingdon: Sutton Courtenay, 1978).
Beadle, Richard, 'Plays and Playing at Thetford and Nearby, 1498–1540', *Theatre Notebook*, 32 (1978), 4–11.
Bevington, David (ed.), *Medieval Drama* (Boston: Houghton Mifflin, 1975).
Blackburn, Ruth, *Religious Drama under the Tudors* (The Hague: Mouton, 1971).
Blatt, Thora Balslev, *The Plays of John Bale* (Copenhagen: G. E. C. Gad, 1968).
Butler, Michelle M., 'Baleus Prolocutor and the Establishment of the Prologue in Sixteenth-Century Drama', *Tudor Drama before Shakespeare, 1485–1590: New Directions for Research, Criticism, and Pedagogy*, ed. Lloyd Edward Kermode, Jason Scott-Warren and Martine van Elk (Basingstoke: Palgrave Macmillan, 2004), pp. 93–109.
Cavanagh, Dermot, *Language and Politics in the Sixteenth-Century History Play* (Basingstoke: Palgrave Macmillan, 2003).
Cawley, A. C. (ed.), *The Wakefield Pageants in the Towneley Cycle* (Manchester: Manchester University Press, 1958).
Christianson, Paul, *Reformers and Babylon: English Apocalyptic Visions from the Reformation to the Eve of the Civil War* (Toronto: Toronto University Press, 1978).
Cox, John D., *The Devil and the Sacred in English Drama, 1350–1642* (Cambridge: Cambridge University Press, 2000).
Craig, Hardin, *English Religious Drama of the Middle Ages* (Oxford: Clarendon Press, 1955).
Davis, Nicholas, 'The Meaning of the Word "Interlude": a Discussion', *Medieval English Theatre*, 6/1 (1984), 5–15.
Dillon, Janette, *Language and Stage in Medieval and Renaissance England* (Cambridge: Cambridge University Press, 1998).
Erler, Mary C., 'Spectacle and Sacrament: a London Parish Play in the 1530s', *Modern Philology*, 91 (1994), 449–54.
Fairfield, L. P., *John Bale: Mythmaker for the English Reformation* (West Lafayette, Indiana: Purdue University Press, 1976).
Firth, Katharine R., *The Apocalyptic Tradition in Reformation Britain* (Oxford: Oxford University Press, 1979).

Frith, John, *A pistle to the Christen reader The revelation of Antichrist. Antithesis, wherin are compared to geder Christes actes and oure holye father the Popes* ([Antwerp]: [Hoochstraten], 1529).

Griffin, Benjamin, *Playing the Past: Approaches to English Historical Drama, 1385–1600* (Woodbridge: D. S. Brewer, 2001).

Haigh, Christopher, 'The Recent Historiography of the English Reformation', *The English Reformation Revised*, ed. Christopher Haigh (Cambridge: Cambridge University Press, 1987), pp. 19–33.

Happé, Peter, ' "Erazed in the booke": the Mystery Cycles and Reform', *Tudor Drama before Shakespeare, 1485–1590: New Directions for Research, Criticism, and Pedagogy*, ed. Lloyd Edward Kermode, Jason Scott-Warren and Martine van Elk (Basingstoke: Palgrave Macmillan, 2004), pp. 15–33.

— *John Bale* (New York: Twayne Publishers, 1996).

— 'John Bale's Lost Mystery Cycle', *Cahiers Élisabéthains: Late Medieval and Renaissance English Studies*, 60 (2001), 1–12.

— 'The Protestant Adaptation of the Saint Play', *The Saint Play in Medieval Europe*, ed. Clifford Davidson (Kalamazoo, Michigan: The Medieval Institute Publications, 1986), pp. 205–40.

— '*The Temptation of Our Lord*: Bale's Adaptation of the Scriptural Narrative', *Theta*, 2 (1995), 57–78.

Harris, Jesse W., *John Bale: a Study in the Minor Literature of the Reformation* (Urbana, Illinois: University of Illinois Press, 1940).

Kemp, Anthony, *The Estrangement of the Past: a Study of the Origins of Modern Historical Consciousness* (Oxford: Oxford University Press, 1991).

King, John N., *English Reformation Literature* (Princeton: Princeton University Press, 1982).

Le Huray, Peter, *Music and the Reformation in England 1549–1660* (London: Herbert Jenkins, 1967).

Leland, John, *The laboryouse journey and serche of J. Leylande for Englandes antiquitees* (London: Richard Jugge for John Bale, 1549).

Lepow, Lauren, *Enacting the Sacrament: Counter-Lollardy in the Towneley Cycle* (Rutherford: Fairleigh Dickinson University Press, 1990).

Markus, R. A., *Saeculum: History and Society in the Theology of St. Augustine* (Cambridge: Cambridge University Press, 1970).

Miller, E. S., 'The Antiphons in Bale's Cycle of Christ', *Studies in Philology*, 48 (1951), 629–38.

Pineas, Rainer, 'The Polemical Drama of John Bale', *Shakespeare and the Dramatic Tradition: Essays in Honor of S. F. Johnson*, ed. W. R. Elton and William B. Lang (Newark: University of Delaware Press, 1989), pp. 194–210.

Potter, Lois, 'John Bale', *The Revels History of Drama in English: Volume II 1500–1576*, ed. Norman Sanders, Richard Southern, T. W. Craik and Lois Potter (London: Methuen, 1980), pp. 177–85.

Rex, Richard, 'John Bale, Geoffrey Downes and Jesus College', *Journal of Ecclesiastical History*, 49/3 (1998), 486–93.

Roston, Murray, *Biblical Drama in England: From the Middle Ages to the Present Day* (London: Faber & Faber, 1968).

Tjernagel, N. S., *Henry VIII and the Lutherans: a Study in Anglo-Lutheran Relations from 1521 to 1547* (Saint Louis: Concordia, 1965).

Trueman, Carl, *Luther's Legacy: Salvation and English Reformers, 1525–1556* (Oxford: Clarendon Press, 1994).

Tyndale, William, *Doctrinal Treatises and Introductions to Different Portions of the Holy Scriptures*, ed. Rev. Henry Walter, The Parker Society (Cambridge: Cambridge University Press, 1848).

— *Exposition and Notes on Sundry Portions of The Holy Scriptures together with The Practice of Prelates*, ed. H. Walter, The Parker Society (Cambridge: Cambridge University Press, 1849).

— *Tyndale's New Testament: a Modern-Spelling Edition*, ed. David Daniell (New Haven: Yale University Press, 1992).

Watkins, John, 'The Allegorical Theatre: Moralities, Interludes, and Protestant Drama', *The Cambridge History of Medieval English Literature*, ed. David Wallace (Cambridge: Cambridge University Press, 1999), pp. 767–92.

White, Paul Whitfield, *Theatre and Reformation* (Cambridge: Cambridge University Press, 1993).

Wickham, Glynne, *Early English Stages 1300–1600*, 3 vols (London: Routledge & Kegan Paul, 1959–81).

Wyclif, John, *Iohannis Wyclif Tractatus de apostasia*, ed. Michael Henry Dziewicki (London: Trübner for the Wyclif Society, 1889).

Zakai, Avihu, 'Reformation, History, and Eschatology in English Protestantism', *History and Theory*, 26/3 (1987), 300–18.

4

Seneca and the Early Elizabethan History Play

Michael Ullyot

The history plays of Christopher Marlowe, George Peele, Henry Chettle and William Shakespeare are indebted to their forebears' Senecan ambles. Thomas Norton and Thomas Sackville's *Gorboduc* (1561/2) and Thomas Legge's Latin *Richardus Tertius* (1579) are both Senecan in style and conventions, in their narratives of high-born and ambitious characters brought low. Both adapt historical subjects to the forms and conventions of Senecan tragedy, owing to their common origin in academic settings, where their authors witnessed performances and read translations and imitations of Senecan plays: Norton and Sackville were students of the Inns of Court, while Legge was a fellow of Trinity College, Cambridge. Each of these plays reflects its academic origins by combining domestic history with a Senecan form. And Norton, Sackville and Legge's choices of Seneca as a model of style and conventions influenced the development of the English history play later in the century.

Senecan drama offered these three playwrights not only a platform to classicize domestic history, but a means to appropriate elements beyond its five-act structure and its fascination with lurid violence. These elements are Seneca's deliberative, declamatory and descriptive rhetoric – his methods for presenting the consultations, positions and actions that comprise the workings of history. In sum, they are Seneca's means of situating known narratives in the unrecorded arguments, emotions, alternatives, doubts and regrets surrounding them as they unfold. These are the stuff of history plays, combining the historian's 'particular truth of things' with the philosopher's 'general reason of things', in Sir Philip Sidney's phrase.[1] Seneca's essential feature for these two plays, and for the histories they influence, is his focus on the processes of decision-making and the tensions between ambition and uncertainty. Seneca's tyrants display doubt and remorse as they weigh the potential and actual ramifications of their decisions. This forensic element makes history plays compelling. Audiences are privy to the debates and arguments surrounding matters of state, and to the alternative histories that might have obtained. Seneca focuses on the civic and public functions of learning through rhetoric in scenes of counsel and advice. His plays often discuss the dynastic origins and aftermath of their immediate events, which suited them to the Elizabethan history plays' predilection for long-range narratives, not least in Shakespeare's two tetralogies.

The Senecan context

In the mid-sixteenth century, long before Christopher Marlowe and Thomas Kyd's Senecan characters entertained audiences in the public theatres, Seneca was largely an academic's playwright. In the 1540s, the humanist revival of classical texts and culture provoked imitations of his style by Latinists in the schools and universities (Thomas Watson; Nicholas Grimald; Alexander Nowell), and a smattering of translations by courtiers and academics (Henry Howard, Earl of Surrey; Thomas Wyatt; Richard Edwards), many of which were printed in Tottel's *Songs and Sonnets* or 'Miscellany' (1557).[2] In the late 1550s and 1560s this trickle became a torrent, as Jasper Heywood, Alexander Neville, John Studley and Thomas Nuce translated nine of the ten tragedies – all but *Thebäis*, which Thomas Newton would translate himself before compiling his *Tenne Tragedies* (1581). This anthology made Seneca the first classical poet whose complete dramatic works appeared in English translation.[3]

In Heywood's 1560 quarto of Seneca's *Thyestes*, the poet's ghost appears in a dream-vision, which Newton did not reprint, to appeal to poets to 'make me speake in straunger speeche and sette my woorks to sight', thereby earning for the English tongue 'greater grace, by pure and paynfull pen'. Heywood could point to a number of highly competent potential translators. Surprisingly, he mentions none of the above-mentioned translators among 'the witts that can display thy Tragedies all ten', but rather, those he perceives as the next generation of 'Mineruaes men, | And finest witts', all members of the Inns of Court: Thomas North, Thomas Sackville, Christopher Yelverton, William Baldwin, Thomas Blundeville, William Bavand and Barnabe Googe.[4] None would publicly translate a word of Seneca, but each contributed to a literary culture of translating Continental sources like Plutarch, and writing plays heavily influenced by Seneca, which circulated among them in manuscript before being printed.[5] Meanwhile, Norton and Sackville collaborated on *Gorboduc*, the first of a series of Inns of Court plays modelled on Senecan tragedy.[6] This play had perhaps more influence than any of the Senecan translations and learned writings at the Inns of Court in these decades: *Gorboduc*'s formal, structural, historical and political significance were each considerable.

In their eight years of study at the Inns of Court, the law students wrote and performed their dramatic and musical compositions, particularly at Christmas. The plays served many purposes: as festive entertainments; as experiments with classical forms and rhetoric; and as opportunities to improve elocution.[7] Outside of term, students studied the sciences and liberal arts: anatomy, astronomy, languages, history, geography and theology. John Fortescue describes these less formal studies with reference to their reading material:

> On the woorkyedayes the moste parte of them applye themselues to the studye of the lawe. And on the holyedays to the studie of the holye scripture: and out of the tyme of diuine seruice to the readynge of chronicles. For there in deed are vertues studyed, and all vices exiled.[8]

Readers of chronicles gain valuable knowledge without the inconvenience of first-hand experience, learning to emulate good examples while shunning bad ones. In his preface to Richard Grafton's *Chronicle at Large* (1568), Norton expressed the humanist commonplace that such histories were 'a glasse to see things past, whereby to iudge iustly of thinges present and wisely of things to come: To beholde the beautie of vertue and deformitie of vice', and to learn among other lessons how 'euill doings and wrongs [be] reuenged' by God's judgement.[9] It is this conception of history that Norton and Sackville and Legge have as their guide when making their dramatic forays.

The genres of neo-Senecan drama

Chaucer and Lydgate's tragic biographies, the stories of falls from prosperity into wretchedness, were more effective when historical, using the veneer of 'truth' to add weight to their moral.[10] Lydgate owed his sense of tragedy's historical character to Boccaccio's *De Casibus Virorum Illustrium*, on which the English poet based his *Falls of Princes*.[11] In the 1550s William Baldwin revived Lydgate's project with *A Mirror for Magistrates* (1559), an anthology of historical biographies of the falls of men from prosperity and happiness – and until the *Mirror's* final expansion of 1610, it emphasized the historicity of its tragic figures.[12] Against Aristotle's unities and more explicit warnings,[13] dramatists from the fourteenth century onward retold sweeping histories of vicious tyrants to urge audiences to shun their examples. The first recorded Senecan imitation was a history play, Albertino Mussato's *Ecerinus* (c. 1315), based on the tyrannical reign of Ezzelino III of Padua.[14] And in England, *Gorboduc* was the first, Norton and Sackville adapting chronicle material about the Saxon king Gorbodugo/Gorbodian. The second English Senecan drama was Legge's *Richardus Tertius* (1579), about the reign of the previous century's Richard III. They were among the first English history plays, and the only domestic histories between John Bale's plays on King John and Thomas Beckett in the 1530s, and *The Famous Victories of Henry V* (1586).[15]

In 1557, one of *Gorboduc's* authors, Sackville, wrote the Induction to William Baldwin's *The Mirror for Magistrates* (1563), to which he also contributed a celebrated conversation between 'Sorrow' and Henry Stafford, the Duke of Buckingham betrayed by Richard III.[16] This is an apprenticeship which is evident in *Gorboduc's* first Chorus:

> And this great king, that doth divide his land
> And change the course of his descending crown
> And yields the reign into his children's hand,
> From blissful state of joy and great renown,
> A mirror shall become to princes all
> To learn to shun the cause of such a fall.[17]

This educative purpose is explicitly stated in Baldwin's 'Address to the Nobilitye' which prefaces the 1559 *Mirror*:

> I humbly offer [this book] unto your honors, beseeching you to accept it favorably. For here as in a loking glas, you shall see (if any vice be in you) howe the like hath bene punished in other heretofore, whereby admonished, I trust it will be a good occasion to move you to the soner amendment. This is the chiefest ende, whye it is set forth, which God graunt it may attayne.[18]

The use of examples, historical or philosophical, to point up morals is something that Thomas Newton's *Tenne Tragedies* associates not just with plays in the Senecan tradition, but also with Seneca's own plays.

The 'Epistle Dedicatory' makes a case that amongst all the 'Heathen wryters' it is Seneca who,

> with more gravity of Philosophical sentences, more waightynes of sappy words, or greater authority of sou[n]d matter beateth down sinne, loose life, dissolute dealinge, and unbrydled sensuality... which is the dryft, whereunto he leveleth the whole yssue of ech one of his Tragedies.[19]

Geoffrey Bullough has noted that *Gorboduc* and *Richardus Tertius* 'show the possibility of combining Senecanism with English chronicle' but he does not ask why one would wish to do so.[20] As Philip Sidney famously noted, historians are often tempted to become poetical to enforce morals from things they cannot otherwise explain – and at least tragedy, with its poetical licence, will not become a 'terror from well-doing, and an encouragement to unbridled wickedness', as historical examples which reward the bad and punish the good may be forced to be.[21]

This hybridization of the *de casibus* and Senecan traditions became an accepted model for history plays later in the century. For instance, Bullough is sure that Shakespeare used *A Mirror* as a source for at least some of *Richard III* and he has also identified parts of translations of *Hercules Furens* as influential on the Richard–Lady Anne wooing scene and on wooing scenes in Legge's version of the story.[22] We do not know whether Shakespeare knew Legge's play, which circulated widely in manuscript, and it has been pointed out that similarities between the two plays could be on account of their shared sources.[23] But we do know that Shakespeare knew *Gorboduc*, and so it is apparent that he was familiar with at least one of the early history plays which combined Senecanism and the English chronicle, giving him a model of historical drama which he went on to make his own. The hybrid model these plays offered encouraged the use of Seneca in the later Elizabethan history play, culminating, it has been argued, in *Macbeth*, Shakespeare's most obviously 'Seneca and chronicle' play.[24]

Richardus Tertius has been traditionally designated the first English history play, due in part to Shakespeareans defining the genre in Shakespearean terms. George B. Churchill wrote in 1900 that Legge 'first perceived that English history as related by the chroniclers possessed as great a store of dramatic material as the classical saga, or Biblical story'. Frederick S. Boas concurred in 1914, rejecting both John Bale's *King Johan* and *Gorboduc* as polemical and political moralities, respectively.[25] It is an argument that Legge's late-century editors gladly repeat. Robert J. Lordi claims that *Richardus Tertius* is the first play to use English history 'for its own sake', that is, 'without the religious polemics of Bale or the political didacticism of Sackville and Norton'. Dana Sutton echoes Churchill in his critical translation of the play: 'its basic premise is that events of national history are no less worthy of serious dramatization than incidents from the Bible, classical mythology, or Graeco-Roman history'.[26]

These claims are predicated on an essentialist notion of the history play that is never precisely or explicitly defined; for instance, Boas has recourse to a 'strict' definition of the genre, which Lordi terms the 'regular' history play. The notion that national history is worth 'serious dramatization' predated Legge by four decades, unless Bale is mere frippery. Owing largely to Bale's polemical aims in *King Johan*, the English king's proto-Protestant opposition to papal authority made him less foreign than Gorboduc, whose paganism underscored his historical distance. Writing *Richardus Tertius* in the late 1570s, Legge might have foreshadowed later Elizabethan adaptations of his 'regular' history play, but he could not have foreseen them. Following Bale's lead, he chose post-Conquest history as the subject of his Senecan imitation, and fused this classical model with the polemical Tudor histories of Richard's reign.

To categorize any play as a 'history' is to distinguish the genre from tragedy, comedy, romance, pastoral and their hybrids. It is easier to define genres on the basis of form than on the basis of source or contents: a history play is a play about history, but so are many tragedies. Paulina Kewes astutely dismantles each of the criteria that modern critics – who take up these categories from Elizabethan sources – typically use to distinguish histories from tragedies and comedies: their Englishness; their didacticism; and their open-endedness.[27] She defines histories in broad formal and narrative terms, as 'any play, irrespective of its formal shape or fictional element, which represents, or purports to represent, a historical past, native or foreign, distant or recent'. In terms of their social function, only histories reflect theatregoers back to themselves; 'a society saturated with history, and turning to it instinctively to interpret the present, looked to the theatre for both instruction and entertainment'.[28]

Because of the regular traffic between Latin and vernacular drama one should treat *Gorboduc* and *Richardus Tertius* on equal terms despite their differences of language.[29] Both are also domestic histories – unlike, say, contemporary Roman plays like Stephen Gosson's lost *Catiline's Conspiracies* (1578). This is not to disagree with Kewes's equanimity

between native and foreign histories, but to situate these plays in
D. R. Woolf's emerging 'historical consciousness' in early modern
England, visible in John Foxe's martyrology, Edmund Spenser's epic-
romantic hagiography, and abridgements and epitomes of chronicles
from John Stow to William Camden.[30] So Thomas Nashe praises plays
like Shakespeare's *1 Henry VI* for relating 'our forefathers valiant acts
(that haue line long buried in rustie brasse, and worme-eaten bookes)',
raising them 'from the Graue of Obliuion'.[31] Nashe's nationalism is
an explicit aim of late Elizabethan histories, but the importance of the
native tradition of history had also been apparent in the earlier *A Mirror
for Magistrates*. Baldwin's 'Epistle' tells us:

> I nede not go eyther to the Romans or Grekes for proofe hereof,
> neyther yet to the Jewes, or other nacions: whose common weales
> have alway flourished while their officers were good, and decayed
> and ranne to ruyne, whan noughty men had the regiment, Our owne
> countrey stories (if we read and mark them) will shewe us examples
> ynow, would God we had not seen moe then ynowe.[32]

Lessons from one's own past are more compelling, it seems, than those
from others'.

History compels not only for its details, but for its scale. Seneca was not
primarily a playwright of history, but the teleological scope of his drama
lent itself to the expansive sweep of history plays.[33] His *Thyestes* and its
sequel, *Agamemnon*, tell a story of bloody acts of retribution beginning
with Tantalus and ending four generations later with Orestes. Through
successive plays, Seneca presents this long-range narrative in a way that
still engages his audience's interest, focusing on one generation at a
time. He learned this technique from his Greek sources Euripides and
Sophocles, the latter of whom provided the model for his plays in the
Theban cycle, *Thebais* and *Oedipus*. Seneca's *Hercules Furens* and *Hercules
Oetaeus* concentrate on one man, but in Hercules's deranged murder of
one wife (Megara) and murder by another (Deianeira's shirt of Nessus) he
presents stages of the narrative that surrounds them, both sequentially
and consequentially.[34] It is also an interest that Bullough notices in
Shakespeare's *Richard III*, positing the three generations of queens as
a Senecan device recalling the *Troades*, each generation looking back
over the past with its own memories and griefs.[35] Bullough suggests,
but cannot prove, that Shakespeare took his use of women as historical
storytellers from Legge who used them in *Richardus Tertius*.

Sackville, Norton and Legge and the functions of history

Norton and Sackville each exhibit an interest in studying and interpreting history for the lessons it could impart to present readers or audiences. Their projects and their politics tell us that *Gorboduc*'s authors believed in the civic function of education; in the didactic importance of domestic (medieval) history; and in the need for educated men to use their reason and eloquence to advocate for the public good. This latter theme dominates their play, which is preoccupied with the moral credit or culpability of good and bad counsellors for the consequences of their advice. When they matriculated at the Inner Temple in 1554 and 1555, respectively, Sackville and Norton were following similar trajectories. Though Sackville was of the higher birth, both men were university-educated and intent on using their educations and literary endeavours to political effect. The civic and Continental humanism of their education made them, like many members of the Inns, 'rhetorically trained, critically minded, professionally ambitious, and politically aware', writes Jessica Winston.[36] Thomas Norton (1530x32–1584) was politically active throughout his life, chairing the committee in 1562/3 that urged Elizabeth to marry in order to secure the succession; in 1581 he was imprisoned for 'overmuch and undutiful speaking' about the Queen's courtship with the Duke of Anjou.[37] While in the Tower, Norton began composing two works at Francis Walsingham's request: 'Devices' or proposals for reforming educational practices and institutions including the Inns and universities; and a review of the wars, laws and rebellions of the five centuries since the Norman Conquest.[38]

While we do not know how Norton and Sackville divided the labour of writing *Gorboduc*, the claim of its unauthorized printer William Griffith in 1565 that Sackville composed the latter two Acts may be an attempt to attribute these Acts' explicit political advice to the more influential of the two.[39] The only son of privy counsellor Sir Richard Sackville (d. 1566), Thomas Sackville (*c.* 1536–1608) served as lord treasurer from 1599 and negotiated the accession and then the Spanish peace treaty of James I.[40] His death while sitting at the council table in 1608 was emblematic of a lifetime of public service as 'a scholar, and a traueller, and a Courtier of speciall estimation'.[41] Although Edmund Spenser and others praised his 'golden verse' in the 1590s, Sackville had not written a line of poetry since 1586, when his Horatian verse epistle 'Sacvyles olde Age' (provoked, perhaps, by his father's death) signalled his renunciation of poetry in favour of public service. In the preceding decade, Sackville's literary diversions earned him Jasper Heywood's praise for

'Sackuyldes Sonnetts sweetely sauste' and, as we have seen, produced the celebrated 'Induction' and 'Complaint of Buckingham' printed in Baldwin's second part of *A Mirror for Magistrates* (1563).[42]

Students of the Inns of Court put the lessons of history into practice, in the performative sense, using 'fictional or historical play situations much as they would use legal precedents', to illuminate theories by example.[43] This emphasis on past precedents for present decisions complemented their legal education. The common law system was based on precedents imparting valuable and applicable lessons to the present: case studies helped lawyers make legal arguments, much as past medical experiments helped physicians make diagnoses. '[I]n the historically oriented culture of late humanism', writes Nancy Siraisi, '*cognitio historica* played a role in many disciplinary and professional contexts' that relied on precedents as guides to conduct.[44] But as lawyers were more rhetorically inclined (or trained) than physicians, they wrote more plays than chronicles. Norton and Sackville's *Gorboduc* marked the first time their practices of reading chronicles and writing plays directly complemented one another. In the uncertain early years of Elizabeth's reign, a time of 'political and religious confusion', Norton and Sackville had every reason to believe that the realm's peace and stability relied on the counsel of its common lawyers;[45] the recent consternation over Henry VIII's final will, decreeing that the crown should descend through the Suffolks rather than the Stuarts, reinforced the importance of sound legal interpretation.[46]

Plays in university settings had 'a serious pedagogical purpose', teaching rhetoric and declamation along with knowledge of history.[47] Like the Inns of Court, Cambridge colleges appreciated the purposes of students participating in plays as vacation exercises. The statutes of St John's College admonish their students to undertake activities to develop the rhetorical eloquence and historical knowledge required of future public figures:

> [O]n the eves of festivals during the four short vacations these students shall not waste (their) [*sic*.] time in idleness and games, but they should be occupied in composing poems, letters, or speeches; in the reading of Greek poets, orators, or historians; or in the putting on of dialogues, comedies, or tragedies.[48]

These productions involved considerable numbers of students and fellows to write and perform on temporary stages erected in college halls.[49]

From his matriculation at Corpus Christi in 1552 to his death in 1607, Thomas Legge served in three different capacities: as a civil (Roman) and canon lawyer; as a college master and university vice-chancellor (1587–8 and 1592–3); and as an avid playgoer and playwright.[50] As a scholar and fellow of Trinity College (1555–68), Legge frequently appears in the college Steward's and the Junior Bursar's account books. In 1558–9, two shillings were paid to Legge and Robert West 'for their play*ers*'. In 1560–1, the year Legge's fellowship began, the Bursar noted 33s 7d 'paid to mr legge for ye expen*ces* of aboughte the setting forthe of medea', namely for costumes and for altering candlesticks to use onstage.[51] And between 1560 and 1567, Legge's name was affiliated with no less than six separate productions of Plautus, Terence and Seneca: 'Medea' (1560–1), 'Adelphus' (his own translation, mounted in 1562–3), 'Stichus' (1564–5), 'Asinaria' (1565–6), 'Iephthes' (1566–7), and an unnamed play in 1563–4.[52] As a rule there were no fewer than five plays produced at Trinity each year, so Legge may have restricted his involvement with these performances.[53] After he left Trinity for Jesus College (1568–73), Legge appears in no records connecting him to dramatic productions. In 1573 John Caius chose Legge to be his successor as master of Gonville and Caius College, in which capacity he served until his death. William Moore's tribute to Legge in the *Gonville and Caius College Annals* (1656–9) reflects the esteem in which he was held, and the fame of his *Richardus Tertius*:

> A man otherwise serious-minded and extremely busy with continuous matters of business, he was accustomed to refresh his tired spirit by attending and composing plays, especially tragedies, one of which, in which he represented the fierce manners of Richard III, had been put on publicly at one time in the hall of St John's College, Cambridge, with the greatest approval of the academics.[54]

This occasion was a dinner held in Legge's honour at St John's College in 1579. The performance of Legge's neo-Senecan trilogy over three evenings at the Bachelor's Commencement in March 1579 was the culmination of his dramatic career. Widely praised and copied into at least eleven extant manuscripts, *Richardus Tertius* also cemented Legge's reputation as 'our best for Tragedie' as late as 1598.[55] In 1591 John Harington praised the play's cautionary moral as exemplary among tragedies, as it would 'terrifie all tyrannous minded men, from following their foolish ambitious humors'.[56] Thomas Nashe recalled one of the players of 'the Latine Tragedie of K. *Richard*' in his 1596 invective against Gabriel

Harvey, *Have with yov to Saffron-Walden*.[57] Apocryphal stories about this 1579 performance circulated well into the next century, including Thomas Fuller's claims in his 1662 that Queen Elizabeth was indeed in the audience, and that John Palmer, the actor who played Richard, was thereafter 'so possest with a Princelike humor' that 'he did what then he acted', living a profligate life before dying in debtor's prison.[58]

It is evident that the education of all three of the playwrights left them with a predisposition in favour of the use of historical examples as moral instruction, coupled with a deep familiarity with the works of Seneca and the English chronicle. Their early efforts to combine the two in dramatic form became unknowing prototypes for a much more readily recognizable form of English historical drama, the 'plays about Barons' of the 1590s of Shakespeare and his exact contemporaries. In *Gorboduc* and *Richardus Tertius* we can see how the Senecan influence in the sixteenth century encouraged early Elizabethan history plays to emphasize the processes and the implications of kingly decisions, particularly as their poor or tyrannical decisions impact on the lives of others. These plays glimpse behind the curtain of history, into the minds of those creating and effecting it, into their deliberations before and doubts after they have made decisions. These are questions in which the static declamations of Senecan drama and the moralizing of the chronicle histories share an interest. The emphases on effective rhetoric and counsel (the civic function of learning) and on descriptive rhetoric and self-analysis (especially of moral weakness and uncertainty) can be traced through all three kinds of writing: in Seneca himself, in the chronicle histories and in their product, the neo-Senecan history plays.

Gorboduc

The essence of good government is good advice, 'Guiding so great estate with great renown' as Gorboduc says to his advisers when soliciting their 'faith and wisdom' in the matter of dividing and divesting his kingdom (I.ii.4, 6). He implores them to speak plainly, 'Lest as the blame of ill-succeeding things / Shall light on you, so light the harms also' (I.ii.31–2). In true Senecan style, much of the play consists of lengthy declamations of advice and warning, punctuated by breathless yet protracted descriptions of the violent spectacles unfolding offstage. When Gorboduc follows the poor advice to divest himself of power and divide his kingdom among his sons, 'the fraud ... Of flattering tongues corrupt[s] their tender youth' (I.ii.351–2). Bad counsellors incite an internecine war that culminates in the king's death. At the close of the play, Gorboduc's 'good counsellor' Eubulus laments that 'This is the end when in fond princes' hearts / Flattery prevails and sage rede hath no place' (V.ii.236–7). Eubulus declares 'the end of *Brutus* royal line' with the devastation visited on the royal family (V.ii.180). But they had been warned: when the king's eldest son Ferrex prepares for his brother and rival Porrex's incursions, his good counsellor Dordan rightly foretells that 'civil hate shall end the noble line / Of famous *Brute*' (II.i.195–6). Yet when the play's chorus reiterates that these events will serve as a warning to those who follow in the office, 'A mirror ... to Princes all, / To learn to shun the cause of such a fall' (I.ii.388–93), the story's legacy promises a form of posthumous fulfilment as a lesson to be learned. In this pleasing piece of metahistorical self-referentiality, by ignoring Brute's historical example, *Gorboduc* becomes a cautionary tale. Norton and Sackville thus create a doubly negative example who neglects the wisdom both of good men and historical precedents.

The play's 'stately speeches' befit its moral exemplarity, its teaching that territorial divisions and uncertain successions would lead to ruin, and that unless flatterers were removed from the court they would bring princes to violent ends. *Gorboduc*'s 'well-sounding phrases' rein-forced these moral lessons with Seneca's trademark *sententiae* or quotable maxims. These distillations of political advice received special emphasis in John Day's 1570 quarto edition, printed under Norton and Sackville's close supervision to correct William Griffith's unauthorized and error-laden quarto of 1565:

> Wise men do not so hang on passing state
> Of present princes, chiefly in their age,
> But they will further cast their reaching eye,
> To view and weigh the times and reigns to come.[59]

These sentences impressed one reader enough to transcribe them into his commonplace book a few decades later.[60] Norton and Sackville's use of this Senecan device, offering maxims for application to other questions in other contexts, underscores their aim to offer domestic history as both advice and entertainment for spectators and readers.

The play's engagement with the immediate political question of Elizabeth's marriage, advocating for a match with Robert Dudley, Earl of Leicester, has been well documented, though recent studies of eyewit-ness accounts and explicit political valences suggest that this topical interpretation is less than definitive.[61] *Gorboduc*'s subject suited Dudley, the Inner Temple's Christmas Prince and Master of the Revels for 1561.

Succession is the main concern of *Gorboduc*, which adapted chronicle accounts of the Saxon king to rewrite a story of fraternal strife as an equally cautionary tale of foreign influences on royal succession.[62] The play's political importance is best understood in the context of other Inns of Court plays offering political counsel during this period, including *Jocasta* by George Gascoigne and Francis Kinwelmersh; two masques on marriage by Thomas Pound; and *Gismond of Salerne* by Henry Noel, Christopher Hatton, Roger Wilmot and others.[63] Safe political plays made only glancing references to contemporary affairs. Yet by contributing historical and topical observations to problems of governance, they expanded the very definition of the Elizabethan 'political nation'.[64]

Gorboduc's political topicality implied that medieval and pre-Conquest historical *exempla* had a direct bearing on public affairs. Its use of precedents to influence immediate political questions was not unique in itself, but Norton and Sackville's choice of form was. As this chapter has argued, in combining a historical subject with the structure and mood of Senecan tragedy this highly innovative play would have lasting effects on English historical drama for decades to follow. Furthermore its metrical form – blank verse – would be customary for English drama until the end of the seventeenth century. This was a tradition that began with Norton and Sackville's decision to turn the Earl of Surrey's blank verse (first used in English for his translations from Virgil's *Aeneid*, printed in 1554) into a medium for the theatre.[65] Sidney, whose test for readable verse was to turn it into prose, famously praised the play's 'skilfull *Poetrie*' for using a verse suiting natural speech to fulfil its Horatian purposes. Sidney described *Gorboduc* as 'full of stately speeches and well-sounding phrases, climbing to the height of Seneca's style, and as full of notable morality, which it doth most delightfully teach, and so obtain the very end of poesy'.[66]

Seneca's plays incorporate a wide range of action within their immediate confines, through their narrative descriptions of events occurring offstage. Authors of history plays also found this a serviceable model. In *Gorboduc*, the royal family descends into internecine wars when princes are misled into bad decisions – most often due to their misperceptions of others' intentions. Speculation, rumour and news circulate with scant regard for the distinction. The word 'tale' describes both prophecies of bad events and their descriptions when they inevitably follow. When the bad counsellor Tyndar reports that 'monstrous tales' of the royal family are circulating, his good counterpart Philander warns Porrex against 'traitorous tales' and 'false reports' (II.ii.24, 31, 32). Marcella later tearfully reports the same prince's murder by his mother, a 'woeful tale' that collapses rumour into actual events (IV.ii.177). Her description of this murder resembles others in the play, including Clotyn's brief description of the king and queen's deaths at the hands of their rebellious subjects. They are affairs that Senecan drama does not linger over, but describes in brief before dealing exhaustively with their excruciating consequences. These include the dire results of various errors that Eubulus recites:

> This is the end, when in fond princes hearts
> Flattery prevailes and sage rede hath no place.
> These are the plagues when murder is the mean
> To make new heirs unto the royal crown.
> Thus wreak the gods, when that the mother's wrath
> Naught but the blood of her own child may 'suage.
> These mischiefs spring when rebels will arise,
> To work revenge and judge their prince's fact.
> This, this ensues when noble men do fail
> In loyal troth, and subjects will be kings.
>
> (V.ii.236–45)

The catalogue of events and their moral causes is a reference-card for *Gorboduc* as a whole. The play's horror at civil strife resonates through later history plays, as does its preoccupation with the fullest possible range of cautionary lessons to be learned from these errors.

Richardus Tertius

When Legge wrote *Richardus Tertius* he confronted the difficult task of dramatizing events that had transpired less than a century earlier, events in which one dynasty ended and the Tudor dynasty began. Legge's fealty to historical accuracy, despite his interest in the play's ideological value, suggests that he appreciated the difficulties of adapting history for the stage.[67] His chief sources for Richard's reign were chronicles and biographies by Edward Hall, Sir Thomas More and Polydore Vergil.[68] More's *History of King Richard III* (1513) was the first to characterize Richard as a murderous tyrant. The Tudor propagandist Vergil wrote his *Historia Angliae* (1534) explicitly for the approval of Henry VIII. Hall is suited to dramatic adaptation because his *Union of the Two Noble and Illustre Families of Lancaster and York* (1548) depicts history in a Tacitean style, vividly 'quoting' speeches and dialogues at length.

Bad government applies as much to the tyrant's moral constitution as to its outward manifestations, a balance that Seneca achieves by situating his tyrants in the middle of things, provoking and responding to their circumstances.[69] Many of their conventional elements mapped onto chronicle accounts of Richard's downfall: his suffering victims; his introspection; his violent end.[70] Dana Sutton identifies specific parallels between Legge's Richard and Seneca's tyrants: his murder of the young princes, as Atreus killed (and served at dinner) the sons of Thyestes; his courtship of Lady Anne, as Lycus courted Megara in *Hercules Furens*; his reliance on terror and threats of violence, as shared by Nero in *Octavia* and Atreus and Eteocles in *Phoenissae*.[71] Legge omits a few of Richard's crimes, including the murder of Henry VI, but he is the first explicitly to charge Richard with direct responsibility for the death of his wife, Lady Anne.[72] He also deviates from many of Seneca's conventions, in ways that Norton and Sackville did not. He diminishes the role of the chorus in favour of characters' commentaries (though there are choric songs at the end of each *Actio*); he casts aside the dramatic unities; and he puts more than three actors on stage at once.[73]

Legge's Richard combines Senecan tyranny with the characteristics his Tudor historiographers had used to vilify him, including his vacillation and subordination to advisers.[74] Richard's decisions to do what is necessary to secure the crown often require not only counsel but the convincing words of his counsellors. When he agrees to prosecute Lord Hastings for treason, for instance, it is only after Catesby urges him to set aside his fears. *Richardus Tertius* tells the story of Richard's rise and fall, but not through a history of a domineering character brought low by bad circumstances. Rather, it is the story of how a weak character creates circumstances adverse to his success, or how his show of strength masks moral weakness. Queen Elizabeth complains early in the play about Richard's ambitions with the metaphor of poison in a golden cup, a timeworn image that also appears in *Gorboduc*; and references to the evil lurking behind Richard's pleasant front recur throughout the play. But this is more than a front that Richard offers to others: it signals his internal division between ambition and doubt, strength and weakness. Legge interleaves Richard's commandments with these confessions of weakness, to underscore the division between Richard's ambitions and his doubts: '*Spes concutit mentem metusque turbidam*'.[75] Late in the play, when a remorseful Brackenbury prays for God's mercy, it is because he has witnessed the king's 'burning' fear making him cruel: '*Metu Richardus aestuat ferox*' (2781). Tyrell confirms in the next scene that fear, not anger, makes Richard cruel: '*Regem metus non ira crudelem facit'* (2899). Richard makes these fears explicit when he bemoans the circumstances they have created: Richmond's rebellion, buoyed by the people's hatred of their tyrant (3578f.) Shortly before he learns of Richmond's approach to England, Richard laments his torment by a 'flood' of cares: *'Torqueor metu miser, / Disrumpor aestuante curarum salo'* (3773–4).

The notion that history has lessons for future princes is common enough, but Legge uses Senecan teleology to reveal how the effects of historical change are felt for generations. Legge appreciated that the dynastic histories of his chronicle sources are best told in a Senecan sequence – that teleological history takes a long time to unfold, and culminates in the present. *Richardus Tertius* tells the story of Richard's violent rise and overthrow in fifteen Acts, divided into three *Actiones* performed on successive evenings. The story extends from the death of King Edward IV, and his brother Richard's murder of his heirs, to the defeat of King Richard, after lamenting the death of his own son. Shakespeare's historical tetralogies are indebted to a similarly thorough understanding of Seneca's sense of time and dynastic history. Familiarity with *3 Henry VI* illuminates a host of references to recent history in *Richard III*, and Henry V's victories redeem his father's usurpation of Richard II.[76] Similarly, the success of the Tudor dynasty is implicitly predicated on the villainy of its predecessor. Legge explicitly addresses his queen, Henry's granddaughter, in the play's epilogue: *'Elizabetham, patre dignam filiam / canosque vincentem seniles virginem'* [Elizabeth, a daughter worthy of her father, a virgin who overcomes the hoary locks of age] (4696–7).

Like Sackville and Norton, Legge's neo-Senecan drama relies upon narrative descriptions of events occurring offstage. This is particularly evident in the play's third *Actio* when these events come thick and fast: Buckingham's capture (3698); Richmond's approach (3788f.) and then his escape from capture (4084f.); and Richard's death in battle (4589f.). These descriptions and commentaries have the cumulative effect of diminishing Richard's self-determination, making him appear (like Gorboduc) the victim of his own bad government loosing forces beyond his control. And Legge uses this reportage in a very sophisticated fashion by depicting the circulating rumours and conversations about the king's real and perceived crimes. When Prince Edward approaches London, a crowd of citizens ('artificers') expresses alarms about his wellbeing under Richard, the Lord Protector (579f.), and in the next Act Buckingham reports that this 'idle rabble' will accuse them of the same: *'Vulgus probris futile lacessit improbis'* (714). Legge charts Richard's descent from suspected to actual tyranny through the realization of these accusations and rumours, much as Norton and Sackville create a sense of foreboding with their counsellors' explicit predictions of precisely the dire outcomes that will obtain. When Buckingham and the Bishop of Ely finally turn away from Richard, they hesitantly voice their doubts to one another before Ely rehearses his misdeeds at length (3073f.). Similarly, before King Richard's coronation Legge presents a citizen of London and a visitor in conversation about the 'princely sin' of confining the princes to the Tower: '*O scelus!*' the visitor exclaims; '*Sed principis tamen*', the citizen replies ironically (2681–2). Later, at Lowell's urging, Richard attempts to manipulate the news by circulating rumours of his wife's death (3866), shortly before she is reported dead (4129).

Legge's admixture of rumour, speculation, misinformation and foreboding into the historiographic techniques of description and debate summarizes the playwright's poetical freedoms: to speculate about both the workings of recorded history and its alternatives, to posit the accidents that combine into its substance. The aim of these freedoms, as Sidney prescribes and his contemporaries practise, is to propagate not merely the historiographer's well-knowing but the poet's well-doing. Richard's inner weakness and outward tyranny are manifested through Legge's range of rhetorical modes, all of them directed to the rhetoric of exemplarity that is an essential function of historical drama.

Conclusion

History refuses to repeat itself, so its vices are easier to shun than its virtues are to imitate. Thus tragedy suits history's exemplary function better than comedy; thus among the troublesome reigns and tragical falls of Elizabethan history plays, there are comparatively few pleasant conceited comedies. History has also preserved more of the materials of tragedy – the kingly decisions and international conflicts – into which playwrights can interpolate the private thoughts and agendas that are the engines of recorded history. As Sidney describes the pitiably circumscribed historian, 'Many times he must tell events whereof he can yield no cause; or if he do, it must be poetically.'[77]

In Senecan drama, these three playwrights found a means not merely to fuel nationalist sentiments or advise their immediate audiences, but to investigate the inner workings of history. They viewed its agents as both familiar and distant, moved by common emotions and by the reprehensible motives of division or ambition. Norton, Sackville and Legge were each educated in the traditions of historical precedent and neo-Senecan drama, both of which had strong pedagogical and moral purposes. Their combination of the two for forensic and rhetorical ends is not surprising. What is surprising is how profound their effects were on later writers of historical drama.

Notes

Research for this essay was funded by the Social Sciences and Humanities Research Council of Canada. I am grateful to Paulina Kewes, Jessica Winston and this volume's editors and anonymous reader for their comments on previous versions of its argument.

1. Philip Sidney, *Miscellaneous Prose*, ed. Katherine Duncan-Jones and Jan van Dorsten (Oxford: Clarendon Press, 1973), p. 351.
2. See H. B. Charlton, *The Senecan Tradition in Renaissance Tragedy* (Manchester: Manchester University Press, 1921; repr. 1946), p. 154. More recently, see Howard B. Norland, 'Adapting to the Times: Expansion and Interpolation in the Elizabethan Translations of Seneca', *Classical and Modern Literature*, 16 (1996), 241–63; Don Share, ed., *Seneca in English* (London: Penguin, 1998), p. xx; and Bruce R. Smith, 'Toward the Rediscovery of Tragedy: Productions of Seneca's Plays on the English Renaissance Stage', *Renaissance Drama*, 9 (1978), 3–37.
3. Share, *Seneca in English*, p. xxi; see pp. 3–63 for excerpts from translations from Surrey to Neville. Jessica Winston divides Seneca's Elizabethan reception into two phases, before and after Newton's anthology ('Seneca in Early Elizabethan England', *Renaissance Quarterly*, 59 (2006), 29–55; pp. 30–1). Senecan drama and translations in the 1560s inaugurated 'the domestication of tragedy as a genre for cultivating political consciousness', before playwrights like Kyd, Marlowe and Shakespeare engaged more 'comprehensively' with his tragedies (pp. 54–5).
4. Seneca, *The seconde tragedie of Seneca entituled Thyestes faithfully Englished by Iasper Heywood* (London: the house of the late Thomas Berthelette, 1560), sigs. *6ʳ, ℞6ʳ, *8ᵛ, *7ᵛ. (In this octavo there are two preliminary quires – *8 and ℞8 – before the main run of signatures. '℞' is an approximation of the horizontal clover leaf sign used on the second of these quires.)
5. Winston describes this community of writers in 'Seneca in Early Elizabethan England', pp. 32–4; see also Norland, 'Adapting to the Times', p. 246.
6. *Gorboduc's* direct imitators were George Gascoigne and Francis Kinwelmershe, *Jocasta* (1566); and Roger Wilmot et al., *Gismond of Salerne* (1566).
7. Jessica Winston, 'Expanding the Political Nation: *Gorboduc* at the Inns of Court and Succession Revisited', *Early Theatre*, 8 (2005), 11–34; p. 13.
8. John Fortesque, *A Learned Commendation of the Politique Lawes of England* (London: 1567), fol. 115ʳ.
9. Richard Grafton, *A Chronicle at large and meere History of the affayres of Englande and Kinges of the same* (London: Henry Denham for Richarde Tottel and Humfrey Toy, 1568; 2nd edition, 1569), sig. 7ʳ. (There is one preliminary numbered quire before the main run of signatures.)

10. The medieval definition of tragedy associated it not (exclusively) with the theatre but with exemplary rhetoric, or the recitation of brief biographies for moral effect. Chaucer presents a series of tragedies in his 'Monk's Tale', and describes *Troilus and Criseyde* as 'litel myn tragedye', by which he means any cautionary tale, historical or not (Chaucer, *Troilus and Criseyde*, in *The Riverside Chaucer*, ed. Larry D. Benson et al. (Boston: Houghton Mifflin, 1987), V.1786). Robert Henryson similarly calls his *Testament of Cresseid* a tragedy. Though Ranulph Higden credited Seneca with 'bokes of benefites, of clemency, declamacions, and tragedies', it is unclear whether he had the classical or medieval definition of tragedy in mind (*Polychronicon Ranulphi Higden monachi cestrensis*, ed. J. R. Lumby. *Rolls Series*, 9 vols (London: Longman, 1865–86), vol. 4, p. 403).

11. Lydgate also underscores tragedy's historical and performative qualities in his *Troy Book*, when he describes the Trojans inventing tragedies to entertain one another during the siege. Suitable exempla for these tragedies are 'historial, / Of kynges, princes', as they are in his *Falls of Princes* (Lydgate, *Troy Book. AD. 1412–20*, ed. Henry Bergen (London: Early English Text Society, 1906–75), vol. 2, ll. 869–70).

12. See Paul Budra, *A Mirror for Magistrates and the* de casibus *Tradition* (Toronto: University of Toronto Press, 2000). On the *Mirror's* relevance to contemporary politics see Winston, 'Expanding the Political Nation'.

13. In the *Poetics* Aristotle warns that history cannot be intelligible as the plot of a play, because it describes not a single action but a single period of time. See D. W. Lucas's Introduction to *Aristotle: Poetics* (Oxford: Clarendon Press, 1968), p. 119. Benjamin Griffin thus defines 'formlessness' and 'the plot's immersion in a historical continuum' as defining features of history plays in *Playing the Past: Approaches to English Historical Drama, 1385–1660* (Cambridge: D. S. Brewer, 2001), pp. 135, 146.

14. *Ecerinus* was 'freely embellished with horrors in an attempt at Senecan sensationalism' and didactic effect (Irving Ribner, *The English History Play in the Age of Shakespeare* (London: Methuen, 1957; repr. 1965), p. 40). John W. Cunliffe notes that four MSS of this play survive in English libraries, testifying to its international influence (*Early English Classical Tragedies* (Oxford: Clarendon Press, 1912), p. xxii).

15. See Alfred Harbage and Samuel Schoenbaum (eds), *Annals of English Drama, 975–1700*, rev. Sylvia Stoler Wagonheim (London: Routledge, 3rd edn, 1989). Bale's 'Anti-Catholic Histories' are *King Johan* (1531) and *The Knaveries of Thomas Becket* (1538). Three intervening plays are designated 'Biblical History' (Anon., *Samson*, in 1567); 'Didactic History' (Gosson, *Catiline's Conspiracies*, in 1578); and 'Classical History' (Anon., *Pompey*, in 1582).

16. The composition of the *Mirror* would be passed on to Richard Baldwin and George Ferrers (and printed, in two volumes, in 1559 and 1563).

17. Thomas Sackville and Thomas Norton, *Gorboduc or Ferrex and Porrex*, ed. Irby B. Cauthen, Jr., Regents Renaissance Drama series (Lincoln: University of Nebraska Press, 1970), I.ii.388–93. All quotations are from this edition, and further references are to act, scene and line only.

18. William Baldwin, *A Myrroure for Magistrates* (London: Thomas Marsh, 1559), sigs. Ciii[r-v].

19. Thomas Newton, *Seneca His Tenne Tragedies, Translated into English* (London: Thomas Marsh, 1581), sigs. A1ᵛ-A2ʳ.
20. Geoffrey Bullough (ed.), *Narrative and Dramatic Sources for Shakespeare* (8 vols; London: Routledge & Kegan Paul, 1957–75), vol. 3 (1960), 'Introduction: *Richard III*', pp. 221–48 (p. 236).
21. Sidney, *Miscellaneous Prose*, p. 356.
22. Bullough, *Narrative and Dramatic Sources*, vol. 3, p. 236. Bullough is unsure whether Shakespeare borrowed the wooing scene idea from Legge or straight from Seneca.
23. H. R. Woudhuysen has uncovered 180 MSS of some 110 dramatic works from this period, and identifies Legge's play as the most widely copied Cambridge drama (*Sir Philip Sidney and the Circulation of Manuscripts 1558–1640* (Oxford: Clarendon Press, 1996), p. 144). Eleven MSS survive today, at least seven of which were written before 1590. Dana Sutton notes verbal echoes of *Richardus Tertius* in the writings of two Christ Church (Oxford) scholars: William Gager's Senecan plays *Meleager* (1582) and *Ulysses Redux* (1591), and Robert Burton's *Philosophaster* (1617) and *Anatomy of Melancholy* (1621–). See Thomas Legge, *Richardus Tertius*, vol. 1 of *The Complete Plays*, ed. and trans. Dana Sutton, Series XVII, vols. 13–14 of *Classical Languages and Literature* (New York: Lang, 1993), pp. xvii–xxii. Given Gager's appreciation for Legge, the possibility of his having a MS copy of the play is strong; see J. W. Binns, *Intellectual Culture in Elizabethan and Jacobean England: the Latin Writings of the Age* (Leeds: Cairus, 1990), pp. 127–31. Alan Nelson conjectures that Legge influenced Shakespeare through Christopher Marlowe, whose *Tamberlaine* owes its ambition and range to *Richardus Tertius* – though Robert Greene and Thomas Nashe are alternative sources ('Cambridge University Drama in the 1580s', *The Elizabethan Theatre*, 9 (1985), 19–31).
24. See, *inter alia* and most recently, Yves Peyré, ' "Confusion now hath made his masterpiece": Senecan Resonances in *Macbeth*', in *Shakespeare and the Classics*, ed. Charles Martindale and A. B. Taylor (Cambridge: Cambridge University Press, 2006), pp. 141–55. The definitive study is Robert Miola, *Shakespeare and Classical Tragedy: the Influence of Seneca* (Oxford: Clarendon Press, 1992).
25. George B. Churchill, *Richard the Third up to Shakespeare* (Berlin: Mayer & Müller, 1900), p. 269; Frederick S. Boas, *University Drama in the Tudor Age* (Oxford: Clarendon Press, 1914), pp. 111–12.
26. T. Legge, *Richardus Tertius*, ed. Robert J. Lordi, in *Renaissance Drama: a Collection of Critical Editions*, series ed. Stephen Orgel (New York: Garland, 1979), p. 2; Legge, *Complete Plays*, ed. Sutton, vol. 13, p. xiii. Dismissing *Gorboduc* as an 'excursion into fantasy', Sutton concludes that 'Legge comes as close as anybody to being the father of English historical drama' (p. xii).
27. Paulina Kewes, 'The Elizabethan History Play: a True Genre?', in *A Companion to Shakespeare's Works*, ed. Richard Dutton and Jean E. Howard, 3 vols (Malden, MA: Blackwell, 2003), vol. 2, pp. 170–93 (p. 171). For a recent comprehensive survey, see Griffin, *Playing the Past*.
28. Kewes, 'Elizabethan History Play', pp. 188, 189.
29. See Binns, *Intellectual Culture*, pp. 120–40 (pp. 139–40); Martin Spevack and J.W. Binns, 'Prefatory Remarks', in Robert J. Lordi and Robert Ketterer (eds), *Thomas Legge: Richardus Tertius and Solymitana Clades* [facsimiles of Clare

College, Cambridge MS K 3.12; and Cambridge University Library MS Add. 7958, respectively], Series II, vol. 8 of *Renaissance Latin Drama in England* (Hildesheim: Georg Olms, 1989), p. i.

30. D. R. Woolf, *The Social Circulation of the Past: English Historical Culture 1500–1730* (Oxford: Oxford University Press, 2003); Andrew Escobedo, *Nationalism and Historical Loss in Renaissance England: Foxe, Dee, Spenser, Milton* (Ithaca and London: Cornell University Press, 2004); and Philip Schwyzer, *Literature, Nationalism and Memory in Early Modern England and Wales* (Cambridge: Cambridge University Press, 2004). For Stow, see Ian Gadd and Alexandra Gillespie (eds), *John Stow (1525–1605) and the Making of the English Past* (London: British Library, 2004).

31. Nashe, *Pierce Penniless, His Supplication to the Devil* (London: Abell Leffes for John Busbie, 1592), sig.F3^r.

32. Baldwin, *Mirror*, sig. Cii^v.

33. Critics are divided on Seneca's authorship of the 'history play' *Octavia*. Even if it is not his, Daalder argues for a strong interest in history and context in the tragedies, and notes that the banquet scene from *Thyestes* uses not only myth as source but also what he calls the 'real story of the noble Mede Harpagus narrated by Seneca in *De Ira* III, XV' (Seneca, *Thyestes*, ed. Joost Daalder, tr. Jasper Heywood (London: Ernest Benn, 1982), pp. xvi–xvii). Furthermore, he sees in the tragedies useful 'camouflaged presentations of equally true horror stories' perpetrated by Nero (p. xvi). This is, of course, a method used by the Tacitean playwrights of the very late sixteenth century to make political points. See introduction to this collection for discussion of this topic.

34. I am grateful to Jessica Winston for this point.

35. Bullough, *Narrative and Dramatic Sources*, vol. 3, p. 236.

36. Winston, 'Seneca in Early Elizabethan England', p. 34.

37. Described thus by Roger Manners, Elizabeth's esquire of the body; cit. Marie Axton, 'Norton, Thomas (1530x32–1584)', *Oxford Dictionary of National Biography: from the Earliest Times to the Year 2000*, ed. H. C. G. Matthew and B. Harrison, 60 vols (Oxford: Oxford University Press, 2004) [hereafter *Oxford DNB*], vol. 41, p. 194. The crime was appropriate, given Norton's advocacy of speaking publicly 'for mater of justice or of policie' (in *Orations of Arsanes agaynst Philip the Trecherous Kyng of Macedone* (London: 1560), sig. A4^v; cit. Axton, 'Norton', p. 191). For Norton's public life see Michael A. R. Graves, *Thomas Norton: Parliament Man* (Oxford: Blackwell, 1994).

38. BL Add. MS 48023, fols 45–58; fol. 44^v. For the broader ambitions of this unfinished survey see BL Cotton MS Titus F3, fols 271–275^v; cit. Axton, 'Norton', p. 194.

39. Axton, 'Norton', p. 192.

40. Rivkah Zim, 'Sackville, Thomas, first Baron Buckhurst and first Earl of Dorset (c.1536–1608)', *Oxford DNB*, vol. 48, pp. 542–8.

41. Thus George Abbot, in his funeral sermon for Sackville, cited Elizabeth's description of Sackville 'in his yoonger daies'. *A Sermon Preached at Westminster May 26. 1608. At The Fvnerall Solemnities of the Right Honorable Thomas Earle of Dorset, late L. High Treasurer of England* (London: 1608), sig. C2^v.

42. Jasper Heywood, 'The Preface', in Seneca, *Thyestes*, sigs. *4^v–℞ 8^v; *8^v.

43. Marie Axton, *The Queen's Two Bodies: Drama and the Elizabethan Succession* (London: Royal Historical Society, 1977), p. 3.

44. Nancy Siraisi, 'Anatomizing the Past: Physicians and History in Renaissance Culture', *Renaissance Quarterly*, 53 (2000), 1–30 (p. 3). She accounts for the disproportionate number of physicians among Italian historiographers: 'far from being isolated in a specialist, academic, or craft ghetto, they were full participants in a culture in which history had come to be valued.'

45. Norman Jones, *The Birth of the Elizabethan Age* (Oxford: Blackwell, 1993), p. 4.

46. Axton, *Queen's Two Bodies*, p. 11.

47. Alexandra F. Johnston, 'The Inherited Tradition: the Legacy of Provincial Drama', *The Elizabethan Theatre*, 13 (1989), 1–25, p. 9. For an account of academic drama from Eton to the universities, see pp. 5–9.

48. See *Records of Early English Drama: Cambridge*, ed. Alan H. Nelson (Toronto: University of Toronto Press, 1989), hereafter *REED Cambridge*, vol. 1, pp. 132–3 for the statutes in Latin; and vol. 2, pp. 1112–14 for Abigail Ann Young's translation (cited here).

49. Staging plays in college halls usually involved the erection of temporary stages: Queen's College had an elaborate scaffolding built in 1546–9 whose 500 pieces of timber had to be assembled and disassembled each year. For more on academic stages, see Alan H. Nelson's *Early Cambridge Theatres: College, University, and Town Stages, 1464–1720* (Cambridge: Cambridge University Press, 1994); also his 'Early Staging in Cambridge', in *A New History of Early English Drama*, ed. John D. Cox and David Scott Kastan (New York: Columbia University Press, 1997), pp. 59–67, which includes a study of academic stage-conventions in three of Shakespeare's plays.

50. Details of Legge's biography are from Christopher N. L. Brooke, 'Legge, Thomas (*c.* 1535–1607)', *Oxford DNB*, vol. 33, pp. 191–2; and Brooke, *A History of Gonville and Caius College* (Woodbridge, Suffolk: Brewer, 1985; repr. 1996), pp. 79–93. See further John Venn, *Caius College* (London: F. E. Robinson & Co, 1901, repr. 1923), pp. 76–92; and Peter Stein, *The Character and Influence of the Roman Civil Law: Historical Essays* (London and Ronceverte: Hambledon Press, 1988), pp. 197–208. I am indebted to Paulina Kewes for the latter two citations.

51. *REED Cambridge*, vol. 1, pp. 206 and 211.

52. See *REED Cambridge*, vol. 1, pp. 221, 225, 246, 248 and 250. Lordi credits Legge with directing *Medea, Asinaria* and *Jepthes* (Legge, *Richardus Tertius*, ed. Lordi, p. iii).

53. Nelson, 'Cambridge University Drama', p. 20.

54. Cited from Young's translation in *REED Cambridge*, vol. 2, p. 1148. The college commissioned Moore's Latin tribute in 1655. On this performance see Boas, *University Drama*, p. 112.

55. Francis Meres, *Palladis Tamia. Wits Treasvry* (London: 1598), sig. 2O3r. For more on Legge MSS, see Legge, *Richardus Tertius*, ed. Lordi, p. xvi.

56. John Harington, *An Apologie of Poetrie*, cit. Robert S. Knapp, 'The Academic Drama', in *A Companion to Renaissance Drama*, ed. Arthur F. Kinney (Malden, MA: Blackwell, 2002), pp. 257–65 (p. 262).

57. Thomas Nashe, *Have with yov to Saffron-Walden*, in *The Works of Thomas Nashe*, ed. R. B. McKerrow, rev. by F. P. Wilson, 5 vols (Oxford: Blackwell, 1958), vol. 3, p. 13.

58. Thomas Fuller, *History of the Worthies of England*, pp. 276–7; cit. *REED Cambridge*, vol. 1, p. 286. On Fuller's relationship to William Moore, see *REED Cambridge*, vol. 2, p. 1221.

59. II.i.126. Imitating Day's marginalia, Cauthen's edition places this sentence in quotation marks.

60. John Briton (d. 1587) transcribed *sententiae* from this play into his manuscript of Sidney's *Astrophil and Stella*. He also inscribed a number of other literary extracts (from Chaloner's translation of Erasmus's *Praise of Folly*, and from the *Mirror for Magistrates*) alongside household records (Woudhuysen, *Sir Philip Sidney*, pp. 410f.).

61. An eyewitness to the play's premiere performance at the Inner Temple interprets it as explicitly favouring Dudley's claim to Elizabeth over that of his rival King Eric XIV of Sweden. In 'Expanding the Political Nation', Winston revises Axton's case for Dudley, using eyewitness evidence as outlined in Norman Jones and Paul Whitfield White, '*Gorboduc* and Royal Marriage Politics: an Elizabethan Playgoer's Report of the Premiere Performance', *English Literary Renaissance*, 26 (1996), 3–16. See also Mike Pincombe, 'Robert Dudley, *Gorboduc*, and "The Masque of Beauty and Desire": a Reconsideration of the Evidence for Political Intervention', *Parergon*, 20 (2003), 19–44. For Dudley's case see M. Axton, 'Robert Dudley and the Inner Temple Revels', *The Historical Journal*, 13 (1970), 365–78; and *Queen's Two Bodies*, chs 4 and 5.

62. Winston, 'Expanding the Political Nation', p. 15. The story appears in chronicles from Geoffrey of Monmouth (*c.* 1136) to Fabyan (1516), Rastell (1529), Hardyng (1543) and Lanquet (1559); see Norton and Sackville, *Gorboduc*, ed. Cauthen, pp. xiv–xvi.

63. *Jocasta* is a translation of Euripides; for Pound, see Mike Pincombe, 'Two Elizabethan Masque-Orations by Thomas Pound', *Bodleian Library Record*, 12 (1987), 349–80; *Gismond* adapts a tale from Boccaccio's *Decameron*.

64. Winston, 'Expanding the Political Nation', pp. 27–8. This term for the sixteenth century's expanded ruling class is from David Loades, *Power in Tudor England* (New York: St. Martin's Press, 1997), p. 4.

65. W. A. Sessions, *Henry Howard, The Poet Earl of Surrey* (Oxford: Clarendon Press, 1999), p. 189. Perhaps prompted by Surrey, Norton translated Calvin's quotations of Virgil into blank verse in Norton's 1559 translation of Calvin's *Institutiones* (Axton, 'Norton', p. 191). See also H. Baker, 'Blank Verse before *Gorboduc*', *Modern Language Notes*, 48 (1933), 529–30.

66. Sidney, *Miscellaneous Prose*, p. 381.

67. Legge wrote from 'an intellectual conviction that his new kind of historical drama ought to be faithful to the historical record' (Legge, *Complete Plays*, ed. Sutton, vol. 13, p. xii). Sutton draws a contemporary parallel in suggesting that Legge conceived of his dramatization of Hall as modern writers 'novelize' film and television programmes (p. xiv).

68. Boas argues that More and Vergil had been absorbed into Hall, and proposes Richard Grafton's continuation of Hardyng's *Chronicle* (1543) as another influential source. All are outweighed by Hall, he concludes (*University Drama*, pp. 114–15).

69. Howard B. Norland, 'Legge's Neo-Senecan *Richardus Tertius*', *Humanistica Lovaniensia: Journal of Neo-Latin Studies*, 42 (1993), 285–300 (p. 288). Legge represents Richard's rise to power in the first two plays and his downfall in

the third, notes Sutton, arguing that Legge improved on Seneca's sequential plays. But Sutton understates Seneca's nuanced portraits of Hercules and others (discussed above) when he states that 'Seneca [...] can only represent tyranny in full bloom' (Legge, *Complete Plays*, ed. Sutton, vol. 13, p. x).
70. Norland cites Nero in Seneca's *Octavia* as Legge's most direct model for Richard ('Legge's Neo-Senecan *Richardus Tertius*', pp. 288, 294).
71. If Legge knew *Octavia* to be the work of Maternus, the Senecan imitator, he seems unfazed by it: he makes much use of this play, a version of recent Roman history. On this question, see Frank Justus Miller's edition of Seneca's *Tragedies*, 9 vols (Cambridge, MA: Harvard University Press, 1979–87), vol. 2, p. 405; and Norland, 'Legge's Neo-Senecan *Richardus Tertius*', p. 288. For Sutton's parallels, mentioned here, see Legge, *Complete Plays*, ed. Sutton, vol. 13, p. xviii.
72. See Legge, *Complete Plays*, ed. Sutton, vol. 13, ll. 4040–79; also p. xvii.
73. Legge, *Complete Plays*, ed. Sutton, vol. 13, p. xii.
74. Churchill, *Richard the Third*, p. 399; Legge, *Richardus Tertius*, ed. Lordi, p. 3.
75. Legge, *Complete Plays*, ed. Sutton, vol. 13, l. 1488. Further references to this text are to line numbers only. Most of the Latin translations herein are from Sutton's bilingual edition.
76. For the 'contingency' of beginnings and endings in Shakespeare's histories see David Scott Kastan, *Shakespeare and the Shapes of Time* (London: Macmillan, 1982), pp. 37–55.
77. Sidney, *Miscellaneous Prose*, p. 355.

Bibliography

Manuscripts

BL Add. MS 48023.
BL Cotton MS Titus F3.

Printed works

Abbot, George, *A Sermon Preached at Westminster May 26. 1608. At The Fvnerall Solemnities of the Right Honorable Thomas Earle of Dorset, late L. High Treasurer of England* (London: Melchisedech Bradwood for William Aspley, 1608).
Axton, M., 'Norton, Thomas (1530x32–1584)', *Oxford Dictionary of National Biography*, ed. H. C. G. Matthew and B. Harrison (Oxford: Oxford University Press, 2004).
— *The Queen's Two Bodies: Drama and the Elizabethan Succession* (London: Royal Historical Society, 1977).
— 'Robert Dudley and the Inner Temple Revels', *The Historical Journal*, 13 (1970), 365–78.
Baker, H., 'Blank Verse before *Gorboduc*', *Modern Language Notes*, 48 (1933), 529–30.
Baldwin, William, *A Myrroure for Magistrates* (London: Thomas Marsh, 1559).
Binns, J. W., *Intellectual Culture in Elizabethan and Jacobean England: the Latin Writings of the Age* (Leeds: Cairus, 1990).

Boas, Frederick S., *University Drama in the Tudor Age* (Oxford: Clarendon Press, 1914).

Brooke, Christopher N. L., *A History of Gonville and Caius College* (Woodbridge: Brewer, 1985; repr. 1996).

— 'Legge, Thomas (*c.* 1535–1607)', *Oxford Dictionary of National Biography*, ed. H. C. G. Matthew and B. Harrison (Oxford: Oxford University Press, 2004).

Budra, Paul, A Mirror for Magistrates *and the* de casibus *Tradition* (Toronto: University of Toronto Press, 2000).

Bullough, Geoffrey (ed.), *Narrative and Dramatic Sources for Shakespeare* (8 vols; London: Routledge & Kegan Paul, 1957–75).

Charlton, H. B., *The Senecan Tradition in Renaissance Tragedy* (Manchester: Manchester University Press, 1921; repr. 1946).

Chaucer, Geoffrey, *The Riverside Chaucer*, ed. Larry D. Benson et al. (Boston: Houghton Mifflin, 1987).

Churchill, George B., *Richard the Third up to Shakespeare* (Berlin: Mayer & Müller, 1900).

Cunliffe, John W., *Early English Classical Tragedies* (Oxford: Clarendon Press, 1912).

Escobedo, Andrew, *Nationalism and Historical Loss in Renaissance England: Foxe, Dee, Spenser, Milton* (Ithaca and London: Cornell University Press, 2004).

Fortescue, John, *A Learned Commendation of the Politique Lawes of England* (London: Richard Tottel, 1567).

Gadd, Ian and Alexandra Gillespie (eds), *John Stow (1525–1605) and the Making of the English Past* (London: British Library, 2004).

Grafton, Richard, *A Chronicle at large and meere History of the affayres of Englande and Kinges of the same* (London: Henry Denham for Richard Tottel and Humfrey Toy, 1568; 2nd edn, 1569).

Graves, Michael A. R., *Thomas Norton: Parliament Man* (Oxford: Blackwell, 1994).

Griffin, Benjamin, *Playing the Past: Approaches to English Historical Drama, 1385–1660* (Cambridge: D. S. Brewer, 2001).

Harbage, Alfred and Samuel Schoenbaum (eds), *Annals of English Drama, 975–1700*, rev. Sylvia Stoler Wagonheim (London: Routledge, 3rd edn, 1989).

Higden, Ranulph, *Polychronicon Ranulphi Higden monachi cestrensis*, ed. J. R. Lumby, *Rolls Series*, 9 vols (London: Longman, 1865–86), vol. 4.

Johnston, Alexandra F., 'The Inherited Tradition: the Legacy of Provincial Drama', *The Elizabethan Theatre*, 13 (1989), 1–25.

Jones, Norman, *The Birth of the Elizabethan Age* (Oxford: Blackwell, 1993).

Jones, Norman and Paul Whitfield White, '*Gorboduc* and Royal Marriage Politics: an Elizabethan Playgoer's Report of the Premiere Performance', *English Literary Renaissance*, 26 (1996), 3–16.

Kastan, David Scott, *Shakespeare and the Shapes of Time* (London: Macmillan, 1982).

Kewes, Paulina, 'The Elizabethan History Play: a True Genre?', *A Companion to Shakespeare's Works*, Vol. II: *The Histories*, ed. Richard Dutton and Jean E. Howard (Malden, MA: Blackwell, 2003).

Knapp, Robert S., 'The Academic Drama', *A Companion to Renaissance Drama*, ed. Arthur F. Kinney (Malden, MA: Blackwell, 2002).

Legge, Thomas, *The Complete Plays*, ed. and tr. Dana Sutton, 2 vols, American University Studies. Series XVII: Classical Languages and Literature, vols 13–14 (New York: Lang, 1993).

— *Richardus Tertius*, ed. Robert J. Lordi, Renaissance Drama: a Collection of Critical Editions, series ed. Stephen Orgel (New York: Garland, 1979).

Loades, David, *Power in Tudor England* (New York: St. Martin's Press, 1997).

Lucas, D. W., 'Introduction', *Aristotle: Poetics* (Oxford: Clarendon Press, 1968).

Lydgate, John, *Troy Book. AD. 1412–20*, ed. Henry Bergen, 3 vols (London: Early English Text Society, 1906–75).

Meres, Francis, *Palladis Tamia. Wits Treasury* (London: P. Short for Cuthbert Burbie, 1598).

Miola, Robert, *Shakespeare and Classical Tragedy: the Influence of Seneca* (Oxford: Clarendon Press, 1992).

Nashe, Thomas, *Pierce Penniless, His Supplication to the Devil* (London: Abel Leffes for John Busbie, 1592).

— *The Works of Thomas Nashe*, ed. R. B. McKerrow, rev. F. P. Wilson, 5 vols (Oxford: Blackwell, 1958).

Nelson, Alan H. 'Cambridge University Drama in the 1580s', *The Elizabethan Theatre*, 9 (1985), 19–31.

— *Early Cambridge Theatres: College, University, and Town Stages, 1464–1720* (Cambridge: Cambridge University Press, 1994).

— 'Early Staging in Cambridge', *A New History of Early English Drama*, ed. John D. Cox and David Scott Kastan (New York: Columbia University Press, 1997).

— (ed.) *Records of Early English Drama: Cambridge*, 2 vols (Toronto: University of Toronto Press, 1989).

Newton, Thomas, *Seneca His Tenne Tragedies, Translated into English* (London: Thomas Marsh, 1581).

Norland, Howard B., 'Adapting to the Times: Expansion and Interpolation in the Elizabethan Translations of Seneca', *Classical and Modern Literature*, 16 (1996), 241–63.

— 'Legge's Neo-Senecan *Richardus Tertius*', *Humanistica Lovaniensia: Journal of Neo-Latin Studies*, 42 (1993), 285–300.

Norton, Thomas, *Orations of Arsanes agaynst Philip the Trecherous Kyng of Macedone* (London: John Day, 1560).

Norton, Thomas and Thomas Sackville, *Gorboduc, or Ferrex and Porrex*, ed. Irby B. Cauthen, Regents Renaissance Drama Series (Lincoln: University of Nebraska Press, 1970).

Peyré, Yves, ' "Confusion now hath made his masterpiece": Senecan Resonances in *Macbeth'*, *Shakespeare and the Classics*, ed. Charles Martindale and A. B. Taylor (Cambridge: Cambridge University Press, 2006).

Pincombe, Mike, 'Robert Dudley, *Gorboduc*, and "The Masque of Beauty and Desire": a Reconsideration of the Evidence for Political Intervention', *Parergon*, 20 (2003), 19–44.

— 'Two Elizabethan Masque-Orations by Thomas Pound', *Bodleian Library Record*, 12 (1987), 349–80.

Ribner, Irving, *The English History Play in the Age of Shakespeare* (London: Methuen, 1957; repr. 1965).

Schwyzer, Philip, *Literature, Nationalism and Memory in Early Modern England and Wales* (Cambridge: Cambridge University Press, 2004).

Seneca, Lucius Annaeus, *Seneca*, tr. Frank Justus Miller, 9 vols (Cambridge, MA: Harvard University Press, 1979–87).

— *The seconde tragedie of Seneca entituled Thyestes faithfully Englished by Iasper Heywood* (London: the house of the late Thomas Berthelette, 1560).

— *Thyestes*, trans. Jasper Heywood, ed. Joost Daalder (London: Ernest Benn, 1982).

Sessions, W. A., *Henry Howard, The Poet Earl of Surrey* (Oxford: Clarendon Press, 1999).

Share, Don (ed.), *Seneca in English* (London: Penguin, 1998).

Sidney, Philip, *Miscellaneous Prose*, ed. Katherine Duncan-Jones and Jan van Dorsten (Oxford: Clarendon Press, 1973).

Siraisi, Nancy, 'Anatomizing the Past: Physicians and History in Renaissance Culture', *Renaissance Quarterly*, 53 (2000), 1–30.

Smith, Bruce R., 'Toward the Rediscovery of Tragedy: Productions of Seneca's Plays on the English Renaissance Stage', *Renaissance Drama*, 9 (1978), 3–37.

Spevack Martin and J. W. Binns, 'Prefatory Remarks', *Thomas Legge: Richardus Tertius and Solymitana Clades*, ed. Robert J. Lordi and Robert Ketterer, Renaissance Latin Drama in England, Series II, vol. 8 (Hildesheim: Georg Olms, 1989).

Stein, Peter, *The Character and Influence of the Roman Civil Law: Historical Essays* (London and Ronceverte: Hambledon Press, 1988).

Venn, John, *Caius College* (London: Robinson, 1901; repr. 1923).

Winston, Jessica, 'Expanding the Political Nation: *Gorboduc* at the Inns of Court and Succession Revisited', *Early Theatre*, 8 (2005), 11–34.

— 'Seneca in Early Elizabethan England', *Renaissance Quarterly*, 59 (2006), 29–55.

Woolf, D. R., *The Social Circulation of the Past: English Historical Culture 1500–1730* (Oxford: Oxford University Press, 2003).

Woudhuysen, H. R., *Sir Philip Sidney and the Circulation of Manuscripts 1558–1640* (Oxford: Clarendon Press, 1996).

Zim, Rivkah, 'Sackville, Thomas, first Baron Buckhurst and first Earl of Dorset (c. 1536–1608)', *Oxford Dictionary of National Biography*, ed. H. C. G. Matthew and B. Harrison (Oxford: Oxford University Press, 2004).

5

History in the Making: the Case of Samuel Rowley's *When You See Me You Know Me* (1604/5)

Teresa Grant

The deliberate attempts of the Stuart kings to define their rule of reunited Britannia as the fulfilment of all past history seems to have been partly prompted by their anxieties about the effectiveness of *post facto* Tudor propaganda. The early years of James I's reign did include a short honeymoon, but the inevitable comparisons with Queen Elizabeth subtly, and increasingly, undermined his validity as man and monarch, because he was obviously much less good at being Elizabeth than she had been herself. This propaganda on behalf of the now-dead Tudors was curiously widespread, particularly in non-courtly circles, including on the public stage of the period.[1] The Tudor monarchs Henry VIII, Edward VI, Mary I and Elizabeth I are severally represented in six plays written between 1602 and 1611: *Sir Thomas Wyatt* (pr. 1607), the two parts of *If You Know Not Me You Know Nobody* (pr. 1605 and 1606), *When You See Me You Know Me* (pr. 1605), *The Whore of Babylon* (pr. 1607) and *Henry VIII* (perf. 1612/13). The citizen dramatists were working to a different remit from those historians, such as William Camden, more nearly concerned with the Jacobean court.[2] Not only did their dramatizations need to work as plays, but they were also going to be played in front of a London audience notable for its strong Protestantism, relative to other sections of English society.

All five of these plays rely to a greater or lesser extent on John Foxe's *Acts and Monuments* for at least some of their source material and, as Thomas S. Freeman has pointed out, many of the other sources they use, including Holinshed and Speed, also derive in part from Foxe's great tome.[3] The influence of *Acts and Monuments* in the seventeenth century is more pervasive and important than scholars have even yet discovered, though it has increasingly become apparent from the sheer number of copies in circulation that its influence was profound.[4] The work became in some sense a statement of Elizabethan national purpose, deliberately bolstering the Protestant Elizabethan religious settlement by representing the status quo as the culmination of all past religious history which, until Foxe corrected it for a grateful public, had been misrepresented by the Catholics: '[those who] altogether delight in untruths, and have replenished the whole Church of Christ with fained fables, lying miracles, false visions, miserable errors contained in their Missals and Portuses, Breviars, and Summaries, and almost no true tale in all their Saintes lyves and Festivals'.[5] This kind of Protestant polemic was as popular on the London stage as it was in its source, and dramatists cherry-picked the most famous and dramatic episodes on which to base their plays. We see developing, then, in the ten years from about 1600, a competition between rival theatre companies to mount the 'best' bits of Foxe, staging plays which deliberately refer to each other's contents, message and, in some cases, even title.

The earliest extant effort is Thomas Dekker and John Webster's *Sir Thomas Wyatt* which, though first printed (as a 'bad quarto') in 1607, is probably a shortened version of the two parts of the 'playe called Ladey Jane' for which Chettle, Dekker, Heywood, Wentworth Smith and Webster received money from Henslowe in October 1602.[6] These plays may also be related to the lost *The Overthrow of Rebels*, payments for the costumes of which also appear in Henslowe's diary in 1602.[7] Reportedly all these plays intermeshed the stories of Lady Jane Grey and Sir Thomas Wyatt the younger, as the extant but mangled text we have does, but the title page of the printed version promises more than it delivers – for instance 'the Coronation of Queen Mary, and the coming in of King Philip'.[8] Mary Foster Martin has noticed that Heywood's involvement in these plays influenced his own two-part Tudor history play, *If You Know Not Me You Know Nobody*, Part 1 of which reuses some material from the earlier collaborative effort.[9] *Sir Thomas Wyatt* and *If You Know Not Me* were written for the same company, the Earl of Worcester's Men, which was assigned to Queen Anne's patronage on the Stuart accession. The contents of Part 1 of *If You Know Not Me* (pr. 1605) are accurately reflected in its subtitle, 'The troubles of Queen Elizabeth', detailing the treatment Princess Elizabeth receives at her sister's hands during Mary's reign and culminating in Elizabeth's triumphant accession procession and her receiving an English Bible from the Mayor of London. Part 2 of *If You Know Not Me* (pr. 1606) mixes the story of Sir Thomas Gresham's founding of the Royal Exchange with a city comedy plot featuring his nephew John as the 'prodigal son' and culminates in the successful English defence against the Spanish Armada in 1588. It is clear in title and content that *If You Know Not Me* and *When You See Me You Know Me* (pr. 1605, written for the Prince's Men acting at the Fortune theatre) are directly responsive to one another, but we do not yet have secure evidence to indicate which was written first. The early Jacobean fad for Foxean history plays seems to have been finished off by the lack of success of Thomas Dekker's *The Whore of Babylon* (pr. 1607), an allegorical response to the Gunpowder Plot figuring Elizabeth as 'Titania' and representing the Catholic threats to her life during her long reign. Dekker claimed in the epistle *Lectori* that it failed because the acting was so bad, but the play itself is messy, overly spectacular and rather lacking in human interest.[10]

So, in 1605 Nathaniel Butter printed a play by Samuel Rowley about Henry VIII with the following description on its title page: '*When you see me, You know me*. Or the famous Chronicle Historie *of king Henry the eight, with the* birth and vertuous life of Edward *Prince of Wales*. As it was playd by the high and mightie Prince *of Wales his servants*.' The action of the play is a collection of disparate and unhistorical episodes from Henry VIII's long reign and since most readers will not be familiar with the play, and Rowley has altered so much of the history, it seems only sensible here to give a brief summary of the plot. The play opens with Cardinal Wolsey receiving French Ambassadors, with whose king he has struck a secret deal to persuade King Henry to peace in return for French support for his candidacy for the papacy. As the royal party awaits the Ambassadors, Henry's heavily pregnant queen, Jane Seymour, goes into labour, after a brief comic interlude where we first meet the king's Fool, Will Somers. The queen's progress is reported upon from off-stage during the ensuing negotiations over the marriage of Henry's sister Mary to the king of France. When events off-stage take a turn for the worse, Henry is finally asked to choose between the life of the child and his wife, opting heroically for the latter despite his previous excitement at the prospect of a son. He is overruled by Queen Jane who says that she cannot bear to see her child die, and the boy is named Edward as his mother expires.

Wolsey and the French Ambassadors lament the spread of Lutheran doctrine and Wolsey makes patronage promises in advance of his expected elevation to Pope. The loss of the queen has made Henry particularly bad-tempered and all his courtiers and Will Somers are too afraid to approach him; in fact, Wolsey bears the brunt of the royal temper when he presumes upon the king's patience to try to bear the news to him that the Pope has proclaimed Henry 'Defender of the Faith'. Will finally makes the king laugh by tricking Patch, Wolsey's simple-minded jester, into creeping up behind Henry and shouting 'Boo'; not unsurprisingly, Henry boxes Patch's ears and, with the ice broken by such hilarity, Will and the courtiers are finally able to confess to the king the effect his grief is having on court and country. Finally Henry listens to Wolsey's news and the normal business of the council is resumed. The king outlines his plan to visit the watches of London *incognito* and solicits Compton and Dudley's company in his attempt to uncover injustices. This is based on an actual event, Henry's 1510 city night-walk in disguise.[11] The mere mention of this story in Stow's *Annals* does not do justice to the strong ballad and chapbook tradition which incorporated several folk motifs and eventually became the source for the following extended section of the play. *When You See Me* has a comedy watch very much along the lines of Dogberry and Verges in *Much Ado*, and we see them getting ready for their nightly duties, having a quick illicit sleep and letting through obviously suspicious characters because they are too timorous to deal with trouble. Fortunately the king is perfectly capable of dealing with both localized and international threats to his authority and the interlude ends with the disguised Henry worsting Black Will, thief and murderer, in a duel (1062–1385).[12]

On our return to court we learn that the death of the French king has left Princess Mary a widow, and foiled Wolsey's plans for securing the papal throne; Henry also announces plans to marry again, this time to Lady Catherine Parr, whom Wolsey calls the 'hope of Luthers heresy' (1490). Indeed, in the following scenes Queen Catherine Parr does lend support to those, including Will Somers, Prince Edward and his tutor Cranmer, who oppose Wolsey's corrupt papal faction and doctrine. Charles Brandon, Duke of Suffolk, returns from France with the king's sister as instructed; unfortunately, and not as part of his remit, he has also married her. King Henry uses this to trick Bonner and Gardiner (Wolsey's evil side-kicks) into exposing themselves as yes-men when he asks them to condone his threatened execution of Brandon as punishment. The next part of the play allows Prince Edward to demonstrate to the audience the minutiae of his life, his schooling and his views on religious matters. Cranmer, Dr Tye the music master, Will Somers and Edward's whipping boy Ned Browne all appear as foils to show Edward's good sense, kindness and Protestantism. Back in Henry's court Queen Catherine defends Cranmer and the reformers against accusations that they are heretics and wins arguments with Bonner and Gardner about the reading of Scripture and the supremacy. She also champions the English Bible; on her exit the bishops strongly represent to the king the error of her ways and suggest that she must be got rid of before she imperils his soul. In Prince Edward's rooms, we find him reading aloud letters from his two sisters, Mary and Elizabeth, which show Mary's Catholicism making her superstitious and deluded and that Elizabeth is full of Protestant virtue. Queen Catherine has been excluded from the king's presence ever since her disputation with the bishops and seeks Edward's help in reconciliation with the king. The king has become convinced that Queen Catherine is guilty of treason and it is only Edward's intervention on his knees which persuades him to let her speak for her life. Of course the queen soon convinces him that they have both been the victims of ill-wishing gainsayers and, reconciled with his wife and her friends, Henry recalls the banished Cranmer to court. When Bonner and Gardiner try to arrest the queen, Henry has the guard haul them off to the Fleet instead. Will and Patch expose Wolsey as having been salting away the money given as tribute to Rome for his own personal use, storing it in his cellar in wine barrels; the Cardinal is finally disgraced, Henry revealing that he has had suspicions about his behaviour all along. The final scenes of the play stage the ceremonial arrival in England of the Emperor Charles V, and his reception and investiture with the Order of the Garter by Prince Edward. Wolsey is dismissed from the king's service and the play ends with a rhyming competition between the Emperor and Will Somers.

Indeed, this play has received most of its critical attention on account of its approximate representation of historical fact; in F. P. Wilson's words, 'Rowley flouts chronology with a freedom unusual even in the chronicle plays of his age'.[13] The example that Wilson gives to show the play's historical inaccuracy is that Wolsey (d. 1530) is still alive in the world of the play in 1546. He could well have added that, as a result, between them Rowley's Cardinal Wolsey and Bishop Stephen Gardiner have to rewrite substantially the religio-political events of the 1530s:

> *Gard.* You saw how soone his majestie was wonne,
>   To scorne the Pope, and Romes religion,
>   When Queene *Anne Bullen* wore the diadem.
> *Wool.* Gardner tis true, so was the rumor spread:
>   But *Woolsie* wrought such means she lost her head.

(526–30)

The historical King Henry, not to mention Thomas Cromwell, would have been very surprised by the 'history' detailed above. Of course, it is obvious that historical accuracy is not the main point of Rowley's play, nor indeed even a real point at all. In this chapter I will try to tease out what *was* the point of the piece, something which can be partly deduced from the decisions Rowley made to wrench certain historical facts in specific ways. In the Stuart period historical nostalgia was often appropriated for polemical purposes not necessarily indicative of criticism of the incumbent ruler, though this was often a feature of the discourse.[14] This essay, therefore, will look at the year when Rowley wrote the play, 1604, to try to trace the political impulses to which Rowley was responding – these range from issues of national importance (such as the fall-out from the Hampton Court Conference in January) to those more localized for Rowley's theatrical company (on whom their change of patronage from the Lord Admiral to Prince Henry had a profound effect, not least for their repertoire).[15] Though *When You See Me* is certainly a play written primarily for Prince Henry, Rowley's choice of topic and the gloss he puts on it is also specifically targeted at King James, and the relationship between king and prince. It also tries to take courteous note of the interests of Queen Anne.

This choice of topic, the history of Henry VIII, shows a deliberate correspondence, common in the literature of the reigns of Elizabeth and James, between the history told and contemporary politics. *When You See Me* replays past religious negotiation, mapping it onto present discussions with a deliberate congruence; it exploits similarities of position to the full in hortatory anticipation of the kind of prince England will have; and its celebration of the past argues for a particular kind of future. *When You See Me You Know Me* is the most misleading of titles, unless one understands its tricksiness from the beginning: the historical characters in the play are ciphers for current political figures and the title warns an audience that looking and seeing are not the same thing. When Black Will, reluctant robber and murderer, fails to identify his disguised king, this is a minatory gesture and advises an audience not to take the play at face value. Of course, though those works of literature which used this so-called 'Tacitean' history often did so for critical purposes, comparative examples might also work as flattery or encouragement.[16] *When You See Me*, and other early Jacobean plays, employ a complimentary/critical approach in their historical drama, where the audience decides how to read the gap between historical example and present parallel.[17] In the very first years of James's reign, it is most likely that the playwrights intended their examples as exhortatory or minatory. But many of these plays were reissued later, especially at times of particular ill-feeling between crown and city, and this argues for warning essentially as proleptic criticism.[18] In 1604/5, James had already revealed his hand, particularly with regard to religious policy, in such a way as to suggest that these plays were responses to Stuart policies with which the playwrights disagreed.

Whose history, which fact?

The idea, indeed, of a historical 'fact' is a difficult starting-point for *When You See Me*. It is obvious that Rowley was using Holinshed and Foxe as his main sources,[19] but these accountants of the period, respectively state-approved chronicler and Protestant polemicist, each had his own agenda. The events which actually took place may roughly correspond in these two accounts but the ascriptions of their motivation and meaning are often subtly, and sometimes blatantly, different.[20] In Rowley's play, furthermore, the emphases must be traced largely through what he used and altered from the sources rather than what he altered from 'fact'. To ascribe to Rowley identical motivations to Foxe is to misrepresent both his method – considerably less faithful to 'fact' – and his meaning, determined by the contemporary events and concerns of 1604, just as Foxe's several editions were shaped to respond to specific sixteenth-century political shifts.[21]

Historical accuracy is clearly not the playwright's main concern. The stories of Queen Jane and of Henry's night-walk, on which some of the play is based, were already memorialized as ballads. Having 'sucked in so much of the sad story [...] from [their] cradle',[22] the London audience might invest the rest of the play with the same status of 'general know-ledge'. Equally, though, *Acts and Monuments* had been widely read for some forty years and might be assumed to provide a veneer of historical accuracy to the material from ballads. So Rowley's association of the communal memory of the ballads and the extracts from Foxe might imply a claim for mutual veracity, but Rowley carefully avoids making any direct assertion of the truth of anything: his very title is based on the notion of communal recollection which goes beyond, and behind, 'truth' or 'history'. Shakespeare's and Fletcher's famous dig at Rowley in their subtitle to *Henry VIII*, 'All is True', exposes not incompetence, but his calculated, and successful, dramatic risk.

Recent critics have termed *When You See Me* a Foxean history play because of its dependency on *Acts and Monuments* for many of its epis-odes and its strong Protestant allegiance. But Foxe, I would argue, is more often the source for the play's events than of the spin put upon them. A good example of this is the celebratory stress Rowley's play puts on the importance of a male heir – something in which Foxe is less interested – which keys in directly to the relief with which England had greeted a new monarch who had already provided two healthy boy children.

Forming Prince Henry's players

The most obvious event to which Rowley's play responds has been noted by F. Nostbakken:[23] over the Christmas period 1603/4, the Lord Admiral, Charles Howard, Earl of Nottingham, transferred his patronage of the Alleyn/Henslowe-run theatre company based at the Fortune Theatre in Golding Lane to Prince Henry.[24] This was probably by royal command, at the instigation of the Master of the Revels, Edmund Tilney. Nottingham continued to be close to Prince Henry and possibly acted as a *de facto* patron of the company during the latter's minority.[25] The early date of *When You See Me* could easily mean that it was the first new play presented by the Prince's Men after the death of Elizabeth in March 1603, as the London theatres were closed through almost all of that year in mourning and on account of the plague. Gurr notes that the company played at court five times over the Christmas season 1603/4,[26] presumably with tried and tested plays since it was their debut. The most likely date of a first court performance for *When You See Me* is the other end of 1604, when the company played in front of the queen on 23 November and the prince on the 24th. This would have given the playwright time to conceive and write his new play, and the company a chance to give it a dry-run in front of a fee-paying audience after the reopening of the theatres on Easter Monday 1604.

That it is a tributary play for Henry is, I think, beyond question. Nostbakken has noted that some of the imagery in the play is the same as in Jonson's later masques, *Oberon* and *Prince Henry's Barriers*, particularly in the sections drawing attention to Prince Henry as the ninth king of that name, and in the use of Arthurian motifs to connect Henry VIII, Prince Henry and England.[27] Furthermore, the concentration in the play on the life and education of Prince Edward is calculated not only as a political gesture of association, but also as material which is likely to interest a ten-year-old prince.[28] The company had been sworn in as Prince Henry's servants and it was to him they were to look for their future patronage. This play marked their first attempt to negotiate their patron's image, but they were negotiating it from a point of relative ignorance of his interests and preferred self-representation.

Forming Prince Henry's image

Of course, by the autumn of 1604, playwrights must have been given hints about specifically acceptable compliments and personations for the prince. Thomas Dekker (a Prince's Company playwright in 1604) had been heavily involved in the entertainments for James's entry into London, and his *Magnificent Entertainment* had negotiated some of these very issues.[29] The same mythology which we see used of Prince Henry in English poetry, masques and art after 1607 (when he began to appear more often in public) had been foisted on him in the cradle in Scotland.[30] To view him as a prince much concerned with chivalry and arms was already part of the image by the time of James's accession to the English throne in 1603; it was a tradition which Williamson alleges was inaugurated in the 1590s by Scottish Presbyterians in the face of James's disapproval and his own attempt to represent Henry as a prince of peace and fecundity.[31] It has been argued that Prince Henry's Protestantism was inculcated by the Earl of Mar, appointed his guardian by James in political circumstances which dictated the wisdom of keeping this powerful nobleman on his side, over and above the fact that James and he were personal friends.[32] By the time James mounted his throne in England, the religious *zeitgeist* had become distinctly Episcopalian, perhaps because James's control of his Scottish kingdom had become more secure and the extreme Presbyterians had been discredited by association with the Gowrie Plot, apparently to assassinate or capture James, in 1600.[33] This change in Scotland's political climate (and the fact that Prince Henry grew up in a Protestant household not keeping pace with James's shifting policy) might explain why the prince's outlook on religion, particularly on 'just' religious wars, seems to have become so at variance with James's own views. When Prince Henry got to England, of course, English Calvinists latched on to this perceived religious difference and clustered around the prince's household.

It has already been noted that *When You See Me* makes very deliberate parallels between Prince Edward Tudor and Prince Henry Stuart.[34] The first half of the play dramatizes the birth of Prince Edward and Jane Seymour's death in childbed (though neither of these actually on stage, of course). King Henry initially intends to give his unborn son his own name, having beseeched Queen Jane to

> Be but the Mother to a Prince of Wales
> Ad a ninth Henrie to the English Crowne.

(266–7)

But on her death, and apparently in fear that he might have fathered another Henry VI (405–6), he changes his mind and calls the son Edward after the saint's day on which the boy was born. Of course, the primary effect of this discussion is to draw attention to the future Henry IX, the patron of the company doing the acting. And the second part of the play – based around Foxe's description of Catherine Parr's disputation with the Bishops and Prince Edward's solid chivalric Protestantism – is much more about the heir to the throne than the incumbent. This dangerous line – given the sensitivity of kings to their heirs' aspirations, and especially King James's sensitivity to Prince Henry's – is carefully negotiated by Rowley and represented brilliantly in Edward's tactful response to the Emperor's speech:

> *Emp.* So well our welcome we accept of thee,
>   And with such princely spirit pronounce the word,
>   Thy father's state, can no more state afford.
> *Prince.* Yes my good Lord, in him theres Majesty,
>   In me theres love with tender infancie.

(2904–8)

Foxe's reading of King Henry's religion is as inaccurate as it is politic. Had Henry only lived longer, he claims, the English church would have been thoroughly reformed. In the end, though, 'God's holy providence [...] reserve[d] the accomplishment of this reformation of his church to the peaceable time of his son Edward and Elizabeth his daughter, whose hands were yet undefiled with any blood, and life unspotted with any violence or cruelty'.[35] This sense of the child finishing the job begun by the father also operates in *When You See Me*: King Henry himself recognizes that the realization of a glorious future belongs to Edward:

> I tell thee Cranmer he is all our hopes,
> That what our age shall leave unfinished,
> In his fair reign shall be accomplished.

(1557–9)

The strength of this formulation is that it can be read several ways in 1604–5: is it King James who will finish Queen Elizabeth's incomplete Reformation? Has James's failure to reform at Hampton Court meant Prince Henry must do it when he becomes king? Is it only religious reforms which will be left half-fulfilled? Though the analogy can work as a compliment to both James and Henry Stuart, it need not necessarily be devoid of critical warning to James. Of course, the future 'fair reign' described is wishful thinking for both the actual and the implied rulers, as both princes' early deaths prevented this glory. But what the representation of Prince Edward tells us, more than anything else, is that this is how Rowley wanted to see Prince Henry: studious, Protestant, chivalric and as the man of the future.

The telescoping of time, shown by Rowley in the unhistorical plot of the play, also has an optative intention and effect, engaging with St Augustine's ruminations on the relationship between past, present and future:

> Who will tell me that there are not three times [...] the past, present and future, but only the present because the other two cannot exist at the same time. Or [perhaps] they do exist; but, when the present is made out of the future, it appears from some hidden place, and returns there when the past is made out of the present.[36]

The manifestation of what, in a different context, Tom Bishop calls the 'ritual of the future perfect' is at work here.[37] Like the masque form of which he is writing, plays which make such specific political statements as *When You See Me* do tend to look forward because their engagement with politics *wills* a certain future. Bishop suggests that 'traditional' rituals are often invented for masques in order to create a 'miraculous stasis' against which the future perfect of the invention can be played. In Rowley's play, in place of Bishop's (invented) ritual, it is the re-enactment of historical material which connects the past and the present and the future. Making this connection was useful for the Stuarts' mythmaking because history's cyclical nature could be used to bolster their hereditary right to the English throne. On 19 March 1604 King James's speech to his first parliament made this very connection: he noted his 'descent lineally out of the loynes of Henry Seventh' and went on to make specific reference to Prince Henry as the 'healthful and hopefull issue of my body [...] for continuance and propagation of that undoubted right which is my person'.[38] *When You See Me*'s curiously unhistorical history, drawing analogies between the Stuarts and the Tudors, reinforces the connection between past, present and future on which hereditary right depends.

But the future perfect is not just the perfected future; it also encourages one to think of the actions described as being somehow in the past. Future perfect deeds have the weight of tradition behind them and accrue the benefit of historical precedent; though they have not yet happened, their 'pastness' offers them as exemplars. And, of course, nothing is so likely to prove the importance of a prince as the idea that he will be, or more accurately 'will have been', a moral example. The past/futureness of the tense also helps to negotiate the separate types of history being employed by Rowley: Foxe's largely providentialist Christian history operates on the notion of the inescapable future; the Classical notions of cyclical history on which exemplarity was based (and which the Renaissance struggled to Christianize) use the past to inform the present.[39]

Furthermore the nature of a play is that it is a present representation of a past action to which the giving of multiple performances introduces a future. The captive audience in a theatre watches time go by on stage so that what started as the future ends up as the past. *When You See Me*'s re-enactment of historical events and its concern with the future echo its own form. The printing of the play in 1605 fixes all three tenses in one place at one time. Past: 'as it was played by the high and mightie Prince of Wales his servants'. Present: 'imprinted for Nathaniell Butter, 1605'. Future: its text provides a notional script for subsequent performances. But the conflated history within *When You See Me* is curiously well suited to the dramatic form, whose very performance confuses history and time themselves. It is possible, as Augustine suggested, for three times to exist concurrently.

Chronicles and ballads

Given that Rowley most often represents Henry VIII as the aged and bad-tempered king of the end of his reign, one of the most curious incidents in the play is the night-walk incident between lines 928 and 1385. This is based on a hint in Stow: 'On Midsommer eve at night, king Henry came privily into Westcheape of London being clothed in one of the coates of his guard [. . .]'.[40] The strong ballad and chapbook tradition which incorporated several folk motifs eventually formed the basis of the extended scene in *When You See Me*. The mysterious comedy cobbler (948–1061) originates in the traditional ballad 'The King and the Cobler', often catalogued under the author name of 'Henry VIII'.

The Henry of the chapbook tradition is not the ageing king in pain of 1546 – he is 'valiant and martial', as Foxe attests.

There are several versions, some of which predate *When You See Me*. An 1825 chapbook reprint summarizes the plot:

> How King Henry VIII used to visit the watches in the City and how he became acquainted with a merry jovial Cobler.

> It was the custom of King Henry the eight, to walk late in the night into the city disguised, to observe and take notice how the constables and watch performed their duty, not only in guarding the city gates, but also in diligent watching the inward parts of the city, that so they might in a great measure prevent those disturbances and casualties which so often happen in great and populous cities in the night; and this he did oftentimes, without the least discovery who he was; returning home to Whitehall early in the morning.[41]

When You See Me makes much dramatic capital of the night-walk. It allows Rowley a chance to include a comic watch scene where all the officers decide to have a nap before they go on duty and then allow everyone through without proper questioning (King Henry because he returns witty answers to their questions, Black Will because they are 'glad [to be] well rid of him' (1127)). This gives Henry a chance to lament

> What bootes it for a King,
> To toyle himselfe in this high state affaires,
> To summon Parliaments, and call together
> The wisest heads of all his Provinces:
> Making statutes for his subjects peace,
> That thus neglecting them, their woes increase.

> (1054–9)

The focus in this section of the play is very much on the contract between government, officers and the populace. The point is made forcefully here, and later when Henry discovers that some of his officers, and Cardinal Wolsey's, have been abusing their positions (1261–72), that everyone in the chain has to perform their role responsibly. In this configuration, as the *vox populi*, the play can be read as informing King James of failures in government which need redressing. By watching the play the new king can discover the wrongs which must be righted;

by pointing up deliberate congruences between him and his glorious ancestor it becomes a book of counsel.

Anne Barton has noted that disguised kings in English histories need to be seen as romantic gestures, and Tudor monarchs enjoyed re-enacting such scenes for their own purposes.[42] But in the case of *When You See Me*, the inclusion of this episode is much more than this: it is also a political gesture which has far-reaching consequences for the meaning of the play. It has been argued that 'oral culture encourages the unobtrusive adaptation of past tradition to present need'.[43] There has always been, of course, heated discussion about the depth of Londoners' 'historical' knowledge; it is not always safe to assume that the stories from the chronicle histories were as widespread as one might imagine.[44] Indeed, some critics are now beginning to see Thomas Heywood's asser-tion that plays were a valuable way of educating their audience as more than simply a slightly disingenuous defence of players' rights. Ian Archer and D. R. Woolf have exposed the fallacy in supposing all Londoners to be the same in this regard, the former pointing out that education varied widely from citizen to citizen. Though there is ample evidence that many citizens owned and read, and compared, historical narratives, not all members of Rowley and Heywood's audience would have done, others relying perhaps more on ballads and fireside tales.[45] Archer also points out that many quite well-educated readers seem to have given nearly as much credence to oral traditions as to written history. Perhaps here a modern understanding of 'truth' is not helpful, for readers and audiences of mayoral pageants were happy to accept the notion of London as Troynovant as having a certain 'moral truth' which underscored its utility and their sense of self, despite scepticism that the city's founding had actually happened as tradition held.[46] Archer also notes Francis Kirkman attesting that, as a young man, he took chivalric romance to be 'true'.[47] The thorny notions of history as 'true' but poetry as a 'true example' with which Sidney struggled in the *Apology* seem to be muddled not only in the heads of London apprentices but also in those of the chroniclers: so, in the popular history plays of the period we would not expect the distinction to be made any more clearly.

Since part of the point of these royal night-walks is to redress wrongs, it is no surprise that the plays with such scenes appear at moments of dissatisfaction with the reigning monarch. Many of them were written in the 1590s, when Elizabeth had famously fallen out with the Commons and the country at large thought she was neglecting them.[48] Outside the theatre too, Archer describes 'the Leathersellers petitioning against Sir Edward Darcy's leather-sealing patent in 1593 [...] cit[ing] Edward

Hall on Henry VIII's respect for the commons, by way of making a point about Elizabeth's neglect of them'.[49] It was clearly acceptable to remind the current monarch by way of a certain type of historical example that they were failing in this duty and Richard Dutton has demonstrated that using ballad material rarely got playwrights into trouble.[50] The 'disguised king' is a Tacitean motif, derived from the *Annals* and detailing Germanicus's eavesdropping on his troops the night before a battle.[51] In this formulation, Tacitean history plays such as *When You See Me* become the equivalent of disguised kings talking to their people. Playwrights' discussion of history through their dramas can be taken as advice by their monarch, should he wish to listen. Crucially both methods are officially sanctioned: Germanicus gives licence to his troops to speak by donning his disguise, and Jacobean playwrights usually receive licence because they disguise their political commentary as history. By both these means kings can learn what is really going on in their realm. Ballads and Tacitean history, it seems, are not so different after all; not only are they mutually reinforcing, but they operate to the same ends.

Two plays of 1604, *Measure for Measure* and *When You See Me*, employ the disguised king device and manage to do so without annoying King James, as far as we can tell. For the appearance of the device, according to J. W. Lever, James I only had himself to blame.[52] Some of James's behaviour upon his English accession in 1603 displays exactly the tendency to romantic gesture that Barton describes. James is well known for fancying himself able to touch for the king's evil and it seems he also sought to reinforce his as a mythic kingship in the Tudor mould by physically engaging with the trope of the disguised king. On about 15 March 1604 James, 'hearing of the preparation [for the coronation pageant] to be great, aswell to note the other things as that, was desirous privately at his owne pleasure to visit them, and accompanied with his Queen in his coach, he came to the Exchange, there to see for their recreation, and thinking to passe unknowne'.[53] The 'other things' (perhaps hidden wrongs) James has come to see, especially in combination with the double meaning of 'recreation', suggests strongly that the new king is modelling himself on the old. However, his attempt at disguise is not very good: though he wants to 'pass unknowne', he wears his own clothes, he turns up in a coach, and brings his wife. Not surprisingly, everyone recognizes him; instead of revealing wrongs that James can redress, the royal appearance engenders a riot: 'the wylie multitude perceiving something, began with such hurly burly, to run up and downe with such unreverent rashness, as the people of the Exchange were glad to shut the staire dores to keepe them out'.[54] An inglorious affair, all in all, about which James will complain later.

The appearance of the disguised king motif in two plays of this year, however, needs further investigation. It might be tempting to read these night-walks as solely prompted by James's attempt to re-create Henry VIII's famous escapade but there are complications caused by the failure of James to pull it off. The 'official' chronicles of Stow make no mention of James's visit or the resulting scramble, but the report above by 'Gilbert Dugdale', was actually written by Robert Armin (or so the latter claimed), the King's Men player, which indicates that the story was current, in theatrical circles at least. We could decide that the actors and playwrights who reused the story were insufficiently 'on message' with the new court to understand that inglorious events such as this should be suppressed rather than recycled in celebration. However, it could be suggested that reusing this trope in 1604 chimes in with this notion of exhortation which can later be read as criticism when the play is replayed and reprinted between 1611 and 1613. Here playwrights use the mythical past as a reminder of what James must do in order to fulfil his destiny; in future editions and performances it becomes criticism by unflattering example.

Indeed, James was only too aware of his responsibilities as lineal descendant of the Tudors, as we have already seen. As well as choosing to model his disguising on Henry VIII, his choice of venue nods at another Tudor monarch, Elizabeth I, whose 'special relationship' with the city culminated in her naming of Sir Thomas Gresham's 'Burse', as shown in Part 2 of Thomas Heywood's *If You Know Not Me You Know Nobody* (1605–6).[55] James knew that a visit to the Exchange was guaranteed to conjure up memories of Elizabeth, just as he must have known that the king-in-disguise motif would associate him with King Henry. Thus, such romantic behaviour begins to seem less whimsical and much more an attempt at political mythmaking on James's part. Interestingly, both Henry's night-walk and the description of Elizabeth's visit to the Exchange given in *2 If You Know Not Me* derive from Stow.[56] *When You See Me* and *If You Know Not Me* are rival pieces which aim at the same audience: Rowley's earlier response to James's disguise incident seems to have prompted Heywood to remember that the venue of the new king's failed night-walk was as significant as the fact that he tried it.

In his portrayal of Black Will, an ex-soldier in stock braggart mould, Rowley both responds to and tries to affect current affairs. Of course, the primary purpose of the duel between King Henry and Will is to entertain the watching Prince Henry, a set-piece guaranteed to amuse any ten-year-old boy, let alone one so well known as Henry for his interest in the military and chivalric.[57] But Black Will, though in some ways a stock character, is also very much a creature of his time. He tells us that 'it is a hard world, when Black Will, for a venture of five pound, must commit such pettie robberies at Mile-ende, but the truth is, the Stewes from whence I had my quartaridge is now grown too hote for me' (1063–6). The Constable has already explained that

> Much theft and murder was committed lately,
> There are two strangers, marchants of the Stillyard
> Cruelly slain, found floating on the Temmes:
> And greatly are the Stewes had in suspect,
> As places fitting for no better use.

> (950–4)

As Lever notes of *Measure for Measure*'s similar interest in the Stews, playwrights were responding to a proclamation of 16 September 1603 which ordered the razing of bawdy houses in a attempt to halt the spread of plague.[58] Furthermore, Peter Holbrook has noted that almost the first thing James did when he arrived in England was to stop English ships attacking Spanish shipping, an action (together with the clear diplomatic efforts at rapprochement) which necessitated sending Ralph Winwood to Holland to assure the Free States they had not been abandoned.[59] This order for cessation of naval activity was given in June 1603; formal peace with Spain came when the Treaty of London was signed in August 1604. But this returned soldiers to London with no means of support and the play sees the exigencies to which Black Will is put as a direct result of the peace policy. Henry VIII insists on Will remaining in prison (though he does give him 'twenty angels' (1371) to keep him) until 'we have further use for ye. If yee can breake through watches with egres and regres so valiantly, ye shal doote amongst your countries enemies' (1373–5). Will responds with the enthusiasm expected of a good subject, and a valiant Englishman: 'The wars sweet King, tis my delight, my desire, my chaire of state, create me but a tattord Corporall, and give me some prehemine[n]ce over the vulgar hot-shots' (1376–8). Henry VIII's promise situates Rowley as a member of the anti-peace camp, at least as far as this peace affected soldiers' livelihoods. King Henry's bellicose example argues for a less pacifist royal military policy for the present and future.

Which King's Great Matter?

By 1546, John Foxe's King Henry, the 'valiant and martial prince' of early in *Acts and Monuments*, is subject to human frailty:

> The king grew, towards his latter end, very stern and opinionate, so that of few he could be content to be taught, but worst of all to be contended with in argument (V.554)

> [...] until, at the last, by reason of his sore leg (the anguish whereof began more and more to increase), he waxed sickly, and therewithal froward, and difficult to be pleased. (V.555)

Rowley takes the character of Foxe's 1546 Henry – where courtiers (and indeed Fools in *When You See Me*) squabble amongst themselves about who is to beard the lion in his den[60] – and intrudes into his narrative the historical issues of the 1520s and 1530s.

The most pressing reason in 1604 to set the play late in Henry's reign is to dramatize the relationship between Catherine Parr (famously Reformed, but calumniated in the play as 'Lutheran'), Henry's bad counsellors in Wolsey, Gardiner and Bonner, and royal ecclesiastical policy.[61] By doing this, and by allowing King Henry to be persuaded at least to listen to 'Luther's heresies', Rowley, writing during the period of its immediate fall-out, is commentating on the Hampton Court Conference of January 1604. Very early in his reign James agreed to meet with all factions of the Anglican church to 'discuss' the religious policy of the new regime. All sides, especially the millenary petitioners, hoped for support from the new king but in the end James, demonstrating his unwillingness to allow others to make the running, chose to maintain the status quo.[62] By that date 'Lutheranism', in England at least, was a spent force, but it does well in the play as a stand-in for the more strongly Puritan doctrines argued for in the millenary petition. Thus Queen Catherine Parr represents the voices of James's moderate Puritan divines and the voice of the party of his ten-year-old son (whose chaplain between 1607 and the prince's death was the moderate Calvinist, Joseph Hall). As the playwright sees it, the important (that is, Catholic versus Protestant) religious controversy of 1604 is summed up in *When You See Me* when Prince Edward receives a letter from each of his sisters. As by imputation Prince Henry does, Edward happily accepts the sensible Protestant advice of Princess Elizabeth but cannot even bear to finish the nonsense that Mary pedals:

> Alas good sister, still in this opinion,
> These are thy blinded Tutors, Bonner, Gardner,
> That wrong thy thoughts with foolish heresies,
> Ill read no farther:

> (2402–5)

Little is known about Samuel Rowley's life, which makes identifying his religious convictions more a matter of reading out from the text than examining external evidence. Certainly, the contents of *When You See Me* seem to celebrate moderate Protestantism. However, the religious tone of the public stage in this period was robustly Protestant, evidenced, as we have seen, in the efflorescence of plays based on Foxe in the early years of the seventeenth century. One must, I think, read Rowley's work as tapping into this vein of polemical Protestantism. The use of Holinshed argues at least for the play as a celebration of England as 'exceptional', its heavy reliance on Foxe for a more committed reformist reading of the history dramatized, and for a Protestant polemic which operates by way of Tacitean historical example. As with *The Whore of Babylon* by Thomas Dekker – one of Rowley's collaborators and another Prince's playwright – the contents of the play suggest a strongly Protestant outlook, but it could be argued that this outlook is conditioned by the reception the playwrights expected from their citizen audience. More compelling evidence can be found, however, to support the religious adherence of the publisher of *When You See Me*, Nathaniel Butter, who also published two more of the Foxean plays, *If You Know Not Me* and *The Whore of Babylon*. His publications between 1603 and 1606 show a fascination with anti-Catholic propaganda, including several works claiming to reveal (and revelling in) the 'shocking' errors of the Catholic faith.[63] Nathaniel Butter also had a hand in publishing almost all the works of Prince Henry's chaplain, Bishop Joseph Hall. These printing stable-mates argue for Rowley as a mainstream-to-hot Protestant.

Some of Rowley's preoccupations in *When You See Me* can be traced back to Foxe's assessment of Henry VIII (my emphases):

> For by him was exiled and abolished out of the realm the *usurped power of the bishop of Rome*, idolatry and superstition somewhat repressed, images and pilgrimages defaced, abbeys and monasteries

pulled down, *sects of religion* rooted out, Scriptures reduced to the knowledge of the *vulgar tongue*, and the state of the church and religion redressed.[64]

Queen Catherine asks of the Bishops 'what Scripture have yee, / To teach religion in an unknowne language' (2254–5); and the Fool, Will Somer, demands in his final assault on Wolsey that he 'speak plaine English, you have deceived the king in French and Latine long enough a conscience' (2813–5). Surely this constant mention is related to the one secure concession which the godly wrung from Hampton Court – the Authorized Version of the Bible.

Luther gets very bad press from almost everyone throughout the play: Charles Brandon notes that one of the things which has upset King Henry is that Luther has 'writ a book against his Majestie' (593); the king complains about the 'upstart sect of Lutherans' (672); and Campeius (Campeggio) makes much of Henry for having defended the Pope 'in learned books gainst Luthers heresie' (838). As well as the compliment to James as a fellow 'Royal Author', it is tempting to read this anti-Lutheranism as Rowley's attempt to dramatize 'sects of religion' being 'rooted out'. But there is a contrast between Catherine Parr's so-called Lutheranism, actually represented in the play as 'common sense', and Luther's doctrines, which are shown to be extreme. Bombarded by the advice of his prelates, the extremities of Luther, and the good sense of his queen, the king has to negotiate a middle way through the conflicting advice. This trope supports James's religious policy of *listening* to (though not necessarily agreeing with) all sides in the debate which was exemplified by the calling of the Hampton Court Conference. But King Henry is forestalled from a definitive decision by the end of the play – a tactful way of intervening in royal policy without proffering 'the right answer', which might turn out to be wrong in James's eyes.

However, in 'the usurped power of the bishop of Rome' the playwright grasps the doctrinal nettle. Rowley introduced an unhistorical Wolsey into the play to embody this usurped power. The dramatic tricks which he employs are interesting, especially in the context of Foxe's own narrative of Wolsey. 'Usurped power' dominates the opening scene and the dramatic use of Wolsey: he meets the French Ambassadors in Henry's stead before the king knows they have arrived; he discloses in soliloquy his devious machinations: 'Now Woolsie worke thy wittes like gaddes of steel / And make them pliable to all impressions' (101–2); and he is aware of his own double-dealing with the king: 'Our private conference must not be known' (39).

In contrast, Foxe's thrust in the Wolsey section (at VI.587ff.) is to open to the reader 'the vain pomp and pride of that ambitious church, so far differing from all pure Christianity and godliness'. Foxe says explicitly that he is using the life of Wolsey as an example to the reader, just as the Lacedaemonians showed drunk men to children to put them off drinking. Foxe does come to note in a later paragraph Wolsey's 'insolent presumption' of Henry's authority in his own household (see pp. 590–1), but the two pages immediately following the opening of the Wolsey story are all taken up by the story of him vying with Campeius in finery and collecting treasure throughout Henry's realm. Foxe is much more exercised about the money, an issue which Rowley deals with in passing when Will and Patch, *When You See Me*'s clowns, discover Wolsey's hidden treasure on a secret drinking raid on his cellar. Foxe does align Wolsey with the Pope specifically, in as much as he draws attention to 'this legate [...] following the steps of his master the pope, and both of them well declaring the nature of their religion, under the pretence of the church, practised great hypocrisy' (p. 590). But what Rowley's Bishops, Catholics of the 1600s, and the hotter sort of the millenary petitioners, in favour of Presbyters, all had in common was a tendency to question the ecclesiastical authority of the king.[65] Wolsey is useful because, in challenging King Henry's authority, he points up the wrongness of doing so to the current king. It is his being a cardinal that circumvents Rowley being suspected of being against episcopacy. Whereas Bonner and Gardiner are usually sufficient as villains in the Foxe-based plays, Rowley's engagement with James's ecclesiastical authority demanded a character who had the status to challenge directly King Henry's jurisdiction. In 1604, at court in front of the family of a Protestant divine-righter who had long resented foreign attempts to interfere in the politics of Scotland, this rejection of outside influence could only play well.

Forming Queen Anne's historical pedigree

It has become clear that much of the play was deliberately angled towards the company's patron Prince Henry, and that, in the detailed description of Prince Edward's schooling, in the knock-about and rhyming scenes involving Patch and Will, and in Queen Catherine's Protestantism there was much for the prince to relate to or admire. But there is lots in the play which would not have been so interesting for the ten-year-old prince, which perhaps cannot be adequately explained by a notion that the audience at the Fortune Theatre also had to find it interesting. Queen Jane's death in childbed, the choice of husband that Henry's sister is allowed to make, and the tricky inter-marital nego-tiations between Henry and Catherine, if not exactly feminist (as Kim Noling might have it),[66] seem to be aimed at a female audience – in this case, almost assuredly Queen Anne.

Noling has noted that one of the most interesting things about *When You See Me* is the handsome coverage it gives to two of Henry's queens – Jane Seymour and Katherine Parr.[67] It is not surprising that Catherine Howard is not mentioned in the play, given that there seems to be a consensus that she was guilty of the adultery of which she was accused. Foxe's narrative, for instance, presents it as 'fact': after a bald statement of the events of the scandal and its outcome, his word order 'the death and punishment of this lady' indicates that Catherine is being punished *after* her death, something only theologically possible if she were guilty as charged.[68] This, in itself, is not terribly flattering to kingly dignity (in which James might be seen to have an interest), but is likely to be even less flattering to Charles Howard, Earl of Nottingham, a cousin of the offending queen. One possible explanation for the silence is that Rowley still has the Prince's Men's powerful ex-patron in mind when writing – Nottingham was also related to Anne Boleyn, which may explain the play's imputation that Wolsey contrived her execution, clearing her of any misdoing (and her innocence of the charges was, of course, taken as read as soon as Elizabeth became queen). Anne of Cleves is only mentioned in Henry's act of sending her home (*WYSM*, l. 1423), and Catherine of Aragon not at all, even in the scenes including her emperor cousin Charles V. Foxe's restraint when dealing with Catherine of Aragon, a Spanish Catholic after all, is symptomatic of the general good feeling in England towards Henry's first wife, perhaps even with a sense that she was misused by him or by her time.[69] Rowley's way of dealing with this seems to be to ignore her, which is all the more remark-able given the amount of time the play spends on Wolsey, in whose urging for the divorce Foxe sees a malicious desire to cross the emperor who failed to assist him to the papal throne. Noling has noted that the function of the two queens to whom Rowley does give full attention is widely different. Jane Seymour is celebrated as the provider of an heir, while Catherine Parr emerges as a religious thinker of a higher sort, and, according to Noling, less submissive than she is in Foxe.[70]

The episodes with Queen Jane also owe something to the chapbook tradition: the choice Henry is asked to make between his son and his queen figures in both Scottish and English traditional ballads. In a Scottish version Queen Jeanie begs both the doctor and Henry to 'rip up [her] two sides to save [her] babie', which they refuse to do until she's 'fallen in a swoon'.[71] A very strong tradition flourished that Jane Seymour died following a Caesarian section, not of puerperal fever as now seems probable. Here, in the inaccuracy of dates at least, Foxe and the ballad tradition concur – Foxe's editor Josiah Pratt alters (practically silently – 'see appendix', he commands) the date of Jane's death because, being unaware of the tradition, he thinks Foxe has 'got it wrong'.[72]

It is clear that celebrating the birth of Prince Edward, and therefore by extension Prince Henry, is a compliment to Queen Anne who had already provided two male heirs, and a princess. In fact, had Rowley but known, as he was mounting the play for the royal household in late 1604 Queen Anne was pregnant yet again, with Princess Mary, born on 8 April 1605 and christened on 5 May. John Chamberlain gossiped to Ralph Winwood on 18 December 1604 that 'yt is generally held and spoken that the Quene is quicke with childe'.[73] One cannot help feeling that, had Rowley been aware of this fact, he might have decided to cut the scenes containing a heavily pregnant, and subsequently dead, queen at the court performances on 23 and 24 November. Celebrating a queen for her previously brave behaviour in risking her life to bring forth heirs is a very different thing to presenting such a possible future for a current pregnancy.

There is another thing to be noted about these court performances which might reinforce the notion that it was *When You See Me* that was given on these two nights. Queen Anne's brother, Ulric, Duke of Holstein paid a long visit to the English court starting on 22 November 1604. According to Chamberlain, he was there for the purpose of 'procuring a levie of men to carie into Hungarie' and he stayed until 1 June 1605.[74] It is a logical inference that the Prince's Men's visit to court just after his arrival was to provide entertainment for him, and it would be fascinating to know how much warning the Company and their playwright had been given about the duke's arrival. There is an alluring possibility that the last few scenes of the play – where Edward welcomes Charles V and presents him with the Order of the Garter – were written with Ulric's visit in mind. Queen Anne and her brothers were part Habsburg, through the marriage of one of Charles V's sisters to Christian II of Denmark, and they were very proud of this heritage, despite Denmark's confessional differences with the Holy Roman Empire.[75] The relationship between Prince Edward and Charles V in *When You See Me* – Charles repeatedly calling the prince such things as 'yong coosen' (2882) – is so close to the uncle–nephew pairing of Ulric and Henry as to make the connection inescapable in a play that so enjoys mapping history on the present. Stow's *Annales* notes that the King of Denmark and the Duke of Wertenberg were elected in their absence to the Order of the Garter on 2 July 1603, and though no mention is made of the same honour being given to Anne's other brother, Duke Ulric, the very specific investiture at the end of Rowley's play might encourage us to suppose that he too was a recipient:

> I here present this collar of estate,
> This golden garter of the knighthoods order,
> An honour to renowne the Emperour:
> Thus as my father hath commanded me,
> I entertaine your royall Maiestie.
>
> (2894–8)

The actual personation of the Garter ceremony at the end of this play surely alludes to a upcoming event, fitting as it would be on the first visit of one of Queen Anne's relatives to James's new kingdom. So, not only does the play present a celebration of Anne as mother of the future king, but it also recalls and honours her Habsburg ancestry in a deliberately flattering gesture.

Conclusions

Samuel Rowley's handling of history in *When You See Me* is an act with specific political purposes. It is not just his treatment of historical facts which is noteworthy but also his historical method, engaging as it does with providential and Tacitean history. In what Rowley chooses from his sources we can trace as localized in the time and place of 1604–5: in comparison to Foxe (on whom he does rely for the 'facts') he gives greater importance to Prince Edward's birth, the importance of the English Bible, and the challenge to the king's ecclesiastical leadership. These changes of emphasis show an engagement with the sensitized topics of the start of the new reign, most notably a celebration of Prince Henry, as heir, as Protestant prince and as theatrical patron. Allied to this is the use the play makes of the re-presentation of the Reformation in England. Old hopes are revived that this will be more thoroughgoing under James I and especially (after the re-dashing of hopes at Hampton Court) when Prince Henry accedes, than under Henry VIII (and by implication Elizabeth). This Protestant fervour identifies the play even more strongly with Prince Henry through the religious outlook he shares with Prince Edward and Queen Catherine.

Rowley's handling of history ties into the hereditary principle: present uses the past to argue for the future. This is especially suitable for 1604–5 because of the way it supports King James's attempts to establish the Stuarts as rightful kings of England. The Tudor history replayed on the stage forcefully maps onto current personalities and events, to persuade of the historical inevitability of the Stuart succession. In connecting past, present and future by showing the correct Stuart re-enactment of Tudor 'myth', the cosmic rightness of the Stuarts' rule is asserted. Rowley's engagement with ballad material associates history and myth, and ostensibly militates them both for Stuart authority. But as Tudor history is being replayed both on stage (in King Henry and Prince Edward) and in real life (by King James and Prince Henry) its comparisons cannot help but assess the fitness of each Stuart for the English crown.

The complication comes in the balancing of Prince Henry's and King James's interests. Rowley's use of the future perfect, ciphered in Prince Edward, both plays out and interrogates the struggle between heir and incumbent. Prince Edward's deft parry of the emperor's comment which challenges kingly authority demonstrates in 1604–5 a playwright 'on message' with the official court line. But there is much in the play which reads like criticism of James's reign, if 'plainly deciphered' in the spirit of the Star Chamber.[76] Certainly by 1611–13, when the play was re-played and reprinted, this should be read as cynically Tacitean. But in 1604–5 offering past example to present king and future king is more ambiguous. What the play shows more than anything else are the benefits of Tacitean method: comparative examples can be criticism, warning, worry, exhortation or praise, depending on which tense is being used.

Notes

1. See D. R. Woolf, 'Two Elizabeths? James I and the Late Queen's Famous Memory', *Canadian Journal of History*, 20/2 (August, 1985), 167–91, where he argues that in the very early years of his reign James encouraged discussion of and comparison with Elizabeth, particularly when it usefully offered a paradigm for his own policies. Curtis Perry notes that this encouragement backfired on James later in his reign: since Tudor–Stuart comparisons had become the norm, the slide from congratulation to criticism was inevitable under the circumstances ('The Citizen Politics of Nostalgia: Queen Elizabeth in Early Jacobean London', *Journal of Medieval and Renaissance Studies*, 23/1 (Winter, 1993), 89–111; p. 92).

2. See Patrick Collinson, 'William Camden and the Anti-Myth of Elizabeth', in *The Myth of Elizabeth*, ed. Susan Doran and Thomas S. Freeman (Basingstoke:

Palgrave Macmillan, 2003), pp. 79–98. Collinson (p. 80) notes that James's interest in reviving the project in 1606, which had been practically forced on Camden by Burghley in 1597, was a desire to rescue his mother's reputation from the description of her reign in Jacques-Auguste de Thou's *Historia sui temporis*, which had become the standard, and deeply unflattering, history.

3. Thomas S. Freeman, 'Providence and Prescription: the Account of Elizabeth in Foxe's "Book of Martyrs"', in Doran and Freeman (eds), *The Myth of Elizabeth*, pp. 27–55; 27. See also Marsha S. Robinson, *Writing the Reformation*: Actes and Monuments *and the Jacobean History Play* (Aldershot: Ashgate, 2002), for a full, if not entirely persuasive, account of the use of Foxe as source for these plays.

4. See Elizabeth Evenden and Thomas S. Freeman, 'Print, Profit and Propaganda: the Elizabethan Privy Council and the 1570 Edition of Foxe's "Book of Martyrs"', *English Historical Review*, 119/484 (November 2004), 1288–1307.

5. John Foxe, *Acts and Monuments* (London: John Day, 1583), sig. §vi^v.

6. See Cyrus Hoy, *Introductions, Notes, and Commentaries to texts in 'The Dramatic Works of Thomas Dekker'*, edited by Fredson Bowers (4 vols; Cambridge: Cambridge University Press, 1980), vol. 1, pp. 311–50; p. 311.

7. Ibid.

8. Thomas Dekker and John Webster, *The Famous Historie of Sir Thomas Wyat* (London: E[dward] A[llde] for Thomas Archer, 1607), sig. A1^r.

9. Mary Foster Martin, 'If You Know Not Me, You Know Nobodie, and The Famous History of Sir Thomas Wyat', *The Library*, 4th series, 13 (1933), 271–81.

10. Thomas Dekker, *The Whore of Babylon* (London: for Nathaniel Butter, 1607), A2^v.

11. For the night-walk see, for instance, John Stow, *The Annales, or Generall Chronicle of England, begun first by maister John Stow*, ed. and supp. Edward Howes (London, Thomas Dawson for Thomas Adams, 1615; STC 23338), p. 489.

12. Samuel Rowley, *When You See Me You Know Me* (1605), ed. F. P. Wilson (Oxford: Malone Society, 1952). All quotations are from this edition, henceforth *WYSM*.

13. *WYSM*, introduction, p. x.

14. See John Watkins, ' "Old Bess in the Ruff": Remembering Elizabeth I, 1625–1660', *English Literary Renaissance*, 30 (2000), 95–116; and Teresa Grant, 'Drama Queen: Staging Elizabeth in *If You Know Not Me You Know Nobody*', *The Myth of Elizabeth*, ed. Doran and Freeman, pp. 120–42.

15. I am very grateful to Lucy Munro for giving me a copy of her unpublished essay 'Plays, Politics and Patronage: the Fortune Repertory, 1603–1625'. I am indebted to her work on the Fortune repertory, especially as it sets *When You See Me* in its proper context. She rightly distinguishes between patrons' self-conscious political use of the theatre (as Buckingham seems to have made with a revival of *Henry VIII* in 1628) and the companies' employment of 'political ideas associated with those patrons' to fashion the substance of their plays. Her work on the 1611/12 revival of *When You See Me* is particularly suggestive: dissatisfaction with James's lack of reforming zeal may have encouraged the later reissue of many of the Protestant plays of the very early years of his reign. One might wish to note, also, that the reformist furore which centred around

the Palatine marriage offered companies a smoke-screen so that they could reissue these plays masquerading as celebration pieces.

16. So-called after the Roman historian Tacitus (*c.* 56–*c.* 117) whose histories were written in the reign of the tyrannical Emperor Domitian. In his accounts of the earlier Caesars contemporaries (and commentators) saw veiled criticism of the contemporary regime. For the widespread use and importance of Tacitean history in this period see the introduction to this collection.

17. Grant, 'Drama Queen', pp. 128–30.

18. Munro, 'Plays, Politics and Patronage', see note 15.

19. Wilson identifies John Foxe, *Acts and Monuments*, and Raphael Holinshed, *The Chronicles of England, Scotland and Ireland*, as major sources for the play, and details the other possible influences at *WYSM*, pp. x–xii. See also Robinson, *Writing the Reformation*.

20. This situation is complicated by the tendency of later editors of Holinshed to assimilate information culled from Foxe. See pp. 47–8 (note 1) of Freeman, 'Providence and Prescription'.

21. See, for instance, Robinson, *Writing the Reformation*, pp. 14–15. Though she does ultimately differentiate between *When You See Me* and the narrative on which it is based – noticing that Foxe is more worried by the dissonances caused by Henry's conservatism – she tends to talk of Rowley as if his sole aim is to portray Foxe's message to the theatrical audience, rather than, more complicatedly, to provide sell-out entertainment and to seek for patronage (happily, of course, these aims are not incompatible with a measure of reforming zeal).

22. Pepys used this expression to describe his relationship with Tudor history after a trip to see a 1667 revival of *If You Know Not Me You Know Nobody*, a 1605–6 play about Queen Elizabeth I. See *The Diaries of Samuel Pepys*, ed. Robert Latham and William Matthews (11 vols; London, 1973), Vol. 8 (1667): 388.

23. F. Nostbakken, 'Rowley's *When You See Me You Know Me*: Political Drama in Transition', *Cahiers Élisabéthains*, 47 (April 1995), 71–8.

24. See Andrew Gurr, *The Shakespearian Playing Companies* (Oxford: Clarendon Press, 1996), p. 246. The choice of the Lord Admiral's Men for Henry also implies the pecking order in the London companies at this time: 'The early choice of the Chamberlain's Men [for James] and the rather belated choice in the middle of the Christmas season of the Admiral's for Henry and Worcester's for Anne appears to be an acknowledgement of the companies' relative status, with the Chamberlain's pre-eminent and the Admiral's a little ahead of Worcester's.'

25. Gurr does comment, however, that Nottingham did not seem to have any say in the allocation of his Company to the prince and his direct involvement in Company matters is not discernible on paper after 1604. For the continuing association, chivalric- and naval-based, between Henry and Nottingham, see Roy Strong, *Henry, Prince of Wales and England's Lost Renaissance* (London: Thames & Hudson, 1986), pp. 57–8, and p. 154, where, at his investiture as Prince of Wales, Henry is supported by the Earls of Nottingham and Northampton.

26. Gurr, *Shakesperian Playing Companies*, p. 255.

27. Nostbakken, 'Rowley's *When You See Me You Know Me*', p. 75.
28. Ibid., p. 74; see Mark H. Lawhorn, 'Taking Pains for the Prince: Age, Patronage, and Penal Surrogacy in Samuel Rowley's *When You See Me, You Know Me*', *The Premodern Teenager: Youth in Society, 1150–1650*, ed. Konrad Eisenbichler (Toronto: Centre for Reformation and Renaissance Studies, 2002), pp. 131–50.
29. As Lucy Munro points out, many of the Prince's Men took part in this entertainment, celebrating the miraculous unification of Britain. But particularly striking is the concentration within the text on the confluence of Time and Fate, typical of early Jacobean writing which stressed the historical inevitability (and rectitude) of the Stuart accession. The implied repetition of history which the use of political ciphering asserts in *When You See Me* has a similar effect: the Stuarts are so like the Tudors that their reign is essentially the same, and therefore cosmically 'right'.
30. See J. W. Williamson, *The Myth of the Conqueror, Prince Henry Stuart: a Study of 17th Century Personation* (New York: AMS Press, 1978), especially ch. 1, 'The Infant and the Myth'.
31. Ibid., pp. 8–10.
32. Walter W. Seton, 'The Early Years of Henry Frederick, Prince of Wales, and Charles, Duke of Albany, 1593–1605', *The Scottish Historical Review*, 13 (1916), 366–79 (p. 377).
33. Ibid., p. 378. He notes that a good way to judge the religio-political climate is to examine the careers of the men into whose care the princes were entrusted in their early years. See also 'Crises of the 1590s and the Gowrie Conspiracy', in Jenny Wormald, 'James VI and I (1566–1625)', *Oxford Dictionary of National Biography*, ed. H. C. G. Matthew and Brian Harrison (Oxford: Oxford University Press, 2004), http://www.oxforddnb.com/view/article/14592, accessed 22 September 2006.
34. Nostbakken, 'Rowley's *When You See Me You Know Me*', p. 75.
35. Foxe, *The Acts and Monuments of John Foxe*, ed. Stephen Reed Cattley; 4th edn, rev. and corr. Josiah Pratt, 8 vols (London: The Religious Tract Society, 1877), Vol. V, p. 692.
36. St Augustine, *Confessions*, The Loeb Classical Library, 2 vols (London: Heinemann, 1912), II, Book XI, chapter XVII, p. 246. My, rather free, translation.
37. Tom Bishop, 'Tradition and Novelty in the Jacobean Masque', *The Politics of the Stuart Court Masque*, ed. David Bevington and Peter Holbrook (Cambridge: Cambridge University Press, 1998), pp. 88–120 (pp. 94–5).
38. Stow, *Annales* (1615), pp. 838–40.
39. For treatments of types of history as discussed in Renaissance humanists and historiographers see, variously, the works of F. J. Levy, F. S. Fussner and, most recently and extensively, D. R. Woolf.
40. Stow, *Annales* (1615), p. 489.
41. Anon., *The History of the King and the Cobler, shewing How Henry VIII used to visit the watches in the city* (Stirling: Macnie, 1825), p. 1.
42. Anne Barton, 'The King Disguis'd; Shakespeare's *Henry V* and the Comical History', *Essays, Mainly Shakespearean* (Cambridge: Cambridge University Press, 1994), pp. 207–33 (pp. 212–13). Monarchs involved in such scenes are clearly indicating their (supposed) willingness to listen to their people, and

to have their best interests at heart. This is the quasi-parental responsibility
of the king/queen, and was a trope of which Elizabeth was particularly fond.

43. Jack Goody and Ian Watt, 'The Consequences of Literacy' (1963), repr. in
Jack Goody (ed.), *Literacy in Traditional Societies* (Cambridge: Cambridge
University Press, 1968), pp. 27–68 (p. 48).
44. Ian W. Archer, 'Discourses of History in Elizabethan and Early Stuart
London', *Huntington Library Quarterly*, 68/1–2 (2005), 205–26.
45. Ibid., p. 210; D. R. Woolf, *The Social Circulation of the Past: English Historical
Culture, 1500–1730* (Oxford: Oxford University Press, 2003).
46. Archer, 'Discourses of History', p. 208.
47. Ibid., p. 213.
48. These include *George a Greene* (1587–93); Peele's *Edward I* (1590–3);
Heywood's *1 Edward IV* (1592–1601); *Fair Em* (1598–1601). See Barton, 'The
King Disguis'd' for details.
49. Archer, 'Discourses of History', p. 213, citing British Library, MS. Lansdowne
74/42, fol. 118^v.
50. Richard Dutton, ' "Methinks the truth should live from age to age": the
Dating and Contexts of *Henry V*', *Huntington Library Quarterly*, 68/1–2 (2005),
173–204.
51. See Barton, 'The King Disguis'd', p. 208; for Tacitus see introduction to this
collection.
52. See *Measure for Measure*, ed. J. W. Lever (London: Methuen, 1965, repr. 1977),
pp. xlix–l.
53. Gilbert Dugdale, *The Time Triumphant* (London: at R. B., 1604), sig. B1^v.
54. Ibid., sig. B1^v.
55. See Grant, 'Drama Queen', pp. 128–30.
56. Archer, 'Discourses of History', p. 210.
57. See note 20 above.
58. *Measure for Measure*, ed. Lever, p. xxxii.
59. Peter Holbrook, 'Jacobean Masques and the Jacobean Peace', in Bevington
and Holbrook (eds), *The Politics of the Stuart Court Masque*, pp. 67–87 (p. 72).
60. See *WYSM*, where Charles Brandon says 'Unless his highnesse first had sent
for me, / I will not put my head in such a hazzard, / I know his anger, and
his spleen too well' (555–7).
61. James Ellison argues convincingly that anti-Catholic plays of 1604 are also
a response to James's crackdown on Catholics who had greeted his accession by displaying their faith too openly. See his '*Measure for Measure*
and the Executions of Catholics in 1604', *English Literary Renaissance*, 33/1
(2003), 44–87.
62. See Wormald, 'James VI and I', and Nicholas W. S. Cranfield, 'Bancroft,
Richard (*bap.* 1544, *d.* 1610)', *ODNB*, http://www.oxforddnb.com/view
/article/1272, accessed 22 September 2006. See also the *ODNB* articles for
the leaders of the millenary petitioners, Stephen Egerton (*c.* 1555–1622) and
Arthur Hildersham (1563–1632).
63. These include Thomas Bell, *The Downfall of Poperie* (1604; STC 1818.5),
Jérôme Bignon, *A briefe, but an effectuall treatise of the election of popes* (1605;
STC 3057, multiple editions), and works of the reformer Daniel Tilenus (later
to emerge as a Pelagian at the Synod of Dort, but in 1605 simply a robust
anti-Catholic writer): *The true copy of tvvo letters, with their seuerall answeres,*

contayning the late apostasie of the Earle of Lauall, after his returne from Italy (1605; STC 24072) and *Positions lately held by the L. Du Perron, Bishop of Eureux, against the sufficiency and perfection of the scriptures* (1606; STC 24071). He also published the Presbyterian Henoch Clapham's *A manuel of the Bibles doctrine for law and Gospell* (1606; STC 5344).

64. *The Acts and Monuments of John Foxe*, ed. Cattley, Vol. VI, pp. 587ff.
65. For the 'millenary petition' see 'The Conference and the Book', in Vivienne Westbrook, 'Authorized Version of the Bible, translators of the (*act.* 1604–1611)', *ODNB*, http://www.oxforddnb.com/view/article/74199, accessed 22 September 2006.
66. Kim H. Noling, 'Woman's Wit and Woman's Will in *When You See Me You Know Me*', *Studies in English Literature 1500–1900*, 33 (1993), 327–42.
67. Ibid., p. 327.
68. *The Acts and Monuments of John Foxe*, ed. Cattley, Vol. V, p. 462.
69. Foxe notes the strength of feeling in favour of Catherine: 'the mouths of the common people, and in especial of women, and such others that favoured the queen...talked their pleasure...and cast out such lewd words, as the king would, "for his own pleasure", have another wife' (ibid., Vol. V, p. 48). Perhaps disingenuously he blames the Spaniards for the first doubt over the legality of Henry and Catherine's marriage: he narrates that the collapse of the match between Charles V and Lady Mary in 1522 was owing to doubts about her legitimacy, a reason also used by the French in 1527 when her match with the Duke of Orleans failed to come to anything (ibid., pp. 46–7). Foxe also has Henry expatiate on Catherine's virtues in his 'Oration to His Subjects': 'beside her noble parentage of the which she is descended (as you well know), she is a woman of most gentleness, of most humility and buxomness, yea, and in all good qualities appertaining to nobility she is without comparison' (ibid., p. 49). This, of course, is the stuff of Shakespeare's *Henry VIII*.
70. Noling, 'Woman's Wit', p. 336.
71. For the ballads see *English and Scottish Ballads*, ed. Francis James Child (8 vols; Boston: Little, Brown and Company, 1889), Vol. 7, pp. 74–8. For a full account of the versions see Noling, 'Woman's Wit', pp. 339–41.
72. Foxe, *Acts and Monuments*, ed. Cattley, Vol. V.148, 814: 'For "twelfth" Foxe improperly reads "second": see Henry's History of England, and Tindals note in Rapin.'
73. *The Letters of John Chamberlain*, ed. and intr. Norman Egbert McClure (2 vols; Philadelphia: The American Philosophical Society, 1939), Vol. I, p. 199.
74. Ibid., p. 198; Maureen M. Meikle and Helen Payne, 'Anne (1574–1619)', *ODNB*, http://www.oxforddnb.com/view/article/559, accessed 28 February 2007.
75. Meikle and Payne, 'Anne (1574–1619)'.
76. See Introduction, pp. 8–9.

Bibliography

Anon., *The History of the King and the Cobler, shewing How Henry VIII used to visit the watches in the city* (Stirling: Macnie, 1825).

Archer, Ian W., 'Discourses of History in Elizabethan and Early Stuart London', *Huntington Library Quarterly*, 68/1–2 (2005), 205–26.

Augustine, St, *Confessions*, The Loeb Classical Library, 2 vols (London: Heinemann, 1912).

Barton, Anne, 'The King Disguis'd; Shakespeare's *Henry V* and the Comical History', *Essays, Mainly Shakespearean* (Cambridge: Cambridge University Press, 1994), pp. 207–33.

Bevington, David and Peter Holbrook (eds), *The Politics of the Stuart Court Masque* (Cambridge: Cambridge University Press, 1998).

Bishop, Tom, 'Tradition and Novelty in the Jacobean Masque', *The Politics of the Stuart Court Masque*, ed. David Bevington and Peter Holbrook (Cambridge: Cambridge University Press, 1998), pp. 88–120.

Chamberlain, John, *The Letters of John Chamberlain*, ed. and intr. Norman Egbert McClure (2 vols; Philadelphia: The American Philosophical Society, 1939).

Child, Francis James (ed.), *English and Scottish Ballads* (8 vols; Boston: Little, Brown and Company, 1889).

Collinson, Patrick, 'William Camden and the Anti-Myth of Elizabeth', *The Myth of Elizabeth*, ed. Susan Doran and Thomas S. Freeman (Basingstoke: Palgrave Macmillan, 2003), pp. 79–98.

Cranfield, Nicholas W. S., 'Bancroft, Richard (*bap.* 1544, *d.* 1610)', *Oxford Dictionary of National Biography* (Oxford: Oxford University Press, 2004), http://www.oxforddnb.com/view/article/1272, accessed 22 September 2006.

Dekker, Thomas, *The Whore of Babylon* (London: for Nathaniel Butter, 1607).

Dekker, Thomas and John Webster, *The Famous Historie of Sir Thomas Wyat* (London: E[dward] A[llde] for Thomas Archer, 1607).

Dugdale, Gilbert, *The Time Triumphant* (London: at R. B., 1604).

Dutton, Richard, ' "Methinks the truth should live from age to age": the Dating and Contexts of *Henry V*', *Huntington Library Quarterly*, 68/1–2 (2005), 173–204.

Ellison James, '*Measure for Measure* and the Executions of Catholics in 1604', *English Literary Renaissance*, 33/1 (2003), 44–87.

Evenden, Elizabeth and Thomas S. Freeman, 'Print, Profit and Propaganda: the Elizabethan Privy Council and the 1570 Edition of Foxe's "Book of Martyrs" ', *English Historical Review*, 119/484 (November 2004), 1288–1307.

Foxe, John, *Acts and Monuments* (London: John Day, 1583).

Foxe, John, *The Acts and Monuments of John Foxe*, ed. Stephen Reed Cattley; 4th edn, rev. and corr. Josiah Pratt, 8 vols (London: The Religious Tract Society, 1877).

Freeman, Thomas S., 'Providence and Prescription: the Account of Elizabeth in Foxe's "Book of Martyrs" ', *The Myth of Elizabeth*, ed. Susan Doran and Thomas S. Freeman (Basingstoke: Palgrave Macmillan, 2003), pp. 27–55.

Goody, Jack and Ian Watt, 'The Consequences of Literacy' (1963), repr. in Jack Goody (ed.), *Literacy in Traditional Societies* (Cambridge: Cambridge University Press, 1968), pp. 27–68.

Grant, Teresa, 'Drama Queen: Staging Elizabeth in *If You Know Not Me You Know Nobody*', *The Myth of Elizabeth*, ed. Susan Doran and Thomas S. Freeman (Basingstoke: Palgrave Macmillan, 2003), pp. 120–42.

Gurr, Andrew, *The Shakespearian Playing Companies* (Oxford: Clarendon Press, 1996).

Holbrook, Peter, 'Jacobean Masques and the Jacobean Peace', *The Politics of the Stuart Court Masque*, ed. David Bevington and Peter Holbrook (Cambridge: Cambridge University Press, 1998), pp. 67–87.

Hoy, Cyrus, *Introductions, Notes, and Commentaries to Texts in 'The Dramatic Works of Thomas Dekker'*, edited by Fredson Bowers (4 vols; Cambridge: Cambridge University Press, 1980).

Lawhorn, Mark H., 'Taking Pains for the Prince: Age, Patronage, and Penal Surrogacy in Samuel Rowley's *When You See Me, You Know Me*', *The Premodern Teenager: Youth in Society, 1150–1650*, ed. Konrad Eisenbichler (Toronto: Centre for Reformation and Renaissance Studies, 2002), pp. 131–50.

Martin, Mary Foster, 'If You Know Not Me, You Know Nobodie, and *The Famous History of Sir Thomas Wyat*', *The Library*, 4th series, 13 (1933), 271–81.

Meikle, Maureen M. and Helen Payne, 'Anne (1574–1619)', *Oxford Dictionary of National Biography* (Oxford: Oxford University Press, 2004), http://www.oxforddnb.com/view/article/559, accessed 28 February 2007.

Munro, Lucy, 'Plays, Politics and Patronage: the Fortune Repertory, 1603–1625', unpublished essay.

Noling, Kim H., 'Woman's Wit and Woman's Will in *When You See Me You Know Me*', *Studies in English Literature 1500–1900*, 33 (1993), 327–42.

Nostbakken, F., 'Rowley's *When You See Me You Know Me*: Political Drama in Transition', *Cahiers Élisabéthains*, 47 (April 1995), 71–8.

Pepys, Samuel, *The Diaries of Samuel Pepys*, ed. Robert Latham and William Matthews (11 vols; London, 1973).

Perry, Curtis, 'The Citizen Politics of Nostalgia: Queen Elizabeth in Early Jacobean London', *Journal of Medieval and Renaissance Studies*, 23/1 (Winter, 1993), 89–111.

Robinson, Marsha S., *Writing the Reformation: Actes and Monuments and the Jacobean History Play* (Aldershot: Ashgate, 2002).

Rowley, Samuel, *When You See Me You Know Me* (1605), ed. F. P. Wilson (Oxford: Malone Society, 1952).

Seton, Walter W., 'The Early Years of Henry Frederick, Prince of Wales, and Charles, Duke of Albany, 1593–1605', *The Scottish Historical Review*, 13 (1916), 366–79.

Shakespeare, William, *Measure for Measure*, ed. J. W. Lever (London: Methuen, 1965, repr. 1977).

Stow, John, *The Annales, or Generall Chronicle of England, begun first by maister John Stow*, ed. and supp. Edward Howes (London, Thomas Dawson for Thomas Adams, 1615; STC 23338).

Strong, Roy, *Henry, Prince of Wales and England's Lost Renaissance* (London: Thames & Hudson, 1986).

Watkins, John, ' "Old Bess in the Ruff": Remembering Elizabeth I, 1625–1660', *English Literary Renaissance*, 30 (2000), 95–116.

Westbrook, Vivienne, 'Authorized Version of the Bible, translators of the (*act.* 1604–1611)', *Oxford Dictionary of National Biography* (Oxford: Oxford University Press, 2004), http://www.oxforddnb.com/view/article/74199, accessed 22 September 2006.

Williamson, J. W., *The Myth of the Conqueror, Prince Henry Stuart: A Study of 17th Century Personation* (New York: AMS Press, 1978).

Woolf, D. R., *The Social Circulation of the Past: English Historical Culture, 1500–1730* (Oxford: Oxford University Press, 2003).

Woolf, D. R., 'Two Elizabeths? James I and the Late Queen's Famous Memory', *Canadian Journal of History* 20/2 (August, 1985), 167–91.

Wormald, Jenny, 'James VI and I (1566–1625)', *Oxford Dictionary of National Biography* (Oxford: Oxford University Press, 2004), http://www.oxforddnb. com/view/article/14592, accessed 22 September 2006.

6
The Stage Historicizes the Turk: Convention and Contradiction in the Turkish History Play

Mark Hutchings

In the summer of 1622 news of sensational events in Constantinople began to reach Western Europe. Christians divided by war rejoiced at reports that the Ottoman Empire was in chaos: defeat by the Poles at Hotin had led to disaffected Janissaries storming the Seraglio and overthrowing the sultan.[1] Informed, well-connected observers such as England's ambassador to Constantinople, Sir Thomas Roe, and pamphleteers anticipated there would be a lively appetite for this news; the title of one London pamphlet proclaims:

> The Strangling and Death of the Great Turk, and his two Sons; with the strange Preservation and Deliverance of his Uncle Mustapha from Perishing in Prison, with Hunger and Thirst; the young Emperor, not three Days before, having so commanded. A wonderful Story, and the like never heard of in our modern Times; and yet, all to manifest the Glory and Providence of God, in the Preservation of Christendom in these troublesome Times. Printed this fifteenth July.[2]

Although it promises a 'wonderful Story [...] the like never heard of in our modern Times', clearly the significance of these events is that God has intervened to effect the 'Preservation of Christendom'. Perhaps unsurprisingly, the text taps into a narrative stretching back to the fall of Constantinople in 1453, the dawn of the 'Ottoman peril'.[3] But if the legacy of 1453 was a cultural memory reawakened periodically, the implied response (for reader as well as pamphleteer) suggested here was by no means the only – or only possible – reaction to the sultan's overthrow. Indeed, such apparently straightforward attitudes to the Ottoman Empire were under pressure from a range of other forces, not least in the dynamic forum where writers and audiences explored their fascination with the Ottoman Empire, the early modern playhouse.[4] In a King's Men play inspired by the events of May, Lodowick Carlell's *Osmond the Great Turk*, the significance of 1453 is apparent, but so too are the stage's own important influences and conventions. This fusion of sources invites a rather more complex range of responses than the pamphlet reportage allows; crucially, it is through its theatre-mediated engagement with the 1453 tradition that the play unsettles the kinds of assumptions found in the pamphlet material.[5]

The Turkish theme was a fixture on the English stage, as scholars now appreciate; but it was not *fixed*: it is increasingly apparent that the playhouse's remarkable fascination for the Ottoman Empire was complex and plural, irreducible to simple formulations or ideological perspectives.[6] Inevitably, the loss of Constantinople looms large in the surviving corpus of plays, a sign, certainly, of its cultural, historical and ideological significance. But its prominence also calls attention to the intersection of cultural memory, sources, conventions, playing and audience perception that underwrites the making of meaning in the theatre. Indeed, it is not only the longevity of the signifier 'Constantinople' that the playhouse acknowledges, but also its flexibility: 1453 is not only recalled but mapped and remapped, registering both its cultural force and, simultaneously, its negotiability.

While accounts of the rise of the Turkish Empire were important sources of information for playwrights eager to exploit the subject, arguably more significant was the myth that came to symbolize the loss of the city, and in turn dovetail with literary and cultural emblems to form a powerful, enduring – and malleable – motif.[7] Indeed, in gendering Constantinople as female – and, according to the myth, as a beautiful Greek captive, Irene, with whom Sultan Mehmed II fell in love[8] – the tale anticipated the later Western fascination with the Seraglio.[9] As the sultan's palace and harem it was both the centre of power and the object of desire and curiosity, with Christians' imaginations being fuelled by its very inaccessibility, as Alain Grossrichard has shown.[10] To Western eyes, then, the Seraglio offered a metonym for the empire – glorious, mysterious, debauched, tyrannical, absolute, decadent; most significantly, its sexual-political make-up not only called up the troubles of sixteenth- and seventeenth-century sultans but evoked the dominant motif of 1453, the tale of the Christian whose tragedy troped the loss of the city itself. Thus the Irene myth is both 'historical', referencing the fifteenth-century fall of Constantinople, and simultaneously contemporary, registering and anticipating post-1453 developments.

The personification of the city as female, the siege and assault a rape perpetrated by a violent, barbaric invader, is a familiar one. Versions of this story were included in William Painter's *The Palace of Pleasure* (1567) and Richard Knolles's *General Historie of the Turkes* (1603).[11] Franz Babinger provides a summary:

> At the capture of Constantinople an exceedingly beautiful Greek girl of sixteen or seventeen was among the numerous prisoners taken. She was brought before the Conqueror, who fell in love with her and so neglected the affairs of state on her account that his advisors made representations to him. Far from taking offense at their audacity, the sultan undertook to prove that he was still master of himself. Summoning his dignitaries to the hall of his palace, he himself, accompanied by the radiant and sumptuously clad Irene, came to meet them. Turning to those around him, he asked whether they had ever encountered more perfect beauty. When all replied in the negative and vied with one another in lauding the sultan's choice, Mehmed cried out, 'Nothing in the world can deter me from upholding the greatness of the house of Osman!' Thereupon he seized the Greek girl by the hair, drew his dagger, and cut her throat.[12]

On one level it is a modern recognition of the link between soldiering and sexual desire, and, however apocryphal, captures in miniature the epidemic of violence that followed sieges. While its primary, primitive force lies in its evocative depiction of Constantinople at the hands of the invaders, it is not only, or completely, a narrative of loss. The city lives on, emblematized as a pure, noble woman: a heroine not as passive victim but as iconic figure, a call to remembrance, and ideally to arms. But crucially the Irene narrative mutates further, retelling later historical events, such as Sultan Suleyman's killing of his son Mustapha at the behest of the increasingly powerful Sultana Roxelana in 1553;[13] indeed, the Irene figure does not only stand for Constantinople in 1453, but calls up literary motifs, notably the Petrarchan figure of the woman besieged. This intertextual fluidity contributed to its longevity on the English stage;[14] it also opened up, rather than closed down, interpretative possibilities.

The Irene narrative features in a range of plays spanning the rise of playing in London inns to the closing of the theatres.[15] From Stephen Gosson's description of the lost play *The Blacksmith's Daughter* (1578) as 'conteyning the trechery of Turkes, the honourable bountye of a noble minde, and the shining of vertue in distresse' we can deduce that this was one of the earliest plays in the narrative.[16] Though lost, the titles of *The Turkish Mahomet and Hiren the Fair Greek* (1588) and *The Love of a Grecian Lady* (1594) leave scholars in little doubt as to their subject.[17] Indeed, the first of these was evidently well known, referred to in *2 Henry IV* (1596–7), *Eastward Ho!* (1605) and *The Old Law* (c. 1618). The story furnished Thomas Kyd with the motif for the inset play in *The Spanish Tragedy* (1587?), and featured in *Soliman and Perseda* (1592?), perhaps also by Kyd.[18] Its flexibility is evident in plays where 1453 is implied, even where the historical context is displaced. Thus it is evoked in the *Tamburlaine* plays, in both the ambush of Zenocrate's caravan and siege of Damascus and in the sequel with Olympia's death after a siege. Further examples include *1 Fair Maid of the West* (c. 1598–1604), *The Turk* (1607), *The Courageous Turk* (1618), *Two Noble Ladies* (1619–23), *Osmond the Great Turk* (1622), *The Renegado* (1624), *2 Fair Maid of the West* (c. 1630–1) and *The Unhappy Fair Irene* (1640).[19] It is in performance, however, that the material releases its fuller 'contexts'.[20] Thus the narrative transparently reworks Mars-Venus, inviting perhaps further links with the Seraglio associations noted earlier; indeed, here the confluence of fear and fascination may well have produced a particular frisson for male spectators, whose gendered ways of seeing logically, perversely, produces the possibility of identification with the sultan, rather than his Christian quarry.[21]

When Lodowick Carlell came to write about the events of May 1622 he had a rich literary and theatrical heritage on which to draw. He was influenced by the pamphlets, and wrote speedily to capitalize on public interest: the play was licensed on 6 September, only a few weeks after the first pamphlets appeared.[22] But more significantly *Osmond the Great Turk* depended on a long-established playhouse motif; while it echoes the pamphlets in places, its key source in fact is its theatrical antecedents. The significance of this is that these diverse influences combine to produce a radical challenge to expectations – a challenge all the starker precisely because the play evokes the 1453 débâcle *and* maps onto this the sultan's assassination, conjoining the original disaster with the desired outcome: the overthrow of the Turks, and 'the Preservation of Christendom in these troublesome times'. Yet remarkably, it offers an endorsement of the Irene narrative only to wrong-foot spectators desirous of an orthodox retelling. Readers of the pamphlets may well have greeted the news with joy, but if they expected to see a dramatic recreation of the 'Preservation of Christendom' they experienced a more complex performance event, one that alternately upholds and undermines convictions and presents an Irene figure redefined by the Jacobean 'theatre of blood'.

Although the title of the play appears to mislead, the playwright clearly expected the audience to recognize the historical contexts – 1453 *and* 1622. While Osmond is *not* the 'Great Turk' but the 'Noble Servant', and his master, Sultan Melcoshus, desires a Christian captive called Despina rather than Irene, the structural and thematic similarities make clear that they are the play's surrogate Mehmed II and Irene. As the title suggests, the sultan's servant is the play's main protagonist, and he is effectively the chorus through which the audience's narrative point of view is focused. The audience's likely inclination to concentrate on Despina – while at the same activating, perhaps, its (male-dominated) desire to view the female character as an *object* (further complicated in turn by the all-male acting convention) – produces the text's dialectic. While the key elements of the Irene narrative are present, Despina is a complex figure whose representation resists the constraints of the Irene convention; the name itself is Greek, meaning 'Lady',[23] but originally it may have signified the Virgin Mary. This suggests intentional irony, signalling an ideological shift from 'Christian' to 'Catholic' – obviously problematic for a Protestant audience, particularly in 1622.[24] Although underpinned by a tragic narrative, the tragedy is not, in fact, Despina's, for her role as a 'femme fatale' figure shifts the narrative focus onto the noble servant. The play's negotiation with the Irene narrative is the pretext for a radical dramatization of the Turk as cultural construct; remarkably, its response to the *coup* is not unambiguous. In explicitly aligning the text's sympathies with the sultan rather than taking a 'Christian' perspective, *Osmond the Great Turk* offers a striking counter-narrative to the Irene convention. Despite transposing 1453 onto 1622, then, the play links the Christian captive's deviousness with the sultan's fall from power. Thus the desired fall of the Turks is here turned on its head: Despina is not only to blame for Melcoshus's death but the catalyst for political unrest. There is little suggestion, as playgoers may have expected, that the play welcomes this Christian-inspired *coup*.

The opening establishes the primal scene. Despina is rescued from the hands of two Janissaries intent on rape by Osmond, who conquers his own desire and loyally presents her to Melcoshus. The subplot to this familiar narrative is then introduced: Orcanes, the sultan's son, is the guest of Callibeus and his wife, Ozaca. The husband's jealousy is justified as Orcanes makes his desire for the complicit Ozaca clear. In Act II the Ozaca/Despina parallel resets the play's co-ordinates. Despina acts not as an innocent victim of the Turks, but as a Jacobean plotter reminiscent of Middleton's Bianca. She expresses her love for Osmond, and in a scene recalling *Women Beware Women* (1621) resists Melcoshus's demands in order to secure her power over him.[25] The subplot dovetails with the play's central narrative as Callibeus tricks Orcanes with a letter purporting to be from his wife, which leads, ironically, to his own cuckolding. While the play makes clear Despina's tactical victory over the sultan, the rivalry between Orcanes and Callibeus is given its political corollary in the pashas' stirrings of discontent over the sultan's obsessive love. When Callibeus discovers Orcanes and Ozaca together, to save her honour she reports she has been raped. The pashas' continued discontent in the next scene is then given material substance when Melcoshus summarily rejects Callibeus's demand for justice for his wife's apparent violation. Odmer, a loyal pasha, expresses to Melcoshus his fears for the empire if the sultan continues his infatuation. This has an immediate effect when Orcanes's misplaced trust in his father is repaid: displacing his guilt onto his wayward son, he has Orcanes blinded and then executed, ironically for the 'rape'. Act V dramatizes the play's internal logic – and the imperative of the 1453 narrative: Melcoshus must choose between the empire and Despina. He kills Despina, and Osmond's pursuit of the sultan as he seeks revenge coincides with the pashas' revolt. In mourning for Orcanes, Ozaca kills herself and wounds Callibeus; the ever-loyal Osmond kills the pashas as they attack Melcoshus; when the latter dies of his wounds, Osmond commits suicide, and Odmer is appointed sultan.

In the opening scenes there is little indication the play will depart significantly from the Irene convention. 'The City reeks with the warm blood of murder'd Christians whose avarice hath made them & their wealth our prey' (I.1.1–4) evokes a familiar image. Later in the play Despina's avarice, and Osmond's honesty, problematize the simplistic anti-Turkish viewing the play initially invites, but her capture, rescue and deliverance to the sultan offers no hint of this later development. The audience may well recognize that her fear of rape foreshadows the threat posed by the sultan, and that his triumphant entrance while his soldiers spoil the city will be symbolically reformulated when he encounters his Christian captive. Osmond's warning to his master, 'you are in danger of your liberty, see not her face [...] if I draw this veil, you then must yield, the thought of all your glories laid aside, and in her heavenly eyes read your captivity' (I.4.29–I.5.2), is conventional, but it alerts the Jacobean audience to the material logic of the narrative which Christian mythology suppresses. This bodily, physical presence at the heart of theatre is given utterance later in Ozaca's aside, 'I find

I am a woman, I long extremely' (I.7.32), and the play begins to realize on stage the narrative tension between desire and ideology. Instead of the ideologically defined (and constrained) Despina stoically resisting the sultan, the material desire lurking beneath articulates itself directly through the Christian icon; ironically, it is Osmond who resists, not the Christian captive:

> What shall I say, I find I am a weak unconstant woman, sure I have lost myself, at least my grief; how pleasure and greatness gains upon our natures! I who wept at first each time their eunuchs did me reverence, thinking they mocked me, now take a great delight in their observance. (II.10.21–6)

Despina does not simply enrapture but recognizes that she does; first, however, she attempts to convert Osmond:

> though I see I shall be able to command *Melcoshus*, and in him the world, yet if you dare apply your courage to the performance of what I shall offer, and that effected become a Christian, I shall think myself happy, to be again wholly at your disposing, as I was when you did unkindly to yourself and me, bestow me on another. (II.11.21–7)

But power, not romance, drives Despina. Melcoshus tells her 'it was ordained I should command' (II.12.17–18) and 'if refused the violence of my affection will compel me to use force' (II.12.21–2);[26] however, Despina shows she is equal to his threats, and responds by suggesting that if he attempts to win her with love his reward will be the greater. Melcoshus's contentment with his delayed pleasure may have been seen as a Christian victory, but it is at considerable cost. No longer outside the play's sexual economy, Despina becomes fully participant in its intrigue.

The following two scenes illustrate this shift. Orcanes, seeking Ozaca – 'I never yet laid siege to any female fort, but either by assault or policy I found a way to conquest' (II.14. 24–5) – discovers Callibeus's forged letter; Osmond then appears on stage with a letter, apparently from Despina, reiterating her plan that they flee and he convert. The first scene parallels Melcoshus's desire for his prisoner in his son's for Ozaca; the second invites spectators to compare Despina with Osmond. While she is swayed by the promise of riches, he resists temptation: 'Hence thou enticing charm, whose witchcraft almost does enforce me, to forsake my faith and virtue' (II.16.22–4). Even here, however, interpretation is complicated when Despina proposes they escape and 'set free a Christian merchant, with his ship and men' (II.18.31) – which gestures in the direction of the audience's likely sympathies. Osmond refuses, declaring, 'Could paradise be gained by crooked paths, I would not tread them' (II.18.36–II.19.1), which challenges Melcoshus's decree that he obey her and ironically inverts the 'turning Turk' motif. The audience might well wonder why the Christian is unable to resist, unlike the Turk – the opposite of the Irene convention. But as if in answer Despina then confirms her new, 'renegade' feelings:

> 'Tis nobly said of *Osmond*; yet, since his denial, I look on him with other eyes. *Melcoshus'* greatness, and his love exceeding that, makes some impression on me. (II.19.31–3)

This portrayal of the captive is disconcerting for the audience, but in keeping with the play's internal logic: spectators know that the conspiratorial pashas' fears that the sultan is infatuated with 'that painted Sorceress' (II.20.11–12) are justified. Odmer, tricked by fellow pashas into risking Melcoshus's wrath – 'were it not madness in any that should tell him, that his dotage on *Despina* makes him neglect his office?' (II.22.29–31), Haly asks – is, like Osmond, empowered by the text's rationale to challenge Despina's power: the dominant narrative is not the Christian imperative to destabilize the Ottoman Empire but the state's attempt to maintain order from external (and internal) threats. These dangers, it makes clear, are not Melcoshus's tyranny but the lust of Despina, Melcoshus, Orcanes and Ozaca. It is the play's redefinition of power as/through sexual desire – replaying the Seraglio convention – that undermines the audience's identification with Despina. Callibeus's discovery of his wife and her lover *in flagrante delicto* reorientates the spectator's knowledge of the relationship between Melcoshus and Despina. Ozaca's 'rape' recalls Melcoshus's desire. The link is cemented when Melcoshus confides in Osmond that 'she's no longer cruel, I have enjoyed her freely, by her own consent' (III.30.14–15).[27] Osmond's expression of loyalty is also one of relief, his conscience tested by Despina's allure: 'there is none living, that sooner could conceive your happiness than I, since none doth more admire and reverence *Despina*' (III.30.26–8).

Melcoshus's denial of justice to Callibeus is framed by a meeting of rebellious pashas, condensing the 1622 revolt and Irene and Seraglio material. A pasha gives voice to sentiments familiar from popular narratives of Turkish tyranny: 'He must not last long, if we be men, and have but sense to see our miseries in him, and what a happy people we should be under some other' (III.32.20–2). Melcoshus's dismissal of Callibeus's plea for justice – 'Degenerate bastard, for could a son of mine commit so base an act; had I used force, where had my joys in *Despina* been?' (III.33.36–III.34.2) – connects the plots, the pashas, overhearing, promising to help Callibeus. It is against this canvas that Osmond functions as a choric figure, putting further torque on the Irene narrative. Not only does the play blame her for both the sultan's neglect of his duty and, implicitly, Orcanes's conduct towards Callibeus and Ozaca – as a foreign pollutant undermining the security of the state – but crucially Osmond's conflict between loyalty and desire clearly leads to the play condemning Despina. Where Osmond battles with – and conquers – his desire for the Christian, Despina has effectively 'turned Turk':

DESPINA
Osmond, how ere the Emperor, in my command o'er him, makes all the empire subject to my will, yet if you kneel I must not be exempt: for well you know I love you.
OSMOND
I fear.
DESPINA
Yet not as heretofore, 'tis now a sisterly affection.
OSMOND
Thanks, heaven.

                                                                        (IV.35.31–IV.36.1)

This comic inversion in turn undercuts Despina's hope that Osmond will use his influence with the sultan to help her free 'some poor prisoners' (IV.36.20). Rather than straightforwardly reminding playgoers of the predicament of captives, Despina's gesture mocks such realities. Indeed, Odmer's brave warning to the sultan underscores the play's recalibration:

I should not need to let you see the peril and dishonour that attends your too much Love (I dare not call it dotage) on *Despina*, if your own judgement were at liberty that better could inform you. (IV.37.14–17)

The play reaches its inevitable crisis. Melcoshus declares: 'ere long thou and those of thy opinion shall know that I am able to govern my passion, perhaps, to their amazement' (IV.39.11–13). Spectators are entitled to expect her death, but Melcoshus's first act is symbolic: the destruction of his surrogate lust in Orcanes. The audience, but not

Orcanes, knows that Melcoshus has changed. Confident that his father will not only do nothing to give Callibeus justice but would 'bring Ozaca to me, nay be content to hold the door, whilst I again enjoy her' (IV.39.27–8), Orcanes ironically signals the flaw in his logic:

> stood my Father as strictly on the point of justice, as heretofore, ere love had softened him, I should fear his frown, but feeling daily the force of beauty in *Despina*, he will look upon my act with favourable eyes. (IV.39.31–5)

Orcanes's behaviour throughout the play signals an empire in decline, perhaps, but Melcoshus's soliloquy reminds the spectator of the Ottomans' former glories and present fascination for playhouse audiences:

> My valour, vigilance, and justice made me Commander over this numerous people, [s]ith when I have acquired an Empire, and made the neighbour world stand amazed fearing my fierce invasion; but by my slothful life I am become hated; nay worse, condemned by my own subjects, as thought unfit to govern, but since by the goodness of our blessed Prophet my eyes are opened, and I see my error, I'll tread those virtuous paths again that did advance me [...] (IV.40.9–16)[28]

He resolves to punish his son, setting up a tragicomic scene reminiscent of Junior's trial in another King's Men play, *The Revenger's Tragedy* (1606).[29] To his father's remark that he 'gain[ed] her by a boisterous way' (IV.40.25), Orcanes glibly admits that 'it were in vain for me to deny it, [...] Sir 'tis true her beauty did compel me' (IV.40.28–30).[30] Melcoshus contrasts his respect for Despina with his son's lust for Ozaca and disinherits him. Orcanes's behaviour, not Melcoshus's, has been in keeping with the Irene narrative's depiction of the sultan as a lusty ravisher of Christians, so it is fitting the sultan should effectively escape censure by displacing the Irene context onto Orcanes. Melcoshus summons his mutes to punish Orcanes: 'these eyes the causes of thy ill, least they again betray thee shall forever lose their light' (IV.43.16–17). Playgoers may have recognized this as an appropriate punishment for Orcanes, since 'historically, in medieval Europe and England blinding and castration were punishments for sexual crimes',[31] but blinding was a Persian, rather than Turkish, punishment: royal offspring, once blinded, could not rule, hence the dispensing with capital punishment.[32] In *Osmond the Great Turk* its function appears designed to add a twist, as it were, to the proceedings. After the loss of one eye, Orcanes pleads: 'Sir, I have belied myself; for know, *Ozaca* was more willing to meet my wished embraces, than I to offer them' (IV.43.30–2). This enrages the sultan, who then decrees the Turkish penalty for his son, death by strangulation.[33]

The play's duality asks much of the spectator, and the collision of the Irene narrative with the play's other concerns – the role of the noble servant Osmond and the fall of the sultan – creates a complex closing act open to multiple interpretation, arguably further destabilizing the Irene text while yet offering Despina as an imperfect Christian martyr. Despina's death is an anti-climax, theatrically, not only expected but overshadowed by the dramatically more resonant blinding of Orcanes. It, too, is an artificially contrived event, inserted from 'outside', as it were, and skilfully stage-managed by the sultan before his credulous subjects:

1ST CAPTAIN
We all acknowledge that your joys are infinite in her, and that it lies not in the power of man to quit such happiness.
MELCOSHUS
To make you know the difference then twixt you and me, and that I value the good of you my subjects and my honour far above fading pleasures, be this my witness, thus cut I from myself such a content, that Mortals ne'r enjoyed.

[*He stabs her.*]

DESPINA
Oh me, my fault lay in my blood, let that expiate my sin against heaven, mercy, mercy.
ALL
Oh cruelty.
ODMER
An act noble above example yet it moves my pity, this was no end of mine, heaven knows. (V.46.12–24)

Visually the scene emblematizes the Irene narrative, but verbally there is dissonance: in her moment of death Despina can only repent that she gave in to her 'blood', and ask heaven for mercy; the play recognizes not her martyrdom but Despina's material desire for power which has resulted in her conversion, not conviction. In echoing Vittoria's 'O my greatest sin lay in my blood. / Now my blood pays for it' in *The White Devil* (1612) Despina is confirmed as a theatrically redefined, Jacobean schemer.[34]

The play's chorus-figure has throughout complicated audience reception. Osmond's resistance to Despina is borne out by the play's description of the corruption of the Turkish court, and his constant struggle with his conscience reinforces rather than undermines the significance of his decision to remain loyal to Melcoshus and reject the Christian's advances. He is vindicated by the play, and remains outside the text's competing plots. His final test of loyalty is to choose, once again, between Despina and his master. Seeing her body, he refuses to believe the emperor is responsible, but is persuaded by a pasha, whose droll remark, 'sure he lov'd her, when he kill'd her' (V.48.17), hints at the sultan's dilemma. At this point Osmond's conflicting loyalties are most acute, before he resolves to exact revenge. But if the play has succeeded in uniting audience with character in Osmond's resolve to kill the sultan, the play then enacts a *volte-face*. Moved by the sultan's words of love for his servant's faithful service, Osmond confides in the audience that 'Me thinks I find my resolution of revenge begin to abate its force' (V.55.10–11). The sultan's explanation that he chose 'state and honour' (V.56.30) over the love which was preventing him rule – which the play has demonstrated in dramatizing Despina's disruptive presence – persuades Osmond of his own treason. Spectators who endorse Osmond's desire for revenge must now negotiate this shift. Indeed, it is apparent at its close, as the play has suggested throughout, that the primary concern in *Osmond the Great Turk* is the noble servant's divided loyalties. If the play underwrites his decision to resist Despina, a residual anti-Turkish sentiment endorses his wish to exact revenge against the sultan. But this he is unable to do. Unable to oppose his master, Osmond's actions are a direct challenge to the authority of the Irene narrative.[35]

The spectator who approves of Osmond's desire for revenge is thus presented with a dilemma a text internally divided cannot reconcile. The play's recognition of this contradiction is, however, confirmed in Osmond's own conclusion – his suicide. Here Osmond signals the play's admission of failure, insofar that it can provide no answer to the questions it puts. With Melcoshus's death Osmond gives vent to his anguish:

Stay, he's gone, and shall I live, he and *Despina* dead? 'twere madness; for what is in the world left that's worthy; or, if there be two such, it is not like, that I shall love the one, and serve the other. The fates ordained me only for this end […] (V.57.27–31)

His dilemma is the crux of the play. Osmond has discovered that he cannot be the servant of two masters; yet neither can he choose. The play has flirted with the simplest option, elopement and conversion to Christianity with Despina: this Osmond rejects.

Nor does the play celebrate Melcoshus's death as the fall of a tyrant; instead, it is the pashas' revolt that is condemned, thus in turn implicating Despina as instigator of the sultan's and the state's decline. Osmond's repudiation of Despina, and his reaffirmed loyalty to his master, is underwritten in a play that mourns the sultan's loss and elevates Osmond, not Despina, at the play's close. Odmer's accession and promise to 'make his name live in eternity' (V.59.21–2) is a clear endorsement of Osmond's faith, not Despina's, and the restitution of order is the play's proclamation. This clear repudiation of political revolution may be regarded as conservative (and may have been seen as a measured reaction to the events of May), but the concomitant destabilization of the Irene narrative is strikingly radical.

This little-known play offers an illustration of how a powerful narrative tradition may be subject to equally strong literary and theatrical influences, the result complicating assumptions and expectations. As a dynamic forum driven by the dual pressures of commerce and creativity, the playhouse was not static.[36] For some playgoers the playhouse may indeed have offered anti-Turk propaganda, but it is unlikely that this is an accurate portrayal of the larger picture.[37] Henry V's anachronistic proposal to Katherine that they should 'compound a boy, half French half English, that shall go to Constantinople and take the Turk by the beard' is undermined by subsequent events, not least Henry VI's reign but also by the interrogative, 'Shall we not?',[38] that history transforms into a statement. A. J. Hoenselaars has argued that the deployment of 'the crusader concept "to go to Constantinople and take the Turk by the beard"' was ironic, 'a repository for vacuous ideals, a phrase that could only be rehearsed with an increasing sense of self-satire'.[39] Indeed, Sydney Anglo has proposed that even ritual Turk-baiting was half-hearted as early as the reign of Henry VIII. In a show performed in 1518, following a papal call for a crusade, the Turks

in this instance, were not at all villainous. On the contrary they seem to have been rather jolly, drum-battering fellows who waited patiently while their enemies celebrated the uncongenial peace within Christendom [...]. There was no serious attempt to denigrate the Turks [...] it was a political allusion without any malice [...]. It is, perhaps, not unfair to see this combat against the Turks as a light-hearted concession to an equally fanciful and insincere prevalent taste for elaborate crusades. The disguising thus made all points clearly, and with a certain measure of, possibly intentional, irony.[40]

It is not necessary to draw a specific parallel between the political situation in 1518 and a century later to recognize that in both cases Europe was divided, and the Ottoman threat a tangible one. But it is interesting that even against the backdrop of a possible crusade the representation of the Turks here is ironic. At a similar performance, when Charles V visited England four years later, there is similarly little attempt to disguise the charade:

> the political realities underlying the expressions of good will, hopes for peace [i.e. among Christian powers], and belief in concerted action against the Turks, must have been patent to all but the most retarded of spectators.[41]

The spectators at these shows will have experienced them differently, of course; not all of them may have noted the irony Anglo identifies, and indeed the irony deployed is politically complex. It is important to bear in mind then that performance does not, of course, always produce the desired meaning, as Keir Elam notes:

> however expert the spectator, however familiar with the frames of reference employed by dramatist and director he [*sic*] may be, there is never a perfect coincidence between the producer's codes and the audience's codes, *especially where the text is in any way innovative.*[42]

In the example explored here, and in others, there was potentially a dissonance between historical contexts, political necessity, and theatrical production and reception: perhaps, in terms of the theatrical representation of Turks, this dissonance was in evidence as early as the reign of Henry VIII; it was even more likely to be so by the later years of his daughter's rule, by which time England had established diplomatic, cultural and commercial relations with the Ottoman Empire.[43]

When Lodowick Carlell wrote *Osmond the Great Turk* Spain was feared and James's court distrusted and ridiculed. This play may be regarded as an allegory of such discontent, and the play may have met with problems from the censor.[44] Although Carlell seems an unlikely critic of James, the portrayal of a corrupt court riven by jealousy may well have given cause for alarm, and spectators may have made a connection between the two political worlds.[45] The pamphlet referred to at the beginning of this discussion stresses the significance of the May events, noting that they come at a time when '*all* Christendom [*is*] *almost in Armes*':[46] much of Europe was, or would become, consumed by the Thirty Years War that had broken out in 1618. Excavating the pamphlets for pointers as to the direction a play drawing on the May events might take provides few clues to Carlell's rationale, however; yet the very precision of the parallel he draws between 1453 and 1622 suggests a conscious and coherent design. Whatever the circumstances of the composition, the text illustrates the elasticity of the Turkish convention, which was no longer moored to the ideological imperative the act of remembrance 1453 signalled. The fusion of sources and contexts both contributes to the play's 'Jacobean' rewriting of the Irene figure and produces a play that is radical in its conservatism: by apparently privileging order over rebellion the play refuses to endorse the figure of Christian myth it has itself re-presented, and out of the ashes of a Seraglio all but sacked, 1453-style, by Janissaries, produces a successor who throughout has demonstrated a fitness for rule. Ironically, then, if *Osmond the Great Turk* may be regarded as at best uneasy about political revolution, it is at the same time the most radical treatment of Turks of the era.

In Hayden White's formulation 'every historical narrative has as its latent or manifest purpose the desire to moralize the events of which it treats': history, that is, depends on, and is structured by literary tropes; there can be no historical meaning other than by and through a narrative telling, and it is this very narration that imposes (moral) meaning on history.[47] 1453 may be regarded as just such a narrative, where the *fall* of Constantinople is narrated as a tragedy. In the playhouse's treatment of the 1453 capture of Constantinople, however, the conventions of tragedy are also subject to other forces. A popular appetite for tales of the Ottoman Empire undoubtedly kept Turkish history plays in the repertory, and led, as with the Irene motif, to plays that drew repeatedly on sensational material. But as *Osmond the Great Turk* suggests, such apparently stable historical narratives are susceptible to alternative interpretations. In transposing 1453 onto 1622 (or vice versa), Carlell produces a palimpsest play that 'updates' the fifteenth-century siege. It does so, however, less by offering a historical parallel in tune with pamphlet propaganda than by revisiting the Irene myth through the lens of Jacobean theatre, lifting the veil and revealing an ambiguous, rather more unsettling portrait.

Notes

1. Godfrey Goodwin, *The Janissaries* (London: Saqi, 1994), p. 157.
2. Anon., *The Strangling and Death of the Great Turk, and his two Sons* (London: by I. D. for Nicholas Bourne and Thomas Archer, 1622).
3. Edward Said, *Orientalism: Western Conceptions of the Orient* (1978) (London: Penguin, 1991), p. 57.
4. For pioneering work in this field see especially Louis Wann, 'The Oriental in Elizabethan Drama', *Modern Philology*, 12 (1915), 423–47; Warner G. Rice, 'Turk, Moor, and Persian in English Literature from 1550–1650, with Particular Reference to the Drama' (unpub. PhD dissertation, Harvard University, 1926); Samuel Chew, *The Crescent and the Rose: Islam and England During the Renaissance* (Oxford: Oxford University Press, 1937); and Orhan Burian, 'Interest of the English in Turkey as Reflected in English Literature of the Renaissance', *Oriens*, 5 (1952), 202–29.
5. Of approximately 3000 plays written during the period 1567–1642 some 600 survive. Of these around one third refer to Turks (including seventeen Shakespeare plays) – a remarkable proportion that may be taken as an indication of the motif's visibility on the stage, and in the audience's imagination. On Persians on stage see Linda McJannet, 'Bringing in a Persian', *Medieval and Renaissance Drama in England*, 12 (1999), 236–67.
6. England's commercial, diplomatic and political relations with the Ottomans pursued by Elizabeth I in the 1580s have been mostly mapped by historians; see for example M. Epstein, *The Early History of the Levant Company* (London: Routledge, 1908); Susan Skilliter, *William Harborne and the Trade with Turkey, 1578–1582* (Oxford: Oxford University Press, 1977); and Lee W. Eysturlid, ' "Where Everything is Weighed in the Scales of Material Interest": Anglo-Turkish Trade, Piracy, and Diplomacy in the Mediterranean During the Jacobean Period', *Journal of European Economic History*, 22 (1993), 613–25. For recent scholarship on Turks and the early modern stage see Nabil Matar, *Islam in Britain* (Cambridge: Cambridge University Press, 1998), and *Turks, Moors and Englishmen in the Age of Discovery* (New York: Columbia University Press, 1999); Daniel Vitkus (ed.), *Three Turk Plays from Early Modern England* (Columbia University Press, 2000), and *Turning Turk: English Theater and the Multicultural Mediterranean, 1570–1630* (Basingstoke: Palgrave Macmillan, 2003); Richmond Barbour, *Before Orientalism: London's Theatre of the East 1576–1626* (Cambridge: Cambridge University Press, 2003); and Matthew Dimmock, *New Turkes: Dramatizing Islam and the Ottomans in Early Modern England* (Aldershot: Ashgate, 2005).
7. Prominent examples would include Peter Aston's 1546 translation *A Short Treatise upon the Turks' Chronicles*; Hugh Goughe, *The Ofspring of the house of Ottomano* (1553); John Foxe, *Acts and Monuments* (1570); Nicholas de Nicolay, *The Navigations, Peregrinations, and Voyages made into Turkey* (1585); George Whetstone, *The English Mirror* (1586); the anonymous *The Policy of the Turkish Empire* (1597); R. Carr, *The Mahumetane or Turkish History* (1600); and the most influential of them all, Richard Knolles, *Generall Historie of the Turkes* (1603).
8. One of the earliest first-hand accounts was by Theodore Spandounes, which first appeared in Italian in 1509; for a modern English edition see *On the*

Origin of the Ottoman Emperors, ed. and trans. Donald M. Nicol (Cambridge: Cambridge University Press, 1997).

9. One such narrative was first published in English by John Withers in 1625. See Ottaviano Bon, *The Sultan's Seraglio: an Intimate Portrait of Life at the Ottoman Court*, ed. Godfrey Goodwin (London: Saqi, 1996).

10. See Alain Grosrichard, *The Sultan's Court: European Fantasies of the East*, trans. Liz Heron (1979; London: Verso, 1998).

11. Ania Loomba, *Shakespeare, Race, and Colonialism* (Oxford: Oxford University Press, 2002), p. 95.

12. Franz Babinger, *Mehmed the Conqueror and His Time*, ed. William C. Hickman, trans. Ralph Manheim (1959; Princeton: Princeton University Press, 2nd edn, 1978), p. 427.

13. This episode is the subject of Fulke Greville's closet drama, *Mustapha* (1596).

14. Babinger, *Mehmed the Conqueror*, p. 428, suggests a close parallel with a seventeenth-century Cossack legend, while affinities with accounts about Alexander the Great published in 1554, 1559 and 1564 suggest the template was highly adaptable. See David Nicol Smith, 'Johnson's *Irene*', *Essays and Studies*, 14 (1929), 35–53 (p. 43). It is then both a narrative drawn from (or *on*) the historical past and a narrative emplotment, or explanation of later, 'similar' events.

15. The Irene narrative is surveyed in Chew, *The Crescent and the Rose*, pp. 479–90.

16. For Gosson see E. K. Chambers, *The Elizabethan Stage*, 4 vols (Oxford: Oxford University Press, 1930), IV, p. 204, and quoted in Chew, *The Crescent and the Rose*, p. 482.

17. Chew, *The Crescent and the Rose*, pp. 484–5.

18. Thomas Kyd is the most likely candidate for the authorship of *Soliman and Perseda*, but the evidence is by no means conclusive.

19. That the list could be further extended – and the Irene narrative shown to be both familiar and culturally evocative, as well as malleable – may be illustrated with the inclusion of plays such as *Edward II*, which also deals with the intrusion of love into affairs of state, and *Antony and Cleopatra*: in both cases the gendering of power moves away from the Irene model, but the motif remains recognizable nonetheless.

20. This is not to suggest that 'text' and '*context*' are separable, merely to point up the ways in which the former may evoke the latter in *plural* form. The problem of distinguishing artificially between the two terms is addressed in Francis Barker and Peter Hulme, ' "Nymphs and reapers heavily vanish": the Discursive Con-Texts of *The Tempest*', *Alternative Shakespeares*, ed. John Drakakis (London: Methuen, 1985), pp. 191–205.

21. On the gendering of seeing in a later age and medium, see Laura Mulvey, 'Visual Pleasure and Narrative Cinema', *Screen*, 16/3 (1975), 6–18.

22. Compare Ben Jonson's claim that he composed *Volpone* (1606) in only five weeks. The play has been misdated *c.* 1637–42 on the basis that the 1657 title page ascribes the play to 'the Queen's Majesty's Servants'; see *Osmond the Great Turk*, ed. Allardyce Nicoll (Berkshire: Golden Cockerel, 1926), p. xi. However, this dating has been challenged by G. E. Bentley, *The Jacobean and Caroline Stage*, 7 vols (Oxford: Clarendon Press, 1941–68), Vol. III, pp. 119–21, who believes the play to date from 1622. All references to the play will be to Nicoll's edition, and Nicoll's lineation, act-page-line,

is followed here (spelling modernized). For a full discussion of the play's date, see Mark Hutchings (ed.), *Three Jacobean 'Turkish' Plays* (Manchester: Manchester University Press, forthcoming).

23. I am indebted to Ioulia Pipinia for this insight. See C. Marlowe, *Tamburlaine*, ed. J. S. Cunningham (Manchester: Manchester University Press, 1981), p. 110, who suggests that Marlowe's 'Zabina', the name in *1 Tamburlaine* of Bajazeth's wife, 'may be an adaptation of "Despina"', the historical wife of the Turkish sultan whom Tamburlaine overthrows.

24. On the crisis precipitated by James's relations with Spain see, for example, Margot Heinemann, *Puritanism and Theatre: Thomas Middleton and Opposition Drama under the Early Stuarts* (Cambridge: Cambridge University Press, 1980); Albert H. Tricomi, *Anticourt Drama in England, 1603–1642* (Charlottesville: University Press of Virginia, 1989); and A. A. Bromham and Zara Bruzzi, *'The Changeling' and the Years of Crisis, 1619–1624: a Hieroglyph of Britain* (London: Pinter, 1990).

25. T. Middleton, *Women Beware Women*, ed. William C. Carroll (London: Black, 1994), II.ii.

26. There are further allusions to the parallel scene in *Women Beware Women* here, and repetition of 'command' is particularly evocative.

27. In fact, Osman II is one of only two seventeenth-century Ottoman sultans who actually married; see Halil Inalcik, *The Ottoman Empire: the Classical Age 1300–1600* (London: Phoenix, 1994), p. 86. Marriage, in Osman's case to a highborn Muslim woman, was unusual and frowned upon: 'when, in 1621, the sultan Osman II married the daughter of the *Mufti* Esad Efendi, scion of the most prestigious *ulema* family in Ottoman history, there was popular opposition to what was perceived to be a harmful violation of political protocol'. Leslie P. Peirce, *The Imperial Harem: Women and Sovereignty in the Ottoman Empire* (Oxford: Oxford University Press, 1993), pp. 106, 71.

28. The play appears to register here two contradictory features of Osman II's rule: he had led a Turkish army into Poland, in contrast to his predecessors; and yet he did not seem to act like a sultan, but 'lack[ed] majesty'; see Peirce, *The Imperial Harem*, pp. 171, 183. Sir Thomas Roe, ambassador from 1621 to 1628, reported of Osman his 'making his person common, cheape, and despised'. T. Roe, *The Negotiations of Sir Thomas Roe in His Embassy to the Ottoman Porte* (London: Strahan, 1740), p. 50; quoted in Peirce, *The Ottoman Harem*, p. 183.

29. *The Revenger's Tragedy*, in *Thomas Middleton: Five Plays*, ed. Bryan Loughrey and Neil Taylor (London: Penguin, 1988), I.ii. Melcoshus's insistence that justice be meted out even to his own son may be contrasted with the Duke's refusal to intervene in the trial of his stepson in Middleton's play. It also recalls Sultan Suleyman's execution of his son Mustapha.

30. Compare Junior's flippancy in *The Revenger's Tragedy*: in reply to the second judge's inquiry 'What moved you to't?', Junior says, 'Why flesh and blood, my lord; / What should move men unto women else'; 'Her beauty was ordained to be my scaffold' (I.ii.47–8, 64).

31. See Jay Halio, 'Gloucester's Blinding', *Shakespeare Quarterly*, 43 (1992), 221–3 (p. 222).

32. For a detailed examination of this Persian practice, see Grosrichard, *The Sultan's Court*, pp. 55–63.

33. This takes place offstage; Melcoshus orders: 'bear him from my sight and strangle him' (IV.44.5–6). The play thus misses an opportunity to dramatize a strikingly visual aspect of the image of the Turk.

34. John Webster, *The White Devil*, ed. John Russell Brown (Manchester: Manchester University Press, 1960), V.vi.240–1. I am indebted to Martin White for this observation.

35. It is interesting that Chew, *The Crescent and the Rose*, p. 488, misreads the conclusion: 'Osmond, to avenge her death, assassinates his master and then commits suicide'.

36. On the economics of theatre see Jean-Christophe Agnew, *Worlds Apart: the Market and the Theater in American Thought, 1550–1750* (Cambridge: Cambridge University Press, 1986), and Douglas Bruster, *Drama and the Market in the Age of Shakespeare* (Cambridge: Cambridge University Press, 1992).

37. For an argument for the playhouse so functioning, see Matar, *Islam in Britain*, pp. 50–72.

38. W. Shakespeare, *King Henry V*, ed. Andrew Gurr (Cambridge: Cambridge University Press, 1992), V.ii.189–91.

39. A. J. Hoenselaars, 'The Elizabethans and the Turk at Constantinople', *Cahiers Élisabéthains*, 47 (1995), 29–42 (pp. 30, 39).

40. Sydney Anglo, *Spectacle, Pageantry, and Early Tudor Policy* (Oxford: Clarendon Press, 2nd edn, 1997), pp. 134–5.

41. Ibid., p. 204.

42. Keir Elam, *The Semiotics of Theatre and Drama* (London: Routledge, 1980), p. 95; italics added.

43. See note 6.

44. On the possible censorship of the play, see Bentley, *The Jacobean and Caroline Stage*, Vol. III, pp. 120–1; Richard Dutton, 'Patronage, Politics, and the Master of the Revels, 1622–1640: the Case of Sir John Astley', *English Literary Renaissance*, 20 (1990), 287–319; N. W. Bawcutt, 'Evidence and Conjecture in Literary Scholarship: the Case of Sir John Astley Reconsidered', *English Literary Renaissance*, 22 (1992), 333–46; Janet Clare, '*Art made tongue-tied by Authority': Elizabethan and Jacobean Dramatic Censorship* (Manchester: Manchester University Press, 2nd edn, 1999), p. 228n; and Hutchings (ed.), *Three Jacobean 'Turkish' Plays*.

45. See Hutchings (ed.), *Three Jacobean 'Turkish' Plays*.

46. 'The Printer to the Reader', sig. A3^r.

47. Hayden White, 'The Value of Narrativity in the Representation of Reality', *The Content of the Form: Narrative Discourse and Historical Representation* (Baltimore: Johns Hopkins University Press, 1987), pp. 1–25 (p. 14). White's influential work was first developed in *Metahistory: the Historical Imagination in Nineteenth-Century Europe* (Baltimore: Johns Hopkins University Press, 1973).

Bibliography

Agnew, Jean-Christophe, *Worlds Apart: the Market and the Theater in American Thought, 1550–1750* (Cambridge: Cambridge University Press, 1986).

Anglo, Sydney, *Spectacle, Pageantry, and Early Tudor Policy* (Oxford: Clarendon Press, 2nd edn, 1997).

Anon., *The Strangling and Death of the Great Turk, and His Two Sons* (London: by I. D. for Nicholas Bourne and Thomas Archer, 1622).

Babinger, Franz, *Mehmed the Conqueror and His Time*, ed. William C. Hickman, trans. Ralph Manheim (1959; Princeton: Princeton University Press, 2nd edn, 1978).

Barbour, Richmond, *Before Orientalism: London's Theatre of the East 1576–1626* (Cambridge: Cambridge University Press, 2003).

Barker, Francis and Peter Hulme, 'Nymphs and reapers heavily vanish: the Discursive Con-Texts of *The Tempest*', *Alternative Shakespeares*, ed. John Drakakis (London: Methuen, 1985), pp. 191–205.

Bawcutt, N. W., 'Evidence and Conjecture in Literary Scholarship: the Case of Sir John Astley Reconsidered', *English Literary Renaissance*, 22 (1992), 333–46.

Bentley, G. E., *The Jacobean and Caroline Stage*, 7 vols (Oxford: Clarendon Press, 1941–68).

Bon, Ottaviano, *The Sultan's Seraglio: an Intimate Portrait of Life at the Ottoman Court*, ed. Godfrey Goodwin (London: Saqi, 1996).

Bromham, A. A. and Zara Bruzzi, *'The Changeling' and the Years of Crisis, 1619–1624: a Hieroglyph of Britain* (London: Pinter, 1990).

Bruster, Douglas, *Drama and the Market in the Age of Shakespeare* (Cambridge: Cambridge University Press, 1992).

Burian, Orhan, 'Interest of the English in Turkey as Reflected in English Literature of the Renaissance', *Oriens*, 5 (1952), 202–29.

Carlell, Lodowick, *Osmond the Great Turk*, ed. Allardyce Nicoll (Berkshire: Golden Cockerel, 1926).

Chambers, E. K., *The Elizabethan Stage*, 4 vols (Oxford: Clarendon Press, 1923).

Chew, Samuel, *The Crescent and the Rose: Islam and England during the Renaissance* (Oxford: Oxford University Press, 1937).

Clare, Janet, *'Art made tongue-tied by Authority': Elizabethan and Jacobean Dramatic Censorship* (Manchester: Manchester University Press, 2nd edn, 1999).

Dimmock, Matthew, *New Turkes: Dramatizing Islam and the Ottomans in Early Modern England* (Aldershot: Ashgate, 2005).

Dutton, Richard, 'Patronage, Politics, and the Master of the Revels, 1622–1640: the Case of Sir John Astley', *English Literary Renaissance*, 20 (1990), 287–319.

Elam, Keir, *The Semiotics of Theatre and Drama* (London: Routledge, 1980).

Epstein, M., *The Early History of the Levant Company* (London: Routledge, 1908).

Eysturlid, Lee W., ' "Where Everything is Weighed in the Scales of Material Interest": Anglo-Turkish Trade, Piracy, and Diplomacy in the Mediterranean during the Jacobean Period', *Journal of European Economic History*, 22 (1993), 613–25.

Goodwin, Godfrey, *The Janissaries* (London: Saqi, 1994).

Grosrichard, Alain, *The Sultan's Court: European Fantasies of the East*, trans. Liz Heron (1979; London: Verso, 1998).

Halio, Jay, 'Gloucester's Blinding', *Shakespeare Quarterly*, 43 (1992), 221–3.

Heinemann, Margot, *Puritanism and Theatre: Thomas Middleton and Opposition Drama under the Early Stuarts* (Cambridge: Cambridge University Press, 1980).

Hoenselaars, A. J., 'The Elizabethans and the Turk at Constantinople', *Cahiers Élisabéthains*, 47 (1995), 29–42.

Hutchings, Mark (ed.), *Three Jacobean 'Turkish' Plays* (Manchester: Manchester University Press, forthcoming).

Inalcik, Halil, *The Ottoman Empire: the Classical Age 1300–1600* (London: Phoenix, 1994).

Loomba, Ania, *Shakespeare, Race, and Colonialism* (Oxford: Oxford University Press, 2002).

Marlowe, Christopher, *Tamburlaine*, ed. J. S. Cunningham (Manchester: Manchester University Press, 1981).

Matar, Nabil, *Islam in Britain* (Cambridge: Cambridge University Press, 1998).

— *Turks, Moors and Englishmen in the Age of Discovery* (New York: Columbia University Press, 1999).

McJannet, Linda, 'Bringing in a Persian', *Medieval and Renaissance Drama in England*, 12 (1999), 236–67.

Middleton, Thomas, *The Revenger's Tragedy*, ed. Bryan Loughrey and Neil Taylor, *Thomas Middleton: Five Plays* (London: Penguin, 1988).

Middleton, Thomas, *Women Beware Women*, ed. William C. Carroll (London: Black, 1994).

Mulvey, Laura, 'Visual Pleasure and Narrative Cinema', *Screen*, 16/3 (1975), 6–18.

Nicol, Donald M. (ed. and tr.), *On the Origin of the Ottoman Emperors* (Cambridge: Cambridge University Press, 1997).

Peirce, Leslie P., *The Imperial Harem: Women and Sovereignty in the Ottoman Empire* (Oxford: Oxford University Press, 1993).

Rice, Warner G., 'Turk, Moor, and Persian in English Literature from 1550–1650, with Particular Reference to the Drama' (unpub. PhD dissertation, Harvard University, 1926).

Roe, Sir Thomas, *The Negotiations of Sir Thomas Roe in His Embassy to the Ottoman Porte* (London: G. Strahan, 1740).

Said, Edward, *Orientalism: Western Conceptions of the Orient* (1978; London: Penguin, 1991).

Shakespeare, William, *King Henry V*, ed. Andrew Gurr (Cambridge: Cambridge University Press, 1992).

Skilliter, Susan, *William Harborne and the Trade with Turkey, 1578–1582* (Oxford: Oxford University Press, 1977).

Smith, David Nicol, 'Johnson's *Irene*', *Essays and Studies*, 14 (1929), 35–53.

Tricomi, Albert H., *Anticourt Drama in England, 1603–1642* (Charlottesville: University Press of Virginia, 1989).

Vitkus, Daniel (ed.), *Three Turk Plays from Early Modern England* (Columbia University Press, 2000).

Vitkus, Daniel, *Turning Turk: English Theater and the Multicultural Mediterranean, 1570–1630* (Basingstoke: Palgrave Macmillan, 2003).

Wann, Louis, 'The Oriental in Elizabethan Drama', *Modern Philology*, 12 (1915), 423–47.

Webster, John, *The White Devil*, ed. John Russell Brown (Manchester: Manchester University Press, 1960).

White, Hayden, 'The Value of Narrativity in the Representation of Reality', *The Content of the Form: Narrative Discourse and Historical Representation* (Baltimore: Johns Hopkins University Press, 1987), pp. 1–25.

7

News Drama: the Tragic Subject of Charles I

Barbara Ravelhofer

The execution of Charles I solicited dramatic responses both in England and abroad. In the second half of the seventeenth century, Continental school plays rehearsed Charles's fall as *de casibus* spectacle. English compositions on the subject of murdered majesty were not granted a legitimate forum on stage, given the closure of the theatres between 1642 and 1660, but they still appeared in print, as the anonymous *The Famous Tragedie of King Charles I* (1649) and *The Tragical Actors, or The Martyrdom of the Late King Charles* (1660) attest.[1] The shift from drama-on-stage to drama-on-the-page in the literary landscape of the 1640s and 1650s has been explained as the result of the work of playwrights who, unemployed in those years, turned their talent to alternative modes of public expression.[2] Many publications of the Interregnum period were advertised in dramatic terms even though they had little or no connection with theatrical performance. Between 1642 and 1660, at least 188 works bore the title 'play', 'theatre', 'droll', '(tragi)comedy', or 'masque'. 'Tragedy', a very popular choice, was often used in a metaphorical sense, but it also referred to various kinds of drama primarily enjoyed through reading.[3] *The Famous Tragedie of King Charles I* and *The Tragical Actors* belong to this latter group. Both works have attracted various labels such as 'dialogue playlet',[4] closet drama, pamphlet play, and indeed 'pamphletheatre', fresh from the '*acting* press'.[5] Pamphlet plays (or play-pamphlets) are commonly defined as small-scale texts which responded to current historical events in a quasi-dramatic fashion. They 'conveyed a satirico-political message through a dialogue between characters real and imaginary', 'mixing [...] drama, reportage, satire, and prose polemic'.[6] They are history plays in an unusual format, and thus the purpose of this chapter will be to examine their genre and material appearance, historical and political orientation, and potential for reading and performance.

The Famous Tragedie of King Charles the First / Basely BUTCHERED (hereafter called *Charles I*) was perhaps penned by Samuel Sheppard, a satirical writer and minister regularly jailed for his share in the production of underground royalist newsbooks.[7] The play is a slender quarto of 26 leaves. Its size corresponds to that of early modern pamphlets, typically consisting of between eight and ninety-six pages in quarto, but it is long for a pamphlet play, the latter being usually between eight and sixteen pages in length.[8] The title page reveals neither author nor place of publication but its liberal plot synopsis demonstrates the ambition of a miniature chronicle:

> The several Combinations and machinations | that brought that incomparable PRINCE to the Block, | the overtures hapning at the famous Seige of Col-| chester, The Tragicall fals of Sir *Charls Lucas* and | Sir *George Lisle*, the just reward of the Level-| ler *Rainsborough, Hamilton* and *Bailies* Treche-| ries, In delivering the late *Scottish* Army | into the hands of *Cromwell*, and the designe | the Rebels have, | to destroy the | ROYAL POSTERITY. | Printed in the Year, 1649.

A long and detailed description of this kind recalls Shakespeare's histories; compare, for instance, the title of the 1594 quarto of Shakespeare's *Henry VI*, part 2, as printed by Thomas Creed:

> The | First part of the Con-|tention betwixt the two famous Houses of Yorke | and Lancaster, with the death of the good | Duke Humphrey: | And the banishment and death of the Duke of | *Suffolke*, and the Tragicall end of the proud Cardinall | of *Winchester*, with the notable Rebellion | of *Jacke Cade*: | *And the Duke of Yorkes first claime unto the* | *Crowne*.

Strong evidence suggests a composition of *Charles I* before May 1649, although we cannot entirely exclude the possibility that the year of Charles's execution appears fictitiously on the title page, chosen for its symbolic portent.[9] Later editions exist as well as a sequel with many borrowings from the original, *Cromwell's Conspiracy* (1660).[10] The action of *Charles I* covers the years 1648 to 1649, moving from the parliamentarian siege of Colchester and the execution of two royalist scions, Sir Charles Lucas and Sir George Lisle, to the fall of Charles I in January 1649 and the decapitation of his followers Lords Capel, Holland and

Hamilton in March of the same year. Outdoor scenes such as the army camp of General Fairfax alternate with private moments; here the anonymous author alleges an illicit relationship between Cromwell and a Mrs Lambert, in the play discreetly managed by Cromwell's subordinate and confidant Hugh Peter.

Already obvious from the title, the play's historical interest and political stance is further developed in the prefatory section. With the political inclinations of the intended readership in mind, the author chose a play in a particular literary tradition as vehicle for an account of the last year under (abortive) Caroline rule. As critics have pointed out, writers of the period regularly employed drama and its associated imagery as a vehicle to target the political adversary. Versions of Jacobean and Caroline drama published during the Interregnum as well as post-1642 'plays' with royalist sympathies routinely invoked the closure of the theatres and emphasized the current regime's lack of literary taste.[11] So too in *Charles I*, where a 'Prologue to the Gentry' deplores the 'Monsters' who 'raze[d] our Theaters to the ground' and appeals to the readers' 'refined Soules' to remember the choice lines of Shakespeare, Shirley, Davenant and other worthies of the early Stuart stage.[12] This has been interpreted as a strategy to 'co-opt *past* cultural icons for royalism'; for Susan Wiseman, 'Jacobean and Caroline playwrights are used here as markers for the continuing cultural importance of the aesthetics of Charles I's court', and hence the play not only establishes a genealogy of martyrs dying for the king's cause but a literary genealogy of pre-Civil War luminaries.[13]

The play's paratext illustrates the argument with politically explicit visual ornament, thus substituting the experience of playgoing by titillating the readerly eye. A dedication to 'To the Sacred MAJESTIE of *Great Britain, France* and *Ireland*, KING CHARLS II' (sig. A2ʳ) is headed by a border of crowned harps and roses, while the text exhorts the king to summon an interfaith coalition and conquer his throne again. This may allude to plans of the Irish Catholic confederacy to levy a royalist army under Charles's lord lieutenant in Ireland, the Marquess of Ormond.[14] (Harp and rose borders are very common in prints of the period, yet the specific content of the publication invites speculation, especially if we assume a publication date of 1649. For Scottish thistles are absent from the design, perhaps because, in 1649, Charles had failed to come to similar agreements with the Scottish parliament and instead authorized the Marquess of Montrose to lead a campaign against Scotland.) The dedication of *Charles I* is appropriately devised in heroic verse, *ottava rima*, taking its cue from Tasso's *Gerusalemme Liberata*, thus making plain that another providential city, London, requires urgent deliverance.

A list of 'persons' helpfully explains the protagonists of the play, neatly divided into factions in visual opposition. A visual distinction of groups in the cast was not uncommon in early Stuart plays; witness, for instance, the division of protagonists into the courts of England and Scotland in John Ford's *The Chronicle Historie of Perkin Warbeck* (in the 1634 quarto). In *Charles I*, the parliamentarian side includes Fairfax, Ireton and Pride (all mentioned by surname only) and is supplemented by allegorical characters such as 'Treason', 'Lust', and 'Revenge'. The royalist party is privileged with extra information on names and titles ('Lord Capell', 'Lord Goring', 'Sir George Lisle' etc.). From the start, non-verbal and textual features direct the readers' interpretation before they even reach Act I.

For early modern English readers the play's characters would have been easily identifiable. To explain briefly the historical background of some of the chief players: Arthur, first baron Capel of Hadham (1604–49) was royal commander-in-chief in East Anglia and thus responsible for towns like Colchester. He was apprehended in 1648 and, after a spectacular escape from the Tower, beheaded outside Westminster Hall in March 1649. His end would have been fresh in the mind of the play's author and its readers, and indeed his corpse is among the bodies brought to the fore in a tableau of royalist martyrs in the final scene. George Goring, first earl of Norwich (1585–1663), ex-courtier and ex-masquer, had served as Henrietta Maria's Master of Horse and royal Vice-Chamberlain.[15] Goring and Capel held Colchester in 1648, together with George Lisle and Lisle's friend Charles Lucas, the brother of the poet and playwright Margaret Cavendish. After the surrender of Colchester to Fairfax both Lisle and Lucas were shot. This death sentence was regarded as particularly harsh, at least in royalist circles. Clarendon called the deed 'barbarous' and 'new and without example'.[16] Such accounts – and the play too – pass over the fact that at least one of the victims had himself offended against the military code of honour. Having been released from imprisonment after Marston Moor in 1644, Lucas had broken his parole of not raising arms again; furthermore, he too had ordered the execution of at least twenty parliamentarian soldiers under similar circumstances on a previous occasion.[17] Even so, Lisle and Lucas instantly became cavalier icons, remembered in broadsides, ballads and poems, and celebrated in *Charles I*.[18]

On the parliamentarian side, the cast of the play was equally prominent. Hugh Peter (also often spelt Peters, *c.* 1598–1660), an independent minister, had laboured to break parliamentary opposition against the trial of Charles I. One day before the king's execution, he preached a grim sermon on Isaiah 14:19–20, biblical verses which, in historical application, not only elucidated Charles's offences against his people ('thou art cast out of thy grave like an abominable branch [...]; as a carcase trodden under feet. [...] Thou [...] hast destroyed thy land, and slain thy people: the seed of evildoers shall never be renowned'), but also offered an action plan for the future of the house of Stuart ('prepare slaughter for his children'). Peter was sentenced to a traitor's death in 1660.[19] Colonel Thomas Pride, Sheriff of Surrey and regicide, is remembered for his role in the political cleansing of the House of Commons in December 1648.[20] Finally, far from playing Bathsheba to Cromwell's sinister David, as the play would have it, 'Mrs Lambert' was Frances, the morally unimpeachable wife of John Lambert, the famous parliamentary military commander who had participated in the Battle of Marston Moor. Lambert later played a key role in establishing the Protectorate, handing the sword of state to Cromwell during the latter's installation; it was rumoured that he would eventually succeed the Puritan from Ely.[21] *Charles I* thus confronted readers with current historical affairs and decision-makers, but in both content and paratext it mingled fact with fiction in the interest of royalist propaganda, thus taking advantage of the seventeenth-century meaning of 'history' as 'story'.[22]

The tragedy itself begins by wheeling out a vice figure in the manner of an old-fashioned morality play, thus channelling readers into the correct understanding of the text. It is, however, a most contemporary villain who gleefully reveals his plottings to his captive audience of readers. Assisted by Hugh Peter, identified as a 'Devill', Cromwell assumes the character of a demonic prophet, declaring his intention to rewrite both history and religion in a new 'English Alchoran' (pp. 1, 4). With this highly topical reference the playlet probably gestures at the first English translation of the Qur'an, published in 1649; the same work was denigrated by its own translator as 'poyson' whose argument prevailed not by 'truth' but the 'sword'.[23] As Nabil Matar points out, a common rhetorical strategy of the period consisted in aligning the Christian convictions of a political enemy with Islam. Thus, for Sir Peter Killigrew, the 1649 *Alkoran* tellingly coincided with the fall of Charles I. In his opinion, Muslim doctrine 'imbued' readers 'with Turkish manners, which have much in common with the actions of the rebels'.[24] Indeed in the play, Sir George Lisle compares Fairfax's army to the 'Ottaman[s]'.[25]

In Act II private colloquy gives way to the camp of Fairfax before Colchester. The long siege of Colchester in summer 1648 was a key event in Civil War history, noted for the bitter misery it inflicted upon both parties.[26] Pamphlets and newsletters of the period across the political spectrum highlighted the plight of Colchester's citizens, who were, from the beginning, 'not glad of their [the royalist forces'] company'.[27] For eleven weeks, Goring, Lisle and Lucas, in command of the town, had been waiting for a fleet to relieve them. With provisions depleted and the water supply cut off by Fairfax, the situation was desperate. Tired of horseflesh infested with maggots, many soldiers deserted. Far from endorsing the king's cause, mutinous troops and civilians finally enforced the surrender of the town. From a parliamentarian point of view, the leaders in charge of the royalist forces appeared out of touch: Lisle 'brought the odium of the countrey upon him, and at last grew harsh to the Towns people [...] when they complained for want of bread'.[28] Allegedly Goring told the inhabitants 'they must eat their children'.[29] Against better knowledge, some royalist pamphlets still upheld the claim that the storehouses were full.[30] In adversity, others insisted, 'the Soldiery [...] makes merry, drinking of healths in water, to King *Charles*, saying, That before they yeald the Town, they will drink their own Urine, and gnaw their fingers to the bone'.[31] *Charles I* turns the siege into a triumphant, if perhaps laboured, demonstration of cavalier defiance. Lucas asserts that Colchester is not destitute of provisions, and unbelievably, sherry can still be found in the town hall. Lisle exclaims 'I shall grow fat with laughter' before all join in a drinking song (p. 16).

Act III switches to a sombre mood. Colchester has fallen, and of all people, it is Goring who now remembers the 'faces black with famine' (p. 26). Cromwell contemplates the doom of Charles ('the Stage growes great with horror', p. 20); the next scene anticipates the king's demise by highlighting the execution of two exemplary royalist commanders for the reader's moral appreciation. Lucas and Lisle, in 1649 the most potent twin emblem of loyal service to the king's cause, must 'lead the dance of death' (p. 27). In his dying speech a Senecan Lisle calls upon the furies for vengeance, and the noble friends expire in an embrace.

Such heroic sacrifice could not contrast more starkly with the ensuing scenes in Act IV. Peter, Cromwell and Mrs Lambert discuss the new order. Perhaps echoing the cheerfully expedient manner in which Shakespeare's Richard III disposed of Henry VI, Cromwell jests that the king he is about to despatch is 'fitter farre for to converse with Saints and

Seraphims, than with erronious and ambitious Mortalls'.[32] (The parallels to Richard III are made even more explicit in the sequel, *Cromwell's Conspiracy*, where Peter observes that Cromwell 'sure was born (as the third *Richard* / Who once rul'd this Land) with his Mouthfull / Of teeth' (p. 4).) Far from endorsing republican values, Cromwell insists on quasi-Caroline protocol: the dress code demands purple, and 'all Heads [are] to stand bare on every shoulder' (p. 33). Cromwell's colour preferences suggest Rome, papal as well as imperial, associations further deepened with references to Nero and Caligula. In Cromwell's Rome, Augustus is dead. Abused by ignoble successors, the Empire has sunk into decadence. Allusions to Cleopatra, Pasiphae and Poppaea in the amorous banter of these scenes leave readers in no doubt as to Mrs Lambert's unbridled sexuality. The highlight of Act IV consists of a masque of the 'six prime Westminsterian Senators', ordered by Cromwell but recalling early Stuart ceremony. It is a scene uneasily pitched between the conventions of revenge tragedy and courtly entertainment: enter 'ambition, treason, lust, revenge, perjury, sacriledge', ominous characters whose dance is joined by Cromwell, Mrs Lambert and Peter. Should readers expect the revellers' comeuppance, as customary in the bloody denouement of the revenge play-within-the-play? Certainly, the combination of grotesque allegorial figures with Cromwell's new elite would have struck readers versed in the conventions of Caroline court theatre as highly inappropriate. As Dale Randall observes, the anti-masque has been conflated with the masque proper.[33] The misshapen entertainment seems a travesty of the noble performance of Lisle and Lucas in Act III. King Oliver's court is indeed, as the 'Prologue to the Gentry' so clearly stated, in need of literary refinement. Its decision-makers have not yet absorbed the subtler points of the spectacle of power.

The discrepancy between erstwhile courtly splendour and the pretender's lack of decorum is sustained in Act V. 'In their night Robes', Cromwell and Mrs Lambert receive a letter with news of the king's death (p. 40). They clear the stage, however, for a tableau of worthier figures. The play's final moments are directed by a Chorus bewailing Cromwell's tyranny. The Chorus 'discovers' the bodies of Charles I and also of Lords Capel, Hamilton and Holland – all three executed in London on 9 March 1649 – 'behind the travers', and explains the victims' exemplary lives to the audience (p. 42). For Dale Randall, this indicates the history genre, for 'history plays, too, generally ended with major scenes involving impressive ceremonies and eye-fixing tableaux'.[34] The play's final lines are dedicated to Capel's corpse:

But here lies one [*Pointing to the L.* Capel.
The glory of his Nation,
A man for valour, virtue, wit,
[...] (had they no more
But this one Devilish Act in store
Of murthering him) the Rebels (sure)
Could not, yet eight yeare more procure,
To Reigne by bloud, by rapines, horrors,
Treason, inexplicable terrors;
But what the Fates allot we must
Submit to, and in them we trust
To see these Monsters fall and rot,
By God and virtuous men forgot. (p. 43)

Insisting on biographical detail in this last scene, *Charles I* didactically directs the reader towards the future, a technique employed in historical drama of the time. In Shakespeare's *Henry V*, the Chorus concludes the play with an outlook on future events under Henry's unfortunate successor. *Charles I* tries very hard. In Wiseman's view, it 'anxiously attempts to control future historical interpretation'.[35] The pamphlet play expresses the hope that providence – or history – will eventually bring down Cromwell's rule.

The other play, *The Tragical / ACTORS / or The / Martyrdome of / the late KING / CHARLES / wherein / Oliver's late falsehood, with the / rest of his gang are described in / their several actions and stations* is a much shorter, undated piece of eight pages, commonly ascribed to the year 1660.[36] The title activates readerly expectations of martyr drama, exemplified in the suffering royal main protagonist. 'Station', a charged term, recalls not only the acts of a pageant or mystery play but also the successive incidents of Christ's Passion, represented in images for the contemplation by churchgoers and pilgrims.[37] The playlet's anonymous author almost seems to invite his readers to turn the king beset by his tormentors into an object of devotional exercise; at the very least, attentive close reading is expected. Although *The Tragical Actors* has no cast list it is easy to identify the protagonists. The action consists of satirical dialogues, mainly between Cromwell, Cornet Joyce, sergeant Bradshaw, Sir Arthur and Sir Harry Vane. The action is confined to January 1649; the protagonists discuss how the law must be bent so as to legitimize the verdict on Charles I. George Joyce was a parliamentarian army officer from London. John Bradshaw (*c.* 1602–59), the lawyer, politician and regicide, already featured prominently as judge in *Charles I* where he presided over the trial of Capel, Hamilton and Holland. Sir Arthur has been identified as Sir Arthur Hesilrige (or Haselrig), second baronet of Noseley (1601–61), a radical opponent of both Charles's Personal Rule and Laud's church policies. In 1660 he was imprisoned in the Tower of London on charges of high treason but died in January 1661 before the trial.[38] Haselrig, historically a fierce opponent of bishops who pleaded for their abolition, is ironically being offered the bishopric of Durham in the playlet (p. 3). While the king's body is envisaged on stage (if only, perhaps, in the reader's mind) at the end of *Charles I*, Charles is completely absent in *The Tragical Actors*, talked about but never 'seen'. As Anne Barton explains, the anonymous author of *Charles I*, 'closer to the pain of the event, could not bring himself to represent the [living] king himself – any more than those dramatists writing before the death of Elizabeth could put the Tudors on the stage'.[39] *Cromwell's Conspiracy*, the pamphlet play printed eleven years later, remained exceptional in calling both masquers and executioner to the stage and showing the monarch's last moments. A Christ-like martyr, Charles meekly submits to his fate – speaking, for once:

> Well then, since there's no remedy I must
> Submit my self to the dispose of God,
> And since it is his pleasure I shal tast
> This bitter Cup, I'le take it.[40]

In 1660, the sad event could be viewed from greater distance; yet, to pull off the scene, *Cromwell's Conspiracy* needed to translate the action from the ignominious scaffold erected before the Banqueting House to the Garden of Gethsemane. In the decade following the restoration of Charles II, playwrights were reluctant to show such glimpses of recent English history, Nancy Klein Maguire has argued: both authors and their audiences preferred to come to terms with the trauma of the Civil War and the king's decapitation in less explicit ways. If plots rehearsed rightful rulers and heirs menaced by usurpers, they took their course in foreign settings (Rome, Madrid, Constantinople, Peru) rather than London. Maguire reads the strong preference for tragicomedy in 1660s repertoire as a response to collective emotional needs to turn the 'tragedy' of the pious martyr Charles I into the tragicomedy of his more worldly and pragmatic successor, Charles II, bereft of royal mystique but at least alive and in charge.[41]

The preferred portrayal of Charles I as a silent hieratic presence (or even absence) in seventeenth-century English playlets may also be connected with the representation of a saintly Stuart beyond action as promoted in *Eikon Basilike* and countless pamphlets of the period.[42] Not for Charles a rousing speech before his ready followers, as with Henry V at Agincourt, or Elizabeth at Tilbury (that favourite moment in Jacobean history plays). At best the distant icon softens to a private family man, a tendency explored in later English drama. William Havard's *King Charles I: An Historical Tragedy. Written in Imitation of Shakespear* (Lincoln's Inn Fields, 1737) introduces Charles reading. Typically, the play dispenses with an onstage execution but instead treats its audience with a sentimental parting scene in which the king takes leave of his children. In Mary Mitford's sumptuous courtroom melodrama *Charles the First: Historical Tragedy* (1834) an impetuous Henrietta Maria contrasts sharply with a bookish, introverted Charles 'poring o'er Shakespeare's page'.[43] William Gorman Hills's *Charles the First: An Historical Tragedy in Four Acts* (first performed 1872) saw Henry Irving in the title role, carrying Prince James on his shoulders. Characteristically, only Shelley's *Charles the First* (fragment, first pub. 1824) redirects attention to Charles's subjects and their performance as subjects. It starts with a masque of the Inns of Court and allows citizens a say about the political situation of the day.

This differs from the representation of Charles in Continental drama of the seventeenth century. In Silesia, the famous Protestant poet Andreas Gryphius wrote a topical school play immediately after the execution in 1649; as he explained in a letter, his work, 'composed within a few days, when the royal corpse had hardly been buried', was intended to 'express the horrid loathsomeness of the crime'. Produced 'almost at the very moment of the callous murder', *Carolus Stuardus* was considered imprudent and tasteless by some critics (which might strengthen Barton's argument for a gingerly dramatic approach to living or recently dispatched monarchs) – yet on the whole the play 'received much recommendation' for its boldness.[44] A dutiful civil servant, Gryphius clearly abhorred the deed as blasphemous. Steeped in the robust tradition of Jesuit martyr drama,[45] he was not as squeamish as his English contemporaries with regard to showing violence against rulers – on the contrary, he assembled as many murdered English monarchs as possible in the full sight of the audience: the play lines up an impressive chorus of luckless rulers led by Mary Stuart.[46] Eleven years before *Cromwell's Conspiracy*, Gryphius makes a public spectacle of the execution of Charles I, which takes place onstage: 'Here I lie. Earth, good night,' says the king on the block before the fatal blow falls.[47]

Reading or performance?

If the character of Charles I preferred reading to speaking in English plays, should we not acknowledge a purpose to his historical drama which includes contemplation as much as action? Are royalist pamphlet plays a covert attempt to undo the outrage of the execution by relocating it in biblical territory or recreating specially private versions of Charles's fate, accessible to the play-reader rather than a gaping audience, in the same way as *Eikon Basilike*? Would the closet format be thus politically charged, substituting private readerly consumption for the public spectacle of shame?

By 1649, theatre could be enjoyed in multiple ways. Certain early editions of Shakespeare's plays are a testament to *Lesedrama*, drama specifically catering for readerly enjoyment.[48] John Jones's *Adrasta* (1635), 'never acted', as the title page asserted, appealed to Caroline readers. According to current statistics, 26 works produced between 1625 and 1641 contained 'closet drama'; between 1642 and 1660, numbers rose to 97; and the period from 1661 to 1685 reveals a respectable 75.[49] Whether these printed or written texts were meant to be read only, or whether they were also meant for acting is still open to debate. Indeed, recent studies have questioned the alleged performance purpose of the larger body of commercial plays printed in early modern England. Were they ever intended as manuals for professional actors, or did they at best serve for (loud) reading?[50] We must acknowledge that the distinction between reading and performance can be fluid, as a work might be used for declamation in a private context.[51] Given the closure of the public theatres, *Charles I* and *The Tragical Actors* could only have been staged in private locations, or in inns on an ad hoc basis. Evidence for clandestine theatre during the Interregnum exists: in one famous case, players were apprehended at Salisbury Court on 1 January 1649 and 'carried to White-Hall with their Players cloathes upon their backs. In the way they [the soldiers] oftentimes took the Crown from his head who acted the King, and in sport would oftentimes put it on again'.[52] It has also been proposed that pamphlet plays may reflect versions of performances at fairs, festivals or markets.[53]

Janet Clare draws attention to the fact that actors involved in such illegal theatre were sometimes mentioned as speakers in Interregnum playlets. These playlets were, she argues, part of an oral popular culture, and, like ballads, 'conceived with performance in mind'. In her view, the textual design of pamphlet plays suggests as much: 'typographically, the plays represent texts for performance, containing as they do the list of dramatis personae, prologues and epilogues, stage directions and details of scene locations'.[54] The presence of quasi-performative features, however, does not prove a performance purpose: famously, the 1605 quarto of Jonson's *Sejanus* filled at least one reader with the hope that 'this publication' would set the author 'free' from the ignorant stage.[55]

Charles I certainly has dramatic potential. Lively changes between private and public scenes might appeal to an audience. Some interesting stage directions could indicate a performance purpose, such as

> Sir *Charles Lucas*, Sir *George Lisle*, Lord *Capell*, Lord *Goring*, &c. appeares as upon the Walls. (p. 9)

Yet others provide readerly information rather than practical instruction:

> Enter *Blackburne* (being the Souldier that escaped from amongst the Fairfaxians, with an intent to kill *Rainsborow*, Act. 3.) with him, three Souldiers, their Pistols and Swords. (p. 37)

Likewise, many stage directions in *The Tragical Actors* are clearly intended to inform a reader, not a prompter or players, as when 'Sir *Arthur* speaks with Sir *Harry* and comes to *Oliver* the next day' (p. 3). How should 'the next day' be indicated in performance? Often so-called stage directions morph into plot synopsis:

> The old Seal is broke and a new one made, and the Court after three daies sitting, gives judgement against the King, and he according to that sentence is beheaded, January the 30. 1648. (*The Tragical Actors*, pp. 7–8)

Pamphlet plays were capable of appealing to readers simply as texts. A dedicatory poem in *Charles I* praises its dramatic qualities from a reader's point of view:

> With a sowre aspect, and a Critick eye
> I have perus'd, thy well writ Tragedie;
> My ravisht soul, grew sicker then the Age
> When as I hastned, to the latter page: [...]
> I wisht thy Play had been more largely writ
> Or I had ne're seene, or perused it. [...]
> He that can read thy Play, and yet forbear

For his late Murthered Lord, to shed a tear,
Hath an heart fram'd of *Adamant* [...].[56]

Such lines evoke affective drama: the reader becomes a protagonist shedding tears. Individual playreading is thus an activity in the true sense of the word. It can become a performance in its own right, and better still, a 'legitimate form of theatrical pleasure [...] imagine[d] as a substitute for playgoing rather than an extension of it'.[57] Pamphlet plays about Charles sought to involve the reader in the experience of history: contemplation might lead to empathy and imitation. *Charles I* prompted at least one reader into a private performance. In Act III, when Sir George Lisle delivers a fine Hamlet-like speech before he is led off to the firing squad, the printer saved space by setting the text as a block of prose. Spoken aloud, however, the lines reveal themselves as blank verse, and indeed, in a copy of the play now held at Cambridge, a seventeenth-century hand inserted caesurae into Lisle's farewell.[58] The anonymous author of *The Tragical Actors* sought the opportunity of communicating directly with his readers in an epilogue:

But now let's merry be, not doubting since
The way is open to bring in our Prince. (p. 8)

The play thus concludes in collective optimism, a common vision of the king's return shared by reader and pamphlet playwright.

The sources

What did the author of *Charles I* know about the siege of Colchester, and how could detailed legal proceedings concerning the king's trial inform *The Tragical Actors*? How did Gryphius, living in Silesia, manage to write a history play on an English monarch so shortly after his fall? The events of 1648 and 1649 were not only communicated in letters and by word of mouth but reflected in the print medium on an unprecedented scale. Statistically the output of items published in Britain increased almost by a factor of ten from an average of 459 titles per annum produced between the 1580s and 1630s to 4038 items in 1642. In 1648 some 67 serial news publications were available to London's readers.[59] At least 81 titles commented on the siege of Colchester, from which the anonymous author of *Charles I* could have learned all about starving children and heroic cavaliers.[60] Gryphius cultivated excellent contacts to exiled courtiers and followed events in England very closely throughout the 1640s. He had even met Elizabeth of Bohemia, Charles's sister, in the Netherlands, and was on excellent terms with Elisabeth, the Palatine princess. But he also relied upon over thirty English and Continental publications: these ranged from histories to newsbooks and polemical literature, including Salmasius's *Defensio Regia* (1649), Thomas Edwards's *Gangraena* (three parts, 1646), *Eikon Basilike* (from which Gryphius may have gleaned the idea of endowing Charles with the triple crowns of king, martyr and saint), as well as other English, German, Dutch and Venetian sources.[61] The availability of news in print even during the Thirty Years War (which ended just one year before Gryphius composed his play) should not be underestimated. *Theatrum Europaeum*, a remarkably well-informed Frankfurt periodical, was issued regularly during the Thirty Years War and was one of the Continental sources which Gryphius was able to consult.[62] Current estimates allege some 30 000 publications across Europe spawned by Charles's execution, and Gryphius made excellent use of some of these.[63]

Given their anomymity, it is impossible to establish whether the authors of *Charles I* and *The Tragical Actors* were directly involved in the events they dramatized, or to what extent they relied on printed sources or hearsay information. Yet the choice of their plot seems significant. The pamphlet plays produced between 1642 and 1660 are not epic histories about conflicts spanning generations, and they do not delve into the distant past. They react quickly to current events. Authors were able to turn to recent or present history for several reasons. They were protected by anonymity and the fact that the sheer quantity of publications rendered any attempt at rigorous censorship futile. But I would also argue that the sources themselves made a crucial difference. For Nigel Smith the newsbooks of the 1640s represented 'a channel of democracy' whose impact on history writing was immense and momentous: looking for historical information, readers found a widely available alternative to the chronicle.[64] The quick and regular provision of a new type of source – news in the shape of pamphlets, newsletters, corantos and newsbooks, up-to-date news covering a wider range of the political spectrum than the heavyweight chronicle – promoted a different kind of history play. If the emerging genre of the periodical turned the drama of King Charles into news, Gryphius and his anonymous English colleagues turned news into drama again.

There seems little point to insist on a canon of historical drama or history plays if we consider hybrid forms such as the pamphlet plays on Charles I. Lines from *Charles I* recall Webster, Shakespeare, Marlowe and Seneca;[65] yet the 1649 and 1660 renderings of royal tragedy captured not only a theatrical space but a new public space to be accessed by news-readers. Feeding on current news, these plays combined the didacticism of martyr drama and morality play with the conventions of histories, revenge tragedy and broad farce, thus appealing to learned as well as popular tastes. They did not chart the course of history in several hours' ponderous traffic but took snapshots of decisive moments with satirical bite. While they did not exclude actual performance they were primarily conceived for private reading. High art these plays were not but effective, aggressive propaganda instruments.

Fast historical drama in smaller format is still a literary art form, lovingly cultivated in newspapers and magazines. In 2000, the pseudo-Shakespearean blank verse documentary *The History of King Tony, or, New Labour's Lost, Love* delighted readers of *The Independent*.[66] And very recently, the *Times Higher Education Supplement* published the short and tragical history of Lear, Vice-Chancellor of the University of Oxford ('Give me the strategic plan [...] 'tis my fast intent to shake all cares of business from our academics, conferring them on outside strengths while we unburden'd crawl towards servitude'). Lear has divided in three his university. As a consequence, the kingdom of academe is usurped by the evil counsellor Lord Hefce ('So Professor Gloucester hast got only a 4 in the RAE? [...] I'll not endure it. I'll pluck out his grants').[67] This kind of satire appeals by rehearsing a long, well-known tradition in a short and savoury manner. Well-established, if not timeless dramatic conventions reduce current affairs to size; they unmask the heroic protagonists of our days as the helpless puppets or feigning actors they are. *Charles I* and *The Tragical Actors* did exactly that: showing us political mimicry, performed by dissembling stage-managers and a monarch beside the plot. We owe to the first experiments in the seventeenth century, the pamphlet plays and their hapless kings, the beginnings of a rich and comically irreverent journalistic crop.

Notes

1. Anon., *The Famous Tragedie of King Charles the First / Basely* BUTCHERED (London?, 1649), Wing F384. *The Tragical Actors, or The Martyrdom of the Late King Charles* ([London]: Printed for Sir Arthur, 1660), Wing T2015; Thomason, E.1019[6*].
2. See Lois Potter, 'Closet Drama and Royalist Politics' and 'Short Plays: Drolls and Pamphlets', *The Revels History of Drama in English*, gen. eds C. Leech and T. W. Craik, 8 vols (London: Methuen, 1975–83), Vol. IV, pp. 263–93; Lois Potter, *Secret Rites and Secret Writing: Royalist Literature, 1641–1660* (Cambridge: Cambridge University Press, 1989); Dale Randall, *Winter Fruit: English Drama, 1642–1660* (Lexington: University Press of Kentucky, 1995).

3. EEBO search as of November 2005. I included spelling variants, and the plural as well as components of these terms (e.g. 'masks', 'playhouse'). If the publication was of indeterminate date I chose the earliest. Multiple editions of the same work were counted as one if they occurred in the same year. 'Tragedy' occurred 59 times. For 'tragedy' in a metaphorical sense, see, for instance, the anonymous *The Tragedy of the Kings Armies Fidelity since Their Entring into Bristol* (1643). 'Tragedy' also denoted texts of a historical or biographical nature, such as Robert Wild's *The Tragedy of Christopher Love at Tower-Hill* (1660). Among actual tragedies (re-)published during the Interregnum was James Shirley's *The Cardinal, A Tragedie* [...] *Not Printed Before*, performed in 1641 but published in 1653.
4. Jonathan Heawood, ' "Never Acted, But...": English Closet Drama, 1625–1685' (unpub. PhD dissertation. Cambridge, 2002), appendix, p. 247.
5. For 'pamphletheatre' see P. A. Skantze, *Stillness in Motion in the Seventeenth-Century Theatre* (London: Routledge, 2003), ch. 3; Elizabeth Sauer coins the term *'acting* press' (her emphasis) in 'Closet Drama and the Case of *Tyrannicall-Government Anatomized'*, *The Book of the Play: Playwrights, Stationers, and Readers in Early Modern England*, ed. M. Straznicky (Amherst: University of Massachusetts Press, 2006), pp. 80–95 (p. 83).
6. Joad Raymond, *The Invention of the Newspaper: English Newsbooks 1641–1649* (Oxford: Clarendon Press, 1996), pp. 201 and 205. See also Nigel Smith, *Literature and Revolution in England, 1640–1660* (New Haven: Yale University Press, 1994), ch. 2.
7. Smith ascribes the play to Sheppard, *Literature and Revolution*, p. 81. See also Andrew King, 'Sheppard, Samuel (*c.* 1624–1655?)', *Oxford Dictionary of National Biography*, ed. H. C. G. Matthew and Brian Harrison (Oxford: Oxford University Press, 2004), http://www.oxforddnb.com/view/article/25347, accessed 20 September 2006.
8. Estimate after Joad Raymond, *Pamphlets and Pamphleteering in Early Modern Britain* (Cambridge: Cambridge University Press, 2003), p. 5, and Raymond, *The Invention of the Newspaper*, p. 201.
9. As Susan Wiseman has demonstrated, Thomason collected the play on 26 May 1649; furthermore, royalist newsbooks gradually disappeared in subsequent months on account of tightened censorship. *Drama and Politics in the English Civil War* (Cambridge: Cambridge University Press, 1998), p. 63. Puzzlingly, however, the final speech alludes to Capel's death in March 1649, following which the 'rebels' are said to reign 'yet eight yeare more [...] by bloud, by rapines, horrors' (p. 43). This would suggest a publication somewhere nearer 1657, a date of crucial importance for a play debating the future of England's rule, as constitutional changes allowed Cromwell to determine his successor in that particular year.
10. W. W. Greg, *A Bibliography of the English Printed Drama to the Restoration*, 4 vols (London: Oxford University Press, 1939–59), Vol. II, n. 680, assumes the play was written after 1649 and appeared in two editions, one dated to 1649, and a later undated version. The later issue, a work of 18 leaves, was printed perhaps about 1660 and reprinted in 1709; it was, according to Greg, ascribed to *c.* 1680 in the British Museum catalogue. *Cromwell's Conspiracy* [...] *Written by a Person of Quality* (London: s. n., 1660) retains the protagonists of *Charles I* within an expanded cast list (Richard Cromwell,

the Mayor of London, and various citizens, among others); it retains features such as the masque of the six Westminster senators and even reuses individual passages, for instance, Cromwell's desire to compose an *'English Alchoran'* (p. 3). On this play see also Randall, *Winter Fruit*, pp. 109–11.

11. The 'ideal reader or spectator' of pamphlet plays 'was assumed to have been a regular theatregoer'; see *Drama of the English Republic, 1649–60*, ed. Janet Clare (Manchester: Manchester University Press, 2002), p. 14. It must be stressed that, irrespective of political orientation, writers used theatrical imagery and allusions; a neat binary of 'parliamentarian' versus 'royalist' struggle did not exist during the Civil War. Wiseman, *Drama and Politics*, pp. 48, 61; and Potter, in *Revels History of Drama*, Vol. IV, p. 264. For Marta Straznicky, closet plays and published stage drama of the Interregnum, particularly those works with a royalist background, often 'transformed playreading into a form of political dissent'. *Privacy, Playreading, and Women's Closet Drama, 1550–1700* (Cambridge: Cambridge University Press, 2004), p. 15.

12. *Charles I*, sig. [A4]^r. See also Randall, *Winter Fruit*, p. 104. References to other plays no longer acted occurred in editions of drama at the time, for instance, in a dedicatory poem in Shirley's *The Cardinal*, sig. [A4]^v, first published in *Six New Playes* (for Humphrey Robinson, 1653), where 'our English Dramma was at hight, | And shin'd, and rul'd with Majesty and might' under Charles I.

13. Wiseman, *Drama and Politics*, pp. 66–7.

14. Ormond had reached this agreement with the Irish Catholics in January 1649; this topical allusion again suggests the play's composition in 1649.

15. Ronald Hutton, 'Arthur Capel, first Baron Capel of Hadham (1604– 1649)', *ODNB*, http://www.oxforddnb.com/view/article/4583, accessed 14 January 2006. Barbara Donagan, 'Goring, George (1608–1657)', *ODNB*, http://www.oxforddnb.com/view/article/11100, accessed 15 January 2006.

16. Edward Hyde, first Earl of Clarendon, *The History of the Rebellion*, ed. W. Dunn Macray, 6 vols (Oxford: Clarendon Press, 1888, rpr. 1958, 1969), Vol. IV, p. 389, bk. 11, 28–31 August 1648.

17. Ian Gentles, *The New Model Army in England, Ireland and Scotland, 1645–1653* (Oxford: Blackwell, 1992), p. 257.

18. David Appleby, *Our Fall Our Fame: the Life and Times of Sir Charles Lucas (1613–1648)* (Newtown: Jacobus, 1996). Barbara Donagan, 'Lucas, Sir Charles (1612/13–64)', *ODNB*, http://www.oxforddnb.com/view/article/17123, accessed 14 January 2006; Basil Morgan, 'Lisle, Sir George (*d.* 1648)', *ODNB*, http://www.oxforddnb.com/view/article/16755, accessed 14 January 2006.

19. Carla Gardina Pestana, 'Peter, Hugh (*bap.* 1598, *d.* 1660)', *ODNB*, http://www.oxforddnb.com/view/article/22024, accessed 13 January 2006. Gentles, *The New Model Army*, p. 309. *KJV*, Isaiah 14: 19–21.

20. Ian J. Gentles, 'Pride, Thomas, appointed Lord Pride under the protectorate (*d.* 1658)', *ODNB*, http://www.oxforddnb.com/view/article/22781, accessed 15 January 2006. Theatre historians note Pride's abolition of bearbaiting in London in 1656, in the course of which the bears were shot and the bulldogs dispatched to Jamaica. For instance, B. Ravelhofer, ' "Beasts of Recreacion": Henslowe's White Bears', *ELR*, 32/2 (2002), 287–323.

21. D. N. Farr, 'Lambert, John (*bap.* 1619, *d.* 1684)', *ODNB*, http://www.oxford-dnb.com/view/article/15939, accessed 13 January 2006.

22. For seventeenth-century definitions of 'history' see Benjamin Griffin, *Playing the Past: Approaches to English Historical Drama, 1385–1600* (Woodbridge: D. S. Brewer, 2001), ch. 1.

23. *The Alcoran of Mahomet* (London: s. n., 1649), sigs. A2^v, A3^v. Anonymous; translated from André du Ryer's French version with a 'caveat' by Alexander Ross appended. Ross was a Scottish royalist.

24. Nabil Matar, *Islam in Britain, 1558–1685* (Cambridge: Cambridge University Press, 1998), p. 46. Sir Peter Killigrew, writing from Venice in 1650, *CSPV 1647–52*, p. 138, in Roger B. Merriman, *Six Contemporaneous Revolutions* (Oxford: Clarendon Press, 1938), pp. 93–4, also cited by Matar.

25. *Charles I*, p. 10.

26. For an account of the siege, see Gentles, *The New Model Army*, pp. 251–7.

27. Hyde, *History*, Vol. IV, p. 359, bk. 11, 12 June 1648. For other important contemporary sources see *Prince Charles His Declaration* [. . .] *Likewise, Strange and Horrible Newes from Colchester* (1648), p. 4; *A True and Perfect Relation of the Condition of Those Noblemen and Gentlemen in Colchester* (1648), p. 5. *A Diary of the Siege of Colchester by the Forces under the Command of Generall Fairfax* (1648), single sheet, 20 and 23 July, 2 and 15 August 1648.

28. Anon., *A True and Exact Relation of the Taking of Colchester* (1648), p. 2. This is, however, a partial account as it seeks to justify the execution of Lisle and Lucas.

29. Donagan's *ODNB* entry on Goring refers to *A Diary of the Siege of Colchester by the Forces under the Command of His Excellency the Lord Generall Fairfax* (1648), 13 June and 15 August. I have not been able to substantiate Goring's notorious statement from the copies of Donagan's source I consulted.

30. *A Letter, from a Gentleman in Colchester, to His Friend in London* (26 June 1648), single sheet.

31. *Another Bloudy Fight at Colchester* (1648), a document signed by Charles P. [Stuart, prince], and others, p. 3.

32. *Charles I*, p. 33; cf. *Richard III*, I.2.109–10, on King Henry VI, now in heaven: 'Let him thank me that holp to send him thither, | For he was fitter for that place than earth.' William Shakespeare, *King Richard III*, ed. Antony Hammond (London: Routledge, 1981).

33. *Charles I*, p. 35. Randall, *Winter Fruit*, p. 108.

34. Randall, *Winter Fruit*, p. 98.

35. Wiseman, *Drama and Politics*, p. 66.

36. A British Library copy bears the date 'March 30 1660' in a seventeenth-century hand on the title page. On the last page it claims to have been 'Printed for Sir Arthur, 1660', which must be a swipe at one of the characters in the playlet.

37. According to the *OED* online, 'station' for 'act of a pageant or mystery play' is not recorded after the late fifteenth century. Yet this particular meaning seems obvious in the context of *The Tragical Actors*, which is, after all, a play.

38. Christopher Durston, 'Hesilrige, Sir Arthur, Second Baronet (1601–1661)', *ODNB*, http://www.oxforddnb.com/view/article/13123, accessed 13 January 2006.

39. Anne Barton, ' "He That Plays the King": Ford's *Perkin Warbeck* and the Stuart History Play', *Essays, Mainly Shakespearean* (Cambridge: Cambridge University Press, 1994), pp. 234–60 (p. 260).

40. *Cromwell's Conspiracy* [...] *Written by a Person of Quality* (London: s. n., 1660), p. 7. In her comprehensive study of the repertoire in the decade following the Restoration of Charles II, Nancy Klein Maguire cites this play as the only example showing the execution directly. Nancy Klein Maguire, *Regicide and Restoration: English Tragicomedy, 1660–1671* (Cambridge: Cambridge University Press, 1992), p. 35.

41. Ibid., pp. 35–6 and ch. 5. According to her statistics, only five out of seventy-odd 'serious' plays written between 1660 and 1671 have unhappy endings.

42. On the image of Charles I, see Potter, *Secret Rites*, ch. 5.

43. Mary Mitford, *Charles the First: Historical Tragedy* (London: Duncombe, 1834), I.ii, p. 10.

44. 'Ut ut enim, quibus cordi fas, decorque rerum atque integritas recti ingente encomio exornarint Poema, quod paucos intra dies attonito, atque vix condito in hypogaeum REGIS cadavere sceleris horror expressit: fuere tamen qui censerent imprudentem me, haud tantum nimis ex propinquo, sed quasi ipso parricidii momento Sontes arguere.' Letter to Gottfried Textor, 13 January 1663. My translation. *Carolus Stuardus*, in Andreas Gryphius, *Dramen*, ed. E. Mannack (Frankfurt am Main: Deutscher Klassiker Verlag, 1991), p. 445; and commentary, p. 1100. *Carolus Stuardus* was first published in 1657. A second version (revised 1660, first published 1663) portrays the regicides in a more differentiated manner. This second version may have been the one performed in the school theatre at Zittau (1665) and the Altenberg grammar school (1671). Gryphius, *Dramen*, commentary, pp. 1076, 1081. See also Eberhard Mannack, *Andreas Gryphius* (Stuttgart: Metzler, 1986), pp. 68–73.

45. Hugh Powell's edition of *Carolus Stuardus* (Leicester: University College Leicester, 1955) pays particular attention to the impact of Jesuit drama upon Gryphius's work.

46. In the earlier version of the play.

47. 'Hir lig ich! Erden gutte Nacht!' *Carolus Stuardus*, Act V, l. 488. Gryphius, *Dramen*, p. 547.

48. Lukas Erne, *Shakespeare as Literary Dramatist* (Cambridge: Cambridge University Press, 2003).

49. Statistics after Heawood, 'English Closet Drama', appendix. Works containing several plays have been counted by Heawood as one single publication. For a general account of the genre see Karen Raber, *Dramatic Difference: Gender, Class, and Genre in the Early Modern Closet Drama* (Newark: University of Delaware Press, 2001).

50. 'Except for the early Tudor interludes, which were advertised on their title pages as scripts for future performances, there is very limited evidence that printed plays from the 1590s on were used with this sort of practical application by professional actors.' Straznicky, 'Introduction: Plays, Books, and the Public Sphere', *The Book of the Play*, ed. Straznicky, pp. 1–19 (p. 14).

51. Straznicky, *Privacy, Playreading, and Women's Closet Drama*, ch. 4; Clare, *Drama of the English Republic*, introduction.

52. Leslie Hotson, *The Commonwealth and Restoration Stage* (Cambridge, MA: Harvard University Press, 1928), p. 40, and Barton, ' "He That Plays the King" ', p. 260.

53. Wiseman, *Drama and Politics*, p. 83.

54. Clare, *Drama of the English Republic*, pp. 10–11.
55. 'This publication sets thee free.' Ev. B., 'To the most understanding poet', in Ben Jonson, *Sejanus His Fall*, ed. Philip J. Ayers (Manchester: Manchester University Press, 1990), p. 69.
56. E. D., 'To the Author, on his Tragedy', *Charles I*, sig. [A3]ᵛ (erroneous pagination).
57. Straznicky, *Privacy, Playreading, and Women's Closet Drama*, p. 70. For Straznicky, this particular passage attests to readerly 'intensity and self-consciousness', connecting 'the reader to public experiences other than the theatrical' (p. 75).
58. *Charles I*, Cambridge University library copy; Wing F384 (UMI reel 491:33); p. 29.
59. Statistics based on figures between 1588 and 1639; in 1640 and 1641 the annual output was higher. Raymond, *Pamphlets and Pamphleteering*, pp. 163–5; *The Invention of the Newspaper*, p. 59.
60. *ESTC* search as of February 2006; variants of the same source excluded.
61. For a comprehensive survey of Gryphius's sources and Gryphius's contacts see Günter Berghaus, *Die Quellen zu Andreas Gryphius' Trauerspiel 'Carolus Stuardus'* (Tübingen: Niemeyer, 1984), especially pp. 40, 46, 145–6.
62. *Theatrum Europaeum* provided a chronicle of the most important European events since 1617; it first appeared in 1633 and kept coming out during the Thirty Years War; its popularity often required multiple reprints. See Berghaus, *Die Quellen*, pp. 230, 290, 296.
63. Gryphius, *Dramen*, commentary, p. 1092.
64. Smith, *Literature and Revolution*, pp. 54, 56.
65. Ibid., pp. 81–3.
66. Miles Kington's serial history parody appeared between 26 February 2000 and 21 July 2001.
67. Terence Kealey's satirical-historical tragedy playlet 'That Way Doth Madness Lie . . .', *THES* (4 November 2005), accessed online. The archived article can be called up under www.thes.co.uk/search/story.aspx. I am very grateful to Richard Sugg for his thoughtful comments on this essay.

Bibliography

The Alcoran of Mahomet [tr. by Alexander Ross] (London: s. n., 1649).
Another Bloudy Fight at Colchester (London: 'Printed for the generall satisfaction', 1648).
Appleby, David, *Our Fall Our Fame: the Life and Times of Sir Charles Lucas (1613–1648)* (Newtown: Jacobus, 1996).
Authorized King James Verson with Apocrypha, ed. Robert Carroll and Stephen Prickett (Oxford: Oxford University Press, 1997).
Barton, Anne, ' "He That Plays the King": Ford's *Perkin Warbeck* and the Stuart History Play', *Essays, Mainly Shakespearean* (Cambridge: Cambridge University Press, 1994), pp. 234–60.
Berghaus, Günter, *Die Quellen zu Andreas Gryphius' Trauerspiel 'Carolus Stuardus'* (Tübingen: Niemeyer, 1984).
Clare, Janet (ed.), *Drama of the English Republic, 1649–60* (Manchester: Manchester University Press, 2002).

Cromwell's Conspiracy [...] *Written by a Person of Quality* (London: s. n., 1660).

A Diary of the Siege of Colchester by the Forces under the Command of Generall Fairfax (London: Tho. Witham, 1648).

A Diary of the Siege of Colchester by the Forces under the Command of His Excellency the Lord Generall Fairfax (s. l.: s. n., 1648).

Donagan, Barbara, 'Goring, George, first Earl of Norwich (1585–1663)', *Oxford Dictionary of National Biography* (Oxford: Oxford University Press, 2004), http://www.oxforddnb.com/view/article/11101, accessed 15 January 2006.

— 'Sir Charles Lucas (1612/13–64)', *Oxford Dictionary of National Biography* (Oxford: Oxford University Press, 2004), http://www.oxforddnb.com/view/article/17123, accessed 14 January 2006.

Durston, Christopher, 'Hesilrige [Haselrig], Sir Arthur, Second Baronet (1601–1661)', *Dictionary of National Biography* (Oxford: Oxford University Press, 2004), http://www.oxforddnb.com/view/article/13123, accessed 13 January 2006.

Erne, Lukas, *Shakespeare as Literary Dramatist* (Cambridge: Cambridge University Press, 2003).

The Famous Tragedie of King Charles the First / Basely BUTCHERED (London?: s. n., 1649).

Farr, D. N., 'Lambert [Lambart], John (*bap.* 1619, *d.* 1684)', *Oxford Dictionary of National Biography* (Oxford: Oxford University Press, 2004), http://www.oxforddnb.com/view/article/15939, accessed 13 January 2006.

Gentles, Ian, *The New Model Army in England, Ireland and Scotland, 1645–1653* (Oxford: Blackwell, 1992).

— 'Pride, Thomas, Appointed Lord Pride under the Protectorate (*d.* 1658)', *Oxford Dictionary of National Biography* (Oxford: Oxford University Press, 2004), http://www.oxforddnb.com/view/article/22781, accessed 15 January 2006.

Greg, W. W., *A Bibliography of the English Printed Drama to the Restoration*, 4 vols (London: Oxford University Press, 1939–59).

Griffin, Benjamin, *Playing the Past: Approaches to English Historical Drama, 1385–1600* (Woodbridge: D. S. Brewer, 2001).

Gryphius, Andreas, *Carolus Stuardus*, ed. Hugh Powell (Leicester: University College Leicester, 1955).

— *Carolus Stuardus, Dramen*, ed. E. Mannack (Frankfurt am Main: Deutscher Klassiker Verlag, 1991).

Heawood, Jonathan, ' "Never Acted, But...": English Closet Drama, 1625–1685' (unpub. PhD dissertation, Cambridge, 2002).

Hotson, Leslie, *The Commonwealth and Restoration Stage* (Cambridge, MA: Harvard University Press, 1928).

Hutton, Ronald, 'Capel, Arthur, First Baron Capel of Hadham (1604–1649)', *Oxford Dictionary of National Biography* (Oxford: Oxford University Press, 2004), http://www.oxforddnb.com/view/article/4583, accessed 14 January 2006.

Hyde, Edward, Earl of Clarendon, *The History of the Rebellion*, ed. W. Dunn Macray, 6 vols (Oxford: Clarendon Press, 1888, repr. 1958, 1969).

Jonson, Ben, *Sejanus His Fall*, ed. Philip J. Ayers (Manchester: Manchester University Press, 1990).

Kealey, Terence, 'That Way Doth Madness Lie...', *THES* (4 November 2005) [http://www.thes.co.uk/search/story.aspx; URL of THES archive].

King, Andrew, 'Sheppard, Samuel (*c.* 1624–1655?)', *Oxford Dictionary of National Biography*, ed. H. C. G. Matthew and Brian Harison (Oxford: Oxford University Press, 2004), http://www.oxforddnb.com/view/article/25347, accessed 20 September 2006.

A Letter, from a Gentleman in Colchester, to His Friend in London [signed by one I. B.] (s. l.: s. n., 26 June 1648).

Maguire, Nancy Klein, *Regicide and Restoration: English Tragicomedy, 1660–1671* (Cambridge: Cambridge University Press, 1992).

Mannack, Eberhard, *Andreas Gryphius* (Stuttgart: Metzler, 1986).

Matar, Nabil, *Islam in Britain, 1558–1685* (Cambridge: Cambridge University Press, 1998).

Merriman, Roger B., *Six Contemporaneous Revolutions* (Oxford: Clarendon Press, 1938).

Mitford, Mary, *Charles the First: Historical Tragedy* (London: Duncombe, 1834).

Morgan, Basil, 'Lisle, Sir George (*d.* 1648)', *Oxford Dictionary of National Biography* (Oxford: Oxford University Press, 2004), http://www.oxforddnb.com/view/article/16755, accessed 14 January 2006.

Pestana, Carla Gardina, 'Peter [Peters], Hugh (*bap.* 1598, *d.* 1660)', *Oxford Dictionary of National Biography* (Oxford: Oxford University Press, 2004), http://www.oxforddnb.com/view/article/22024, accessed 13 January 2006.

Potter, Lois, 'Closet Drama and Royalist Politics' and 'Short Plays: Drolls and Pamphlets', *The Revels History of Drama in English*, gen. eds C. Leech and T. W. Craik, 8 vols (London: Methuen, 1975–83), Vol. IV, pp. 263–93.

— *Secret Rites and Secret Writing: Royalist Literature, 1641–1660* (Cambridge: Cambridge University Press, 1989).

Prince Charles His Declaration [. . .] *Likewise, Strange and Horrible Newes from Colchester* (London: for R. Wells, 1648).

Raber, Karen, *Dramatic Difference: Gender, Class, and Genre in the Early Modern Closet Drama* (Newark: University of Delaware Press, 2001).

Randall, Dale, *Winter Fruit: English Drama, 1642–1660* (Lexington: University Press of Kentucky, 1995).

Ravelhofer, Barbara, ' "Beasts of Recreacion": Henslowe's White Bears', *ELR*, 32/2 (2002), 287–323.

Raymond, Joad, *The Invention of the Newspaper: English Newsbooks 1641–1649* (Oxford: Clarendon Press, 1996).

— *Pamphlets and Pamphleteering in Early Modern Britain* (Cambridge: Cambridge University Press, 2003).

Sauer, Elizabeth, 'Closet Drama and the Case of *Tyrannicall-Government Anatomized*', *The Book of the Play: Playwrights, Stationers, and Readers in Early Modern England*, ed. M. Straznicky (Amherst: University of Massachusetts Press, 2006), pp. 80–95.

Shakespeare, William, *The First Part of the Contention betwixt the Two Famous Houses of Yorke and Lancaster* (London: Thomas Creed, 1594).

— *King Richard III*, ed. Antony Hammond (London: Routledge, 1981).

Shirley, James, *The Cardinal*, in *Six New Playes* (London: for Humphrey Robinson, 1653).

Skantze, P. A., *Stillness in Motion in the Seventeenth-Century Theatre* (London: Routledge, 2003).

Smith, Nigel, *Literature and Revolution in England, 1640–1660* (New Haven: Yale University Press, 1994).

Straznicky, Marta, 'Introduction: Plays, Books, and the Public Sphere', *The Book of the Play: Playwrights, Stationers, and Readers in Early Modern England*, ed. M. Straznicky (Amherst: University of Massachusetts Press, 2006), pp. 1–19.

— *Privacy, Playreading, and Women's Closet Drama, 1550–1700* (Cambridge: Cambridge University Press, 2004).

The Tragical Actors, or The Martyrdom of the Late King Charles ([London]: 'for Sir Arthur', 1660).

A True and Exact Relation of the Taking of Colchester, Sent in a Letter (London: Robert White, 1648).

A True and Perfect Relation of the Condition of Those Noblemen and Gentlemen in Colchester (s. l.: s. n., 1648).

Wiseman, Susan, *Drama and Politics in the English Civil War* (Cambridge: Cambridge University Press, 1998).

Index

Anon., *Captain Thomas Stukeley* (1596), 41

Anon., *The Famous Tragedy of King Charles the First* (1649), 179–93 *passim*, 199

Anon., *A Larum for London* (c. 1594–1600), 41

Anon., *The Love of a Grecian Lady* (1594, lost), 161

Anon., *Mankind* (c. 1470), 61

Anon., *Pathomachia: Or the Battell of Affections* (1630), 14, 26, 27

Anon., *Prince Charles His Declaration* (1648), 200

Anon., *Speculum Sacerdotale* (late 15th century), 68

Anon., *The Strangling and Death of the Great Turk, and his two Sons* (1622), 158, 173, 177

Anon., *The Tragical Actors, or The Martyrdom of the Late King Charles* (1660), 179–93 *passim*, 201

Anon., *A True and Exact Relation of the Taking of Colchester, Sent in a Letter* (1648), 201

Anon., *A True and Perfect Relation of the Condition of Those Noblemen and Gentlemen in Colchester* (1648), 201

Anon., *The Turkish Mahomet and Hiren the Fair Greek* (1588, lost), 161

Anon., *A Warning for Fair Women* (1599), 12, 13, 26, 27

Archer, Ian, 138, 153, 155

Aristotle, *Poetics*, 2, 3, 11, 22, 27, 101, 116, 123

Assman, Jan, 5, 23, 28

Augustine, St, 64–5, 68, 88, 90, 94, 96

Baldwin, William, *A Mirror for Magistrates*, 99–101, 104, 116, 118, 124

Bale, John, 4, 5, 16, 18, 27, 29, 49, 55–6, 58–91 *passim*
   Catalogus, 58–9, 91, 95
   God's Promises, 4, 18, 58, 60, 67–80, 93–4
   John Baptist's Preaching, 18, 58–60, 79–87, 93–4
   King Johan, 33, 47, 49, 55, 62–3, 66, 69, 79, 92, 101–3, 116
   Summarium, 58, 61, 91, 95
   The Image of Both Churches, 62
   The Temptation of Our Lord, 18, 58, 81, 85–91, 93–4, 96
   The Vocacyon of Johan Bale, 58–9, 64–5, 80, 90, 91–2, 95
   Three Laws, 61–2, 66, 68–9, 79, 86, 90, 92, 93

Barton, Anne, 138–9, 152–3, 155, 187–8, 196–8

Bergeron, David, 5, 23, 28

Berghaus, Günter, 198

Bevington, David, 27, 30, 32, 52, 56, 93, 95, 152–3, 155–6

Bishop, Tom, 135, 152, 155

Boccaccio, Giovanni, *De casibus virorum illustrium*, 100
   The Decameron, 120

Bullough, Geoffrey, 15–16, 102, 104, 117–18, 122

Butter, Nathaniel, 127, 136, 143, 150, 155

Camden, William, 15, 104, 125, 149–50, 155

Capel of Hadham, Arthur, first baron, 180, 182, 185–7, 190, 194–5, 199

Carlell, Lodowick, *Osmond the Great Turk*, 3, 17, 20, 159–72 *passim*, 174, 176, 177

Cavanagh, Dermot, 85, 94–5

Cavendish, Margaret, 182

Charles I, King of England, 3, 5, 21, 179, 180, 181, 183–9, 192–3
Charles II, King of England, 187, 197
Charles V, Holy Roman Emperor, 36, 44, 53, 146–7, 154
Chaucer, Geoffrey, 100, 116, 122
Cicero, 3, 14
Clare, Janet, 189, 195
Cranmer, Thomas, 49, 55, 128–9, 134
Cromwell, Oliver, 19, 21, 180–7, 194, 195, 197, 199
Cromwell, Thomas, 49, 55, 59, 129
Cromwell's Conspiracy, 180, 185, 187–8, 194, 197, 199

Davenant, William, 5, 23, 181
Dekker, Thomas, 11, 16, 21, 133, 150, 156
Sir Thomas Wyatt, 126, 150, 155
The Shoemaker's Holiday, 4, 28
The Whore of Babylon, 26, 127, 143, 150, 155
Devereux, Robert, second earl of Essex, 8, 21, 25, 28, 48
Dudley, Robert, earl of Leicester, 24, 109, 120–1, 123, 128
Dutton, Richard, 23–4, 28–9, 52, 56, 117, 122, 139, 153, 155, 176–7

Edward Tudor, Prince of Wales and later Edward VI, King of England, 61, 63, 92, 125–38, 142–9
Edwards, Thomas, *Gangraena*, 192
Eikon Basilike, 188–9, 192
Elizabeth I, Queen of England, 4–8, 32, 38, 47–8, 53, 105, 108, 112, 120, 125–43 *passim*, 134, 138, 140, 143, 146, 173, 187–8
Essex, Earl of, *see* Devereux, Robert
Euripides, 104, 120
Evanthius, 4, 23, 30

Fairfax, Thomas, third Lord Fairfax of Cameron, 181–4, 190, 196, 199
Famous Tragedie of King Charles I, The, 3, 4, 16, 21, 179–93 *passim*
Famous Victories of Henry V, The, 101

Fletcher, John and Philip Massinger, *Sir John van Olden Barnavelt* (1619), 41
Ford, John, *Perkin Warbeck*, 1, 15, 22, 26, 28, 182, 196, 198
Foxe, John, *Acts and Monuments*, 11, 16, 18–19, 27, 29, 66, 104, 125–7, 131, 134, 136–7, 142–8, 150–2, 154–5, 173

Gascoigne, George, *Jocasta*, 110, 115
Googe, Barnabe, 99
Goring, George, 182, 184, 190, 195–6, 199
Gosson, Stephen, 103, 160
Grafton, Richard, *A Chronicle at Large*, 100, 115, 120, 122
Greville, Fulke, *Antony and Cleopatra*, 8
The Life of Sir Philip Sidney, 25, 29
Griffin, Benjamin, 2, 4, 5, 22, 23, 27, 29, 32, 33, 52, 56, 83, 94, 96, 116, 117, 122, 196, 199
Griffith, William (printer), 105, 109
Gryphius, Andreas, *Carolus Stuardus*, 188, 191–2, 197–200

Halbwachs, Maurice, 5, 23, 29
Hall Edward, 111, 120
The Union of the Two Noble and Illustre Families of Lancastre and York, 34–40, 52–4, 56
Hall, Joseph, 142–3
Happé, Peter, 18, 27, 29, 58, 67–0, 73, 79, 91–6
Harington, John, 7, 107, 119
Havard, William, *King Charles I*, 188
Hayward, John, *Henry IIII*, 8–9, 25, 29, 48
Henrietta Maria, Queen of England, 5, 182, 188
Henry Stuart, Prince of Wales, 130–6, 140–9, 151–2, 156
Henry VIII, King of England, 3, 5, 16–20, 34, 41, 44, 47, 53–7, 58, 62, 65, 92, 96, 106, 111, 125, 127, 130–2, 136–43, 148, 150, 152, 154, 170–1
Henslowe, Philip, 2, 22, 28, 125, 132, 195, 200

Herodotus, 2

Hesilrige (Haselrig), Arthur, 187

Hesiod, 6, 24

Heywood, Jasper, tr. of Seneca,
   Thyestes, 99, 105, 115, 118, 123–4

Heywood, Thomas, 21, 126, 138
   The Four Prentices of London, 16, 29
   *The Golden Age, The Silver Age, The
      Brazen Age* and *The Iron Age*, 7,
      13, 15, 26
   *If You Know Not Me You Know
      Nobody*, 4, 5, 6, 24, 29
   tr. of Sallust, *The Two Most Worthy
      and Notable Histories*, 9, 10, 11,
      12, 23, 25, 26, 30
   A Warning for Faire Women, 3, 26,
      140, 153

Hills, William Gorman, *Charles the
   First*, 188

Holinshed, Raphael, 19, 125, 131,
   143, 151

Homer, *The Iliad*, 3

Howard, Henry, earl of Surrey, 99,
   110, 115, 120, 124

Howard, Charles, earl of Nottingham,
   132, 146, 151

Hunter, G. K. 1, 22, 29

James I, King of England, 19–20, 24,
   31, 32, 38, 105, 125, 130, 133–49,
   152–5, 157, 171, 175

Johnson, Samuel, 32, 52, 56–7, 174,
   178

Jones, John, *Adrasta*, 189

Jonson, Ben, *Everyman in His Humour*,
   13, 26
   masques, 132
   Sejanus, 8, 25–6, 29, 190, 198–9
   Volpone, 174

Katherine of Aragon, Queen of
   England, 36, 40, 128–9, 144–6,
   149, 154

Kealey, Terence, 'That Way Doth
   Madness Lie', 193, 198

Kewes, Paulina, 4, 23, 27, 29, 51, 52,
   54–6, 103, 115, 117, 119, 122

Kington, Miles, *The History of King
   Tony*, 193, 198

Knolles, Richard, *The General Historie
   of the Turkes*, 160, 173

Kyd, Thomas, 99, 115, 161, 174

Lambert, Francis, *Exegeseos in sanctam
   diui Ioannis Apocalypsim Libri VII*
   (1539), 66

A Larum for London (c. 1594–1600), 41

Legge, Thomas, 98–115 *passim*, 107,
   117, 119, 120, 121, 122
   Richardus Tertius (1579), 7, 17, 19,
      101, 117–18

Leland, John, 66
   Laboryouse Journey (1549), 63, 92, 96

Lesedrama, 189

Levy, F. R., 24, 29, 152

Livy, 3, 10

Lollards, 83

Lord Mayor's Shows, 5

Love of a Grecian Lady, The (1594,
   lost), 161

Ludolphus, 85

Luther, Martin, 63, 65, 87

Lydgate, John, 100, 116, 123

Machiavelli, Niccolò, 1, 22

Mankind (c. 1470), 61

Marlowe, Christopher, 98, 99, 115,
   117, 192
   Edward II (c. 1592), 174
   The Massacre at Paris (1593), 41, 51
   Tamburlaine (1590), 161, 175, 178

Mary I, Queen of England, 59, 66,
   125, 126
   (as princess), 34, 37, 53, 129, 143,
      154

Mary Stuart, daughter of James I, 147

Mary Stuart, Queen of Scots, 188

Mary Tudor, sister of Henry VIII, 127,
   128

Mason, John, *The Turk* (1607), 161

Medwall, Henry, 61

Mendoça, Don Iñigo de, 37, 40, 44,
   52, 54

Menken, H. L., 1

Middleton, Thomas, 17
   The Revenger's Tragedy (1606), 167,
      175, 178

Women Beware Women (1621), 163, 175, 178
and William Rowley, *The Old Law* (c. 1618), 161
Mitford, Mary, *Charles the First: Historical Tragedy* (1834), 188
Montaigne, Michel Eyquem de, *Essais*, 9, 10, 14, 25, 27, 30
More, Sir Thomas, *The History of King Richard III* (1513), 111, 120
Mussato, Albertino, *Ecerinus* (c. 1315), 101

Nashe, Thomas, *Pierce Penniless his Supplication to the Devil*, 7–8, 24, 30, 104, 118, 123
Have with you to Saffron-Walden, 107–8, 119, 123
Newton, Thomas, *Tenne Tragedies* (1581), 99, 101, 117, 123
Nicolay, Nicolas de, *The Navigations, Peregrinations, and Voyages made into Turkey* (1585), 173
Norton, Thomas, 105, 118, 123
and Thomas Sackville, *Gorboduc* (1561/2), 18, 98–115 *passim*, 116, 123

Ovid, *Metamorphoses*, 6

Painter, William, *The Palace of Pleasure* (1567), 160
Pathomachia: Or the Battell of Affections (1630), 14, 26, 27
Peele, George, 98
The Battle of Alcazar, 41
Plautus, 54, 55, 107
Plutarch, 99
Prince Charles His Declaration (1648), 200
Puttenham, George, *English Poetics and Rhetoric* (1589), 3, 23

Randolph, Thomas, *The Muses Looking-Glass* (1638), 15, 26, 30
Rapin, René, 10, 25
Rastell, John, 61
Ribner, Irving, 12, 22, 26, 30, 116, 123
Roe, Thomas, 158

The Negotiations of Sir Thomas Roe in His Embassy to the Ottoman Porte (1740), 175, 178
Rowley, Samuel, 143
When You See Me You Know Me (1605), 3, 6, 11, 19–20, 21, 125–49 *passim*, 150
Rowley, William, and Thomas Middleton, *The Old Law* (c. 1618), 161

Sackville, Thomas, 98–115 *passim*, 101, 105–6, 118
Gorboduc (1561/2), *see* Norton, Thomas
Salinas, Martin de, 36, 40, 42, 43, 46, 52, 53
Sallust, 3, 9, 11, 15, 23, 25, 26, 30
Salmasius, Claudius, *Defensio Regia* (1649), 192
Seneca, 9, 16–17, 18, 19, 98–115 *passim*, 115, 116, 118, 121, 123–4, 184
Shakespeare, William, 21, 25, 27, 29, 32, 53, 98, 99, 108, 115, 117, 173, 188, 189, 192
Antony and Cleopatra, 174
Hamlet, 3, 23, 30
history plays, 1, 2, 13, 38, 41, 54, 98, 113, 121, 180
Julius Caesar, 51
1 King Henry IV, 53
2 King Henry IV, 53
King Henry V, 53, 170, 176, 178, 186
1 King Henry VI, 104, 180
King Henry VIII, 125, 131, 150, 154
King Richard II, 25, 30, 51
King Richard III, 53, 102, 104, 184–5, 196, 200
Macbeth, 33, 102
Measure for Measure, 139, 141, 153, 156
Much Ado About Nothing, 128
Shelley, Percy Bysshe, *Charles I* (1824), 188
Sheppard, Samuel, 194
possible author of *The Famous Tragedy of King Charles the First* (1649), 179–93 *passim*, 199

Shirley, James, *The Cardinal* (1653), 194, 195, 200
Sidney, Philip, 120
   An Apology for Poetry, 7, 12, 24, 30, 98, 102, 110, 114, 115, 117, 120, 121, 124, 138
Speculum Sacerdotale (late 15th century), 68
Speed, John, 15, 125
Spinelli, Gasparo, 40, 52
Stow, John, *Annales*, 128, 136, 140, 148, 150, 152, 156
   Chronicles, 15, 104, 118
Swinhoe, Gilbert, *The Unhappy Fair Irene* (1640), 161

Tacitus, 1, 8, 9, 10, 14, 15, 19–20, 25, 130, 139, 143, 148, 149, 151, 153
Tasso, Torquato, 182
Terence, 23, 30, 55, 107
Thou, Jacques-Auguste de, *Historia sui temporis* (from 1604), 150
Thucydides, 3, 23, 30
Tilenus, Daniel, 153–4
Tottel's *Miscellany* (1557), 99
Tourneur, Cyril, *The Revenger's Tragedy, see under* Thomas Middleton
Towneley Cycle, 74, 83
The Tragical Actors, or The Martyrdom of the Late King Charles (1660), 179–93 *passim*, 201
A True and Exact Relation of the Taking of Colchester, Sent in a Letter (1648), 201

A True and Perfect Relation of the Condition of Those Noblemen and Gentlemen in Colchester (1648), 201
The Turkish Mahomet and Hiren the Fair Greek (1588), 161
Tyndale, William, 58, 66, 70, 74, 75, 83, 86, 92, 93, 97

Vener, Marco Antonio, 43, 54
Vergil, Polydore, 111, 120
Virgil, 15, 110, 120
Vincent of Beauvais, *Speculum Naturale* (mid 13th century), 68
Vulgate, 69

A Warning for Fair Women (1599), 12, 13, 26, 27
Webster, John, *The White Devil* (1612), 168, 176, 178, 192
   et al., *Sir Thomas Wyatt see under* Dekker, Thomas
Wilmot, Roger *et al.*, *Gismond of Salerne*, 110, 115
Wilson, Robert, *The Cobler's Prophecy* (1594), 13–14, 26, 31
Wolsey, Thomas, cardinal archbishop of York, 37, 44, 45, 46, 52, 54, 55, 127–9 *passim*, 137, 142, 144–5, 146
Woolf, D. R., 1–2, 22, 24, 31, 104, 118, 124, 138, 149, 152, 153, 156
Wyclif, John, 90, 95, 97